A Walk Away

A Novel

First published by Devitt Enterprises LLC 2024

A Walk Away is a work of fiction. All incidents and dialogue, and all characters, with the exception of some historical/public figures, are products of the author's imagination and are not to be construed as real. Where real-life historical/public figures appear, the situations, incidents, and dialogues concerning those persons are entirely fictional and are not intended to depict actual events or to change the entirely fictional nature of the work. In all other respects, any resemblance to actual persons, living or dead, events, or locales is entirely coincidental.

988 Suicide and Crisis Lifeline: If you or someone you know is struggling with depression or suicidal ideation, you can call 988 to access the 988 Suicide and Crisis Lifeline.

First edition

ISBN: 979-8-9914447-0-5

Cover art by Justin Devitt

This book is dedicated to...
My family. You give meaning to my every day.
The thousands I've met along the way. Your stories, both real and imagined,
have enriched my life.

Prologue

One Year Later

"Remember, when I give you the signal, start taking a few quick steps forward," Justin said.

Russell nodded without really thinking. He felt his heart pounding.

"Run, run, run!"

Russell heard the words, leaned forward, and cantered downhill in a slow-motion parody of running. After a few steps the wind passed through the leading edge and filled the cells. Conditions were ideal. The warm air that had collected in the valley during the day rose into the cooling upper atmosphere. The ropes tightened and the wing lifted them gently aloft.

Russell's grin was as wide as his eyes. He may have screamed in excitement, he wasn't sure. Justin reminded him to sit back. Russell adjusted his body and settled into the harness.

"It's magic air tonight, Mr. Russell," Justin said.

Russell could hear the pilot's voice above the gentle woosh of air caressing his face and blowing across the sail. He nodded. It did feel like magic. While the sky remained a vibrant blue, a trace of violet underlined the strand of distant clouds that accompanied the setting sun. Looking down, Russell was surprised by how high they had already climbed. A flutter of fear rose from his stomach. He reminded himself to breathe the way Lil had taught him and refocused his attention on searching for familiar landmarks. Usually, he would survey these mountains from his kitchen, but tonight, as he drifted, he found that he could still identify many of the peaks and ridges. He even recognized Cathedral Rock, the spot he and Lil had visited that day their world had changed.

His reverie was interrupted by the pilot. "Get ready. We'll catch that thermal on the left and core-up to get some more height. Once we level out that would be a good time."

Russell glanced to the side and saw a kettle of broadwings. Beneath their outstretched wings the raptors floated atop the lift, circling along the circumference of the invisible column.

As Justin pressed his feet lightly across the speed bar and lowered the sail's leading edge, Russell felt the acceleration. The tandem curved toward the soaring locals. Passing the birds they spiraled higher and higher. Russell closed his eyes and wrapped his arms in front of him as if embracing the sky. To his surprise he was not afraid.

When he opened his eyes they were no longer ascending. They were gliding slowly along a ridgeline of stable air. "This is the spot," said Justin.

Russell reached into the purple pouch he had strapped to his chest, the one he now took with him whenever he went for a walk. He removed the metal cylinder, the one Lil had wrapped and left for him that final morning. He pressed the engraving against his cheek. He did not feel metal. At that moment he could smell her skin and hear her laugh and see her smile. He removed the cap. Holding the container in one hand, Russell extended his other in front of him and slowly sprinkled the contents. He held the ash briefly before Lil slipped through his fingers one last time.

I

Part One

The Diagnosis

The Family

Lil and Russell

L ifting her eyes from the papers on the kitchen table, Lil said, "I am going to do it."

Russell thought for a moment. He cautiously raised his head and hazarded a glance into Lil's still-blue eyes. "Do you think that is a good idea?" The words crept reluctantly from his mouth. "I mean, it's a long way," he added with a sympathetic nod. There. It was done. Mild as it was he had said his piece. As his mind cycled through her possible reactions, Russell noticed he wasn't breathing. He exhaled slowly. In that moment of silence he hoped that she would find his logic convincing. A lifetime of marriage suggested otherwise.

As he spoke, Lil wordlessly considered the face she had kissed good morning each day for forty-five years. In their early years she often called him her beautiful man. It wasn't true, at least not physically. His bent nose, untamed eyebrows, and angled ears – each feature heading in its own direction – ensured he would never be mistaken for handsome. But it was a dependable face. Always clean-shaven even on weekends. Quick to smile when she was near. And rarely contorted by anger or disappointment. For Lil this was beautiful enough.

"It's a long way," Russell had said. He had misunderstood her intent. She spoke of her fate, not the Tour. A forgivable mistake. They had been discussing a great many decisions recently. She dismissed his error with an

5

imaginary wave of her hand. "A good idea? Perhaps not," she replied with a sympathetic nod of her own. A wry smile emerged beneath her determined eyes. "I am doing it anyway," she declared, referring to both.

Russell recognized the tone. He knew what it meant. His only choice was whether he would join her. The sadness that had crept into his wrinkles over the past two months lifted momentarily. He smiled, her dependable Russell, and nodded.

"And I am asking Sophie and Luke to join us . . ."

Sophie

Sophie said yes before she knew what she was agreeing to. Her mother rarely called, a characteristic Sophie shared. The contact had grown less frequent over the past two years. The distance between them seemed greater than the 100 miles that separated their houses.

After graduating college Sophie moved out as quickly as she could. The demands of her new job provided an easy excuse to limit visits to the obligatory holidays. When Rick appeared on the scene, his schedule as an attorney offered another layer of probable cause for the diminished contact. There was a stretch in her twenties when Sophie was hard-pressed to remember a single visit.

All that changed when Luke was born. Through Luke's elementary years Lil and Russell visited frequently: Holidays, long weekends, major milestones, and minor celebrations, it seemed as if Russell and Lil were there, invited or not. As distant or judgmental Sophie found her as a mother, she recognized Lil's unconditional love for her grandson. Once, after a particularly stressful visit, Rick commented, "I don't understand why you can't get along better with your mother."

Sophie curtly replied with the truth that underlies all sarcasm. "The woman you see with Luke is not my mother."

The pattern changed again when Luke became a teenager. He grew more interested in his friends than his family, including his grandparents. And it went downhill after Rick's exit.

Still, inexplicably, when Lil asked, Sophie immediately accepted. Perhaps she was now ready or needed to be.

"Well, I better see what I just got into," Sophie said after she put the phone down.

Her Googling caused her heart to beat faster.

"*Generally regarded as one of the world's great hikes, the Tour du Mont Blanc, or TMB, is a circular route covering more than 104 miles and passing through three countries: France, Italy, and Switzerland. While the name pays homage to Mont Blanc – at 4800 meters the tallest of the peaks – geologically, it is part of a larger massif that includes a legion of lesser mountains, ridges, and aiguilles. Most hikers complete the tour in 8–10 days. This would typically require walking 6–8 hours a day with elevation gains ranging from 800 to 2000 meters.*"

"'One hundred and four miles . . . ten days . . . eight hours a day,'" Sophie frowned.

She read on. "*A series of towns and villages are connected by established trails which allow determined hikers to circumnavigate the massif with inspiring and ever-changing views at virtually every turn. An array of Alpine huts, small hotels, auberges, or rifugios allow travelers to readily find meals and lodging without the need to carry all the equipment and food required of a traditional through-hike. Most lodging is dormitory style ranging from 8–24 in a room and feature shared bathroom facilities and community dining halls.*"

"Dormitories . . . shared bathroom . . . community dining." Sophie's stomach flipped. She stopped scrolling, unable to read any more. "What am I going to tell Luke?"

Luke

Luke rolled his eyes, recently his go-to response in almost every conversation with his mother. Where are you going? Eye roll. "Out." Who will you be with? Heavy sigh. "With friends." What time will you be back? Head shake. "Later." What do you want for dinner? Shoulder shrug. "I don't care."

"But that's right in the middle of qualifiers," Luke protested, choosing an angle he thought might elicit sympathy from his mom.

His athleticism was a source of pride for his parents. They attended all the meets from when he was a Little Splasher through high school. His dad had been the loudest parent in the stands.

Luke wasn't the best swimmer, but he was okay. As a young boy, he frequently medaled in his division. Then, he was big for his age, skinny but with long arms. When he entered his teens, and the other kids started to catch up in size, the wins grew fewer and fewer. Luke's interest sagged, along with his effort. "Sports burnout," Luke told himself, adopting a phrase he had heard other parents use when confronted with their golden child's lack of success. Now on a good day, when everything was feeling right, he might manage to medal as part of a relay.

For the past year he thought about quitting, at least the school team – those early morning practices especially were a grind. But he kept at it. It was familiar. His friends were there. It was a good distraction. "Gotta go to practice. Back later," also gave him cover to escape.

"If I miss the qualifier, I can't swim in the summer championship," Luke added. "I could stay with Sean – his parents won't mind." Luke remembered what his father, the lawyer, had taught him about negotiation: Provide a solution that addresses the other person's needs.

His mother paused. Luke imagined she was considering the possibility. Despite the differences in their parenting styles, Luke knew his mother appreciated how the Troys had treated him, especially recently. But when she spoke it wasn't about Sean's family.

"I talked to coach," his mother began. "He said it would be fine as long as you are back in the pool by July fifteenth. Summer league is more flexible." Sophie had anticipated the swimming argument and ignored the staying-with-another-family option. She also knew a thing or two about negotiation.

"We leave on June twenty-nine and return on July seventh," Sophie concluded, her tone indicating the end of what was never really a discussion. "It'll be fun. You will see Nan and Russell. Besides, it will give you a chance to practice your photography."

Luke turned away from his mother and headed toward the door. "Fuck this," he mouthed to himself, slamming the door behind him.

8

Two Months Earlier

"Lil, I don't often get to see you. So what brings you in today?" asked Dr. Hsu.

"My husband," Lil offered with a dismissive nod in the direction of Russell.

Dr. Hsu laughed good-naturedly. She had been Russell and Lil's primary for more than twenty years. While she would routinely see them both for an annual physical and bloodwork, it was a rare occasion for Lil to visit otherwise. She never seemed to get sick or, more accurately, to seek treatment if she were. Russell, on the other hand, was a regular. He would come in for his flu shot and never missed an immunization or a booster. He would be quick to call if his knee was bothering him or he'd strained his back or had a high fever. Not a malingerer, just cautious.

Dr. Hsu waited her out.

"I had a choking episode two days ago. A piece of fish tried swimming down the wrong stream. For a few moments I had trouble swallowing. When I did cough it out there was a little bit of blood, that's all." Lil presented the incident quickly.

Russell added, "She was turning blue. I was just about to Heimlich her."

"Hmm," Hsu replied and remained silent. She had found a healthy dose of wait time typically led to new symptoms.

Lil was as good at this approach as her doctor. She responded by considering her fingernails and looking at the diplomas on the wall as if seeing them for the first time. It wasn't that she didn't trust or like the doctor. Far from it. She had great respect for Dr. Hsu. Rather, of all her qualities, Lil worshipped

9

her own independence most.

Russell sighed and folded his arms. The gesture was aimed at both women. He had witnessed this dance before.

Today, Dr. Hsu blinked first. "Have there been any other instances of choking or difficulty swallowing?"

"Not really," Lil replied.

In her years as a healer of people Dr. Hsu had become a student of language. "Not really" was a code. It really meant "Absolutely yes, but I am not ready to tell you yet."

Hsu was about to probe further when Russell scolded Lil with his eyes. With a good-natured pat to her hand, he said, "You are such a secretive liar, my sweet Elizabeth." Russell turned to Hsu and explained, "She has been coughing quite a bit lately, nothing as extreme as two days ago. And since then I have been finding tissue paper with little dots of blood."

"It's not that dramatic," Lil added, pulling her hand away from Russell and looking at Dr. Hsu. "I've been a little careless chewing. There have been a few times lately when it feels like food has been stuck in my throat, and I will cough to clear it out so I can swallow. The blood that my unregistered nurse reports," she said, glancing at her husband, "must be left over from the other day. It was a rough cough to unhook that damn fish, and I must have scraped the inside of my throat. It is less today than yesterday, just a dot, really."

Dr. Hsu nodded and smiled at them each in turn. "Well, you did the right thing by coming in, and I am glad you are here. You are two of my favorite patients and are fortunate to have each other."

Russell and Lil smugly flashed the same self-satisfied smile as if Hsu was referring to them alone and not the other.

"Right, let's have a look at you, Lil." Hsu directed, handing Lil an examining gown.

The doctor methodically proceeded through the standard check-up, devoting added attention to the abdominal area. Lil reported no discomfort from the probing but did acknowledge some recent back and leg pain that she attributed to poor stretching.

"Everything looks good from the outside," Hsu offered. "I wished all my patients took as good care of themselves as you do, Lil." She turned to the computer to enter some notes into Lil's medical file.

Lil smiled at the obvious flattery and looked sideways with an I-told-you-so glance at Russell.

"I see you've lost three pounds since your last visit," Hsu observed while looking at the data on the screen.

"I've been quite busy, actually," Lil began. "There are my usual gym visits..."

Hsu was very aware of Lil's dedication to exercise, having signed off on her yearly fitness reimbursements. It was not uncommon for Lil to log 20 gym visits a month with a regimen that included Pilates, Zumba, yoga, Barre, exercise machines, and even free weights. Hsu counted Lil as one of her fittest patients regardless of age.

Lil continued, "And the weather's been nice, so I have been outside more."

Hsu glanced out the window at the snow cover. Rather than respond to the apparent contradiction, she instead turned toward Russell.

"She's not been eating as much. Last week I made this risotto with leeks, bacon and parmesan cheese," Russell paused as if savoring the dish again. "She ate three bites."

"Too much cheese," Lil suggested. "I've not been hungry, that's all."

"You two are quite the show," Doctor Hsu added. "I would like to schedule an endoscopy to take a look at your throat, and let's do a blood draw to check your levels," she said to Lil. Returning to Russell, Hsu added, "Next time you make the risotto, you invite me over."

* * *

It was a quiet ride home. There was no anger or bitterness in the silence. After all these years Russell knew his wife. He had learned to accept her temporary quiet; it gave her time to think. She would speak when she was ready.

After they arrived home, Lil reached out to Russell's hand. Russell embraced her and then made the appointment. The earliest opening was in two days.

Russell accompanied Lil to the medical center for the endoscopy. The procedure itself was relatively short – less than thirty minutes. But as it required moderate sedation, the docs kept Lil for an extra hour just to make certain there were no complications. They were home before noon.

Early the next morning Dr. Hsu's office called to schedule a visit to review the results. Lil and Russell were back with Hsu the following day.

The next few meetings with Dr. Hsu occurred in quick succession. Looking back, to Russell and Lil it felt like a blur, a pummeling sequence – one round of bad news following another with no time to recover in between.

First..."*The endoscopy revealed some growths in the esophagus. That explains the bleeding and difficulty swallowing. Before discussing treatment options, I would like to do an MRI. Would you be available tomorrow?*"

Then..."*The scan showed some other growths around the bile duct, small intestine, pancreas, and liver. I would like to biopsy some excisions so we know exactly what we are looking at.*"

They did recall more from the third follow-up, the one where the darkest future became indelibly clear. Russell and Lil entered the room. Dr. Hsu was standing with a second doctor, whom neither Lil nor Russell had met before. Dr. Hsu greeted them and introduced Dr. McGinty "from the oncology unit." Hsu inhaled slowly. With an open hand, she gestured the group toward a leather couch and side chairs. The seating was stationed at the sunny corner of the room in front of the wall of medical books. The doctors stood behind the side chairs. Lil and Russell correctly read the cue that the couch was theirs. They sat down.

The wrinkled brow on Dr. Hsu's face overshadowed a tight-lipped attempt at a smile. She reached out a hand to each. Lil and Russell took hold.

"I am afraid it is not good news." Lil and Russell remembered that phrase distinctly. The dozens of overwhelming details were more fragmented: *Pancreatic cancer . . . stage IV . . . metastasized . . . spread to other organs . . . I am very sorry.*

Midway through the diagnosis Lil brought her hand to her face and bit on the middle joint of her index finger. Russell drew her close, wrapping his arm around her shoulder while rubbing her leg with his other hand. He could feel his heart pounding, or perhaps it was Lil's.

"How long?" Lil instinctively asked.

Dr. McGinty, who had been attentive but silent, responded. "Every situation is different, and I don't like to talk about specific times. I would encourage you to think about the quality of life you wish to have."

He may have said more. Lil did not recall. He had lost her at the first pronoun. Lil turned squarely to Dr. Hsu, the woman she had known and trusted for the past 25 years. She tipped her hand slightly to silence the second doc. "How long?" she repeated.

"Without treatment, six to twelve months." Dr. Hsu nodded her head sadly and repeated the information. "Patients with this condition, typically six to twelve months, give or take a few."

Russell gasped. Lil lowered her head and whispered, "Thank you."

After the unfilled pause, Dr. Hsu continued. "There are some options that might slow the progress of the disease, but they are not without side effects. And risks. That is why I asked Dr. McGinty to join us. He is one of the finest specialists in the northeast."

Lil and Russell now turned to Dr. McGinty.

"There are a number of treatments for pancreatic ductal adenocarcinoma, or PDAC. Unfortunately, once the disease has progressed to this point, there are no clinically proven and effective cures," McGinty pronounced.

'No . . . cure.' The piercing words lodged in Lil's head.

McGinty continued to speak: *Try surgery but . . . tumors non-localized . . . complete surgical removal not viable . . . spread to other organs . . . could target larger masses . . . Whipple procedure . . . hope to slow progress . . . surgery presents risks . . . recovery period extensive . . .*"

Lil shook her head and stifled a smile. Her mind recalled the old medical joke: The surgery was successful but the patient died.

McGinty went on: *Chemotherapy another option . . . PDAC more resistant than other cancers . . . usual side effects weakness, nausea, fatigue, and weight loss . . . possibly debilitating . . . minimal impact on one-year survival rate . . .*"

Lil offered another barely perceptible shake of her head. She remembered her father's battle with lung cancer. Suffer through months of chemo just to suffer some more for a little longer. Another lousy option, she quickly concluded.

When McGinty then mentioned clinical trials, Lil allowed herself a flicker of hope: *Experimental immunotherapies . . . the body's own killer-T cells . . .* As he continued Lil felt the flicker fade: *None currently successful . . . an extensive commitment of time and energy . . . help further our knowledge.*

She nodded lightly. Ah, a hero's path. Do it for the good of science. In the next moment Lil caught herself negotiating with a God she didn't believe in.

"Finally, there is palliative care," McGinty said. "Where the goal is to manage pain and keep the patient comfortable, allowing them to function and enjoy life as long as possible."

I don't like any of the options, Lil thought. The words came out as "That's it?"

Dr. McGinty nodded silently and shrugged his left shoulder.

"But I feel fine. I really do," Lil protested. "A little weight loss, not as hungry. That's all. It must be a mistake," she concluded.

Hsu drew a slow breath and pushed back in her chair. "I'm sorry, Lil," the doctor responded, her face sagging as the words slipped out. "We double-checked and triple-checked."

McGinty said hurriedly, as if discussing his favorite hobby, "Pancreatic cancer is notorious that way. The pancreas is deep in the abdomen surrounded by other organs. A regular doctor can't feel any tumors during a standard physical. So any early symptoms are easily missed or dismissed. Most diagnoses don't occur until after the disease has progressed to stage four. If it weren't for your coughing and blood, you might not have been diagnosed for another three or four months when symptoms were more acute and other systems had started to shut down."

Numbed, neither Lil nor Russell asked any more questions.

The First Decision

L il woke at 2:00 AM. She slid silently out from under the quilted comforter she had stitched herself and headed toward the kitchen. Russell did not stir. He hardly ever did when she would arise in the middle of the night or wake before him in the morning. Lil possessed a graceful stealth when moving. On the other hand, she would always awaken when Russell stumbled from bed and clomped across the floor on one of his increasingly frequent night-time bathroom runs. Accommodating in so many other ways, Russell proved immune to Lil's efforts to train him on how to take gentler nocturnal steps.

As a young woman, once she woke, Lil would immediately set to work on a checklist of things she should have done yesterday but didn't or simply had to do today at all costs. However, as she aged she found herself more relaxed. For the better part of the past two decades she followed a similar morning routine: Set the kettle, make the tea, and read the paper. She loved holding the warm mug to her cheek. *Lil seated at the kitchen table scanning the headlines, with a cup pressed against her face and a contented smile on her lips.* This would become one of Russell's everlasting memories of Lil – he even referenced it at her memorial service.

On this particular morning, despite the early hour, she still followed her routine, minus the paper which would not be delivered for another three hours. Freed from the distracting headlines of the outside world, Lil reflected upon her own substantial news. She had always been clear-headed in the morning: "I do my best thinking before the rest of the world shake themselves out of bed," she had been known to tell Russell, the words

15

delivered with an invisible wag of an accusatory finger. And like the familiar cup warming her cheek, this morning was no exception. She was clear-headed.

Like all mortals, Lil had imagined this event from afar, comforted by the presumed luxury of time. Long ago, though, she had decided how she would like the end to unfold – if she were confronted with the uncomfortable choice. Though the abstraction had become horribly, terrifyingly, inescapably real, this morning Lil was still certain.

She sensed Russell's presence in the doorway to the kitchen before she saw or heard him. "It may take my life but I will not let it steal my time. I'll live whatever good days I may have left," she said without preamble before turning to face her husband.

Russell nodded.

She did not speak her other truths. She was not ready for that yet. Though he sensed there was more to be said, he did not press her. He just held her. They stood gently rocking in the middle of the kitchen.

Together, they left before sunrise for a walk on one of their favorite trails. Hand in hand they followed the switchbacks up the hillside, their feet crunching the remaining traces of dry snow underfoot. Their destination lay hidden a short distance off the main trail. A path snaked through dense stands of mountain laurel, now flowerless but with their darkened leaves still clinging to the gray branches even in the cold of winter. The hardened earth gave way to a series of stone pavers worn smooth by countless pilgrims before them. To reach the single granite boulder at the end, you first passed by three columns of vertical rock, like buttresses on some medieval church, which gave the name to the destination: Cathedral Rock.

Early on this winter morning they were alone. They took a seat, a pair of witnesses in the first pew, as the sun graced light and color upon the world around. The wisps of their own breath danced from white to gray before departing to join the breaths of all the others who had passed before.

That afternoon, they received the promised call from Dr. Hsu. Lil shared her decision. There would be no knife, no injections, no informed consent. They scheduled the meeting with the palliative care provider.

Lil would accept whatever time her body would bequeath, and that would be all.

Meet the Team

D r. Hsu was not surprised by Lil's choice. There were no good options. Lil had been medically independent her whole life, avoiding treatment when most others would have long ago visited their doc. For a brief moment Hsu indulged the fleeting series of what-ifs. What if Lil had visited more often? What if Hsu had been a more skilled diagnostician? Perhaps this would have resulted in an earlier diagnosis. She quickly dismissed this idea. Pancreatic cancer is a tricky bastard, remaining silent and hidden, leaving only the slightest breadcrumbs here and there. Besides, nothing to be done about it now. Hsu had learned long ago: There is enough worry in the every day without creating more in the might-have-been. So, she set about assembling the best support team possible. Lil and Russell were going to need one.

An introductory meeting of the palliative care team was arranged for the following week. Over the phone, Hsu had been careful to explain to Lil the differences between palliative care and hospice: "Remember, Lil, while hospice is one form of palliative care, not all palliative care is hospice," Hsu explained. "Palliative care is specialized care for people with a serious illness. The goal is to improve quality of life for both the patient and the family. Yes, it offers some relief from the symptoms, but it also provides an extra layer of support with the stress and uncertainties of a serious illness. We can go over this in more detail when we meet. But the important thing is that *you* are in charge. The team will provide the supports *you* find helpful." It was a script she had used many times before, but for Hsu it was also true.

The introductory meeting was held at South Mountain Medical Center, which, after all of her recent tests, Lil was starting to view as her second home.

When they entered the conference room Russell was struck by the number of people. Beyond Dr. Hsu and Micah, one of the nurses from Dr. Hsu's practice, he did not recognize the other four.

Lil first noticed the layout. Eight chairs, all in a circle. No tables or desks to separate them. Beyond the floral pattern commonly worn by the medical class no one seemed "in uniform." Lil liked the vibe. It reminded her of a Quaker circle she had attended many years ago during a religious studies course. Though she viewed herself as unaligned, if she were spiritually inclined, Lil imagined she would be a Quaker, a Universalist, or maybe a Buddhist.

As Lil scanned the faces around the room her eye was drawn to one individual in particular. Perhaps it was the woman's position in the circle, seated directly opposite Lil. Or, more likely, the woman's Cheshire cat grin, a smile made all the more distinct by sparkling purple lipstick, a color that perfectly matched the scarf draped over her left shoulder. Lil smiled and nodded at the unknown, who silently mouthed back her acknowledgment: "Hello, sister."

Dr. Hsu facilitated the meeting. Each member shared a bit about their background and announced their role on the team. Micah from Dr. Hsu's office would serve as team coordinator. A nutritionist would help with diet. The social worker would advise on community resources. A Sister of Mercy with the HealthCare Chaplaincy could provide compassionate listening. Finally, there was Debbie, the woman in purple, a palliative care nurse with South Mountain Hospice.

The initial session lasted about thirty minutes. The tone was relaxed but professional. To Lil and Russell it also felt sincere.

At the conclusion of the team meeting, Dr. Hsu explained that Debbie would stay a bit longer. "You are in good hands here, Lil," Dr. Hsu said, gesturing toward the palliative care nurse. Standing up, she touched Lil's shoulder and left the room, leaving the three of them alone.

"She has put together a good team for you, Ms. Lil. I work with many docs, and I have a lot of respect for Sandra," Debbie began.

Lil had never heard anyone refer to Dr. Hsu by her first name. She had seen the children's pictures on the desk and the diplomas from Boston University and Johns Hopkins on the wall. But she knew precious little else about her doctor. She briefly considered some of these unknowns: What were her children like? Did she love her husband? Was she happy with her life? Ashamed she had never bothered to ask these questions before, Lil quickly retreated from these thoughts.

"I can tell you all about the services we provide but sometimes I find it best to start with you. What do *you* need, Lil, and how can I help?" Debbie asked.

Lil's eyes widened. Dozens of questions, feelings, and confusions – the surviving remnants of the hundreds that had bombarded her over the past two weeks – swirled in her head. Lil paused before speaking and then said, "I'm not really sure," which both was and was not true. Lil offered a second pause upon which Debbie did not trespass. "This is all so new, and overwhelming . . . I guess I just want someone to be there to walk this path with me, with us," Lil added, gesturing toward Russell. "Someone who has been there before and maybe knows the way, at least a little bit."

Debbie had leaned in slightly while Lil was speaking. She chuckled and said, "Ms. Lil, I may not know all your particular journey holds. But I promise you this: I will be there with you. And it will be an honor to accompany you."

Lil smiled and breathed. She had always kept her own counsel, cautious not to overshare. But even in this first conversation Lil sensed something comforting in Debbie's manner. Perhaps this is a woman I can trust, she thought hopefully.

"Well, let me guide you through some of the highlights. You stop me anytime if you want more detail," Debbie began. "Like was said at the meeting, palliative care is about quality of life. It ain't about dying tomorrow – we all gonna die tomorrow. It is about living today," Debbie said. "And for me, the most important thing is to respect your wishes, Ms. Lil. All that matters is what you want." The emphasis in Debbie's voice matched the determined look in her eye.

"Now, when Sandra called me, she told me which road you chose. No surgery, no chemo, no radiation. I suspect that's why she asked for me to join the team. I hold strong women dear to my heart," Debbie confessed. "But everyone, even the strongest, needs and deserves support. And when you let people in, you help yourself, yes, but you are giving them a gift as well. You are not being a burden, Ms. Lil, oh no. You are relieving a burden. Their burden." As Debbie paused, her eyes seemed drawn to a distant corner of the room. "See, the loved ones, they want to help. But they don't know how. And when you let them in, you are showing them the way. That is a powerful gift."

"Amen to that," Russell said aloud.

Lil wondered how much Dr. Hsu had told Debbie. And how much Russell had told Dr. Hsu.

"Enough preaching, Little Debbie," Debbie said to herself with a laugh. "Now, here's the lowdown. I will schedule a time to come out to you at home. Once every few weeks for now. More frequent as we get further along. There are four pillars of support: The physical, emotional, spiritual, and practical. I'll go over these more at our first home visit. You can tell me which ones are most important to you. At least to start."

Lil found herself nodding.

"When we get closer, somewhere in the final month or weeks, we transition to hospice care. And hospice isn't a specific place. You decide the location – at home, nursing home, assisted living, hospital. But I will still be there with you, as long as you'll have me," Debbie explained.

"You've got some good insurance. Both palliative and hospice care are covered. We don't need to worry about that. And you strike me as a woman who's got some living yet to do, Ms. Lil. So you are going to get your money's worth out of those insurance companies," Debbie added with a smile.

"Thank you," Lil replied and meant it. "I look forward to our visits."

As they all stood to leave, Debbie added, "And you call me anytime. You have a question. Somebody not getting back to you. Something not feeling right. You call me." The tone struck Lil as the sort a mother would give to her daughter going off to college, though she was sure Debbie was a good twenty years her junior. "It's my job, but it's also personal to me," Debbie

21

concluded.

Compassionate Choices

While everyone lives with death, for Lil it was a topic life had provided occasion to consider with some regularity. Both her parents were deceased. Her mother passed first. Lil cared for her father through his cancer chapter. She was now of the age where several friends had recently died. Even as a young woman she had lost those she loved. Yes, Lil had given quite a bit of thought to the topic.

Three weeks out from receiving the unexpected news from Dr. Hsu, two weeks after meeting her palliative care team and one week past her first home visit with Debbie, Lil had not wavered from her first instinct. There would be no prolonged descent, no interminable battle with her terminal foe, no slow walk into fogginess as her body stubbornly ceased to function even while refusing to surrender. The thought of soiling herself with Russell wiping her clean day after day or the prospect of incoherent ramblings distressing those around her was more upsetting than any fear of physical pain. She could endure it, but it was not the life she wanted. Long ago she resolved to live on her own terms. Her death would be no different.

The phone was answered on the second ring by an actual person. In rehearsing the call she had awkwardly imagined the greeting on the automated phone chain: *If you want to kill yourself, press 2 now. If you would like to help a relative to die, press 3. For all other calls press the pound sign and a representative will be with you shortly.* She appreciated the matter-of-fact tone shared by the receptionist: Kind but without pathos. Lil scheduled the appointment with Betsy, a Compassionate Choices counselor, for the following week. Normally the counselor would meet the partner – not patient, Lil had learned – at home. However, Betsy agreed to meet with Lil at a local cafe.

Le Fournil Chamoniard was one of Lil's favorite spots. Rene, the owner, was filled with as much life as his drinks were with chocolate. Lil had met Rene in the long ago. She was quietly instrumental in helping him relocate to the area. Since then, at least once a month, Lil and Russell treated themselves to a visit. Well before it became a trend, Rene partnered with nearby farmers for locally sourced vegetables, meats, and cheeses. His pastries rivaled those from a European cafe. The secret, Rene would say, was "love – and fresh butter." Rene cooked with an abundance of both. Typically, Lil would order a salad with goat cheese and berries, while Russell was partial to the fig, pear, and prosciutto flatbread. On a rare occasion Lil indulged and ordered the *chocolat montagne*. Today was such a day.

Lil arrived first. Rene pressed two fingers to his forehead and nodded – a silent salute he reserved for Lil alone. The cafe was empty. A bit after breakfast but well before lunch, that sweet respite fleetingly nestled between the bustle of the past and the anticipation of the future. Lil settled at a small table next to a window where she was afforded a view of both the parking lot and the Presidential Range.

Lil closed her eyes for a moment. She wandered into distant mountains. She stepped upon a footworn path wending its way to the top of a col, its many twists and turns sending you first in one direction and then another, yet always toward the destination of the other side. She saw the summits, shrouded then unmasked as the winds caressed the stone face, flicking the clouds like wisps of hair. After a few moments or maybe more, Lil's reverie was interrupted by the grating sound of tires on gravel. She opened her eyes abruptly.

The newly arrived car parked next to Lil's older Subaru. An unfamiliar woman in brown corduroys and a faded flannel shirt emerged from the driver's side. The stranger scanned the cafe and walked toward the yellow door. She reached for the oversized whisk that served as a handle and entered. Lil signaled to her with a raised hand. An unnecessary gesture as there were no other customers in the restaurant.

Though she imagined herself a compassionate soul, Lil was not a hugger.

Her preferred greeting was a smile accompanied by a kind word. If she knew you well, she would extend her hand palm up, connecting while also keeping space, and lean back ever so slightly so as not to inadvertently invite a discomforting cheek kiss. Russell, on the other hand, was a frequent and robust hugger. This was another one of the differences they accepted in one another.

Betsy lightly grasped the open hand that Lil had extended. She did not insert herself beyond that boundary. By nature, Betsy was a keen observer of others. By training, she learned to follow their lead.

"I am pleased to meet you, Lil," Betsy began. Her expression suggested she meant it.

Lil had hoped she would like this stranger and was relieved to find she did. "Same here," she replied.

There was no rush to the serious business of the day. They chit-chatted a bit. Each shared a few curated details about their family and life. Even so, it did not feel like small talk; it felt more like two old friends reacquainting with one another after a long absence.

"Shall we get some noshes?" Lil invited with a sparkle in her eye.

"Lead on," Betsy replied. They rose simultaneously from their chairs. Their noses easily followed the invisible strands of deliciousness luring them toward the open display case. Lil caught Betsy closing her eyes. It was not the first time she had seen someone entranced by Rene's baking. Russell had reacted the same way, too.

Betsy lived further upstate and was unfamiliar with this local legend. On Lil's recommendation, Betsy ordered the *chocolat montagne* and a pistachio biscotti. Lil chose an orange scone to accompany her drink.

Chatting with Rene and watching the master at work was half the charm of this magical place. The proprietor was a flirtatious narrator with a sing-song voice. His accent only added to the charm. "The chocolate is from Ghana," Rene began, holding a solid chunk the size of a brick. He used a hand rasp to grate the chocolate into a metal pitcher. "The milk is from Blue Spruce Farms down the road. The steam," he said, using the wand from the most elaborate espresso machine Betsy had ever seen, "makes it silky and oh so good." Rene set the pitcher on the counter, took down a large clear glass, and placed it on the pedestal in front of him. He scooped two dollops of whipped cream into the bottom of the glass and then coated the top inch, both inside and out, with salted caramel. "In life you need a little salt to appreciate the sweetness, *non*?" Using a piping bag, he laced three wiggly strands of mascarpone, connecting the cream on the bottom to the caramel at the top. "Happiness is always a winding path. Is that not true, ladies?" Rene commented before dabbing some espresso molasses along the top rim. By pressing an unseen button with his foot, the maestro then set the glass gently spinning on the pedestal before slowly pouring the milk and chocolate to near overflowing. He then pressed the button a second time and the drink gradually came to rest.

Betsy couldn't help but smile. No one ever could. As she reached toward the glass, Rene wagged his finger. "Not yet," he teased. He hand-shaved one more topping – African dark chocolate with ginger and papaya – and capped the glass with a thin lid of dark chocolate, sealed in place with strands of chocolate ganache. "And the final ingredient, the most important one of all – is love," he announced as he nested a small red candy heart amidst the sea of chocolate atop the glass. Only then did he invite Betsy to claim her prize.

With smiles as wide as their eyes the two new friends returned to their table. "Can we wait just a moment," Betsy requested as she reached into her pocket. "I feel foolish, but I just want to take a picture to send to my kids."

Lil laughed. "What's life without a little foolish fun? Here, give me the phone." While Betsy mugged in the background, Lil snapped a photo of the happy creations. As Lil handed the camera back to her, Betsy felt her squeeze her hand imperceptibly.

"*A ta sante*," Lil offered reflexively, raising her glass. "*A la tienne*," Betsy replied, surprising Lil. Even as they took the first sip, the shavings started to melt and the heart disappeared into the ocean of chocolate.

Over the next twenty minutes, between nibbles and sips, Lil told parts of her story. She began with the shock of the diagnosis and how her symptoms were progressing. Strangely, she felt more comfortable speaking with this recent stranger than with friends and family. Lil spoke of her relationship with Sophie, sharing details she had not shared with anyone besides Russell, and a few not even with him. This freedom was liberating. She felt like a child spinning in an empty meadow after a storm had passed. Then she realized she was speaking quickly and her heart was racing. She abruptly caught herself and changed directions. "I've been talking too much," Lil declared," both to herself and Betsy. "Tell me about you," she said, the flush on her cheeks already fading. "And how this all works," she added with a rolling motion of her hand.

Betsy smiled and took her cue. "I am not a doctor," she began. "I am a social worker by training. UVM a long time ago."

Betsy paused briefly. Sometimes, clients want to know more about their counselor's personal life, marital status, children, where they live, and so on. Lil remained silent. Betsy decided to stick with her work journey.

"I first became involved with Compassionate Choices from the other side, as a client, when my father sought medical aid in dying," she continued. Lil reacted with a light nod. "The people were wonderful. It was still painful but very affirming for my dad. He was a Marine. Wanted things his way, you know." Betsy had shared this story with other clients before. With Lil she added a detail. She wasn't certain why. Perhaps it was Lil's insistence that they meet outside the home or that Lil had come alone. "I felt closer to him when he was dying than at any other time," she confided. "It was one of the most intimate experiences in my life, almost beautiful if you can say that about the death of a parent."

As she was speaking Betsy's gaze drifted out the window. When her eyes returned to the cafe she was warmed by Lil's face. "That's when I knew what I wanted to do. You know, in my professional life. There was an open position at Compassionate Care. Entry level, but that was fine. I enrolled at Larner. Back to school at thirty-five, evenings and weekends. That sort of thing. I got my end-of-life doula certificate and then moved up to a counselor position. I've been doing this for fifteen years now."

Lil was chuckling. "A death doula. Who knew there was such a thing," she said. "When I had Sophie – that was back when birth centers were just starting – we had 'birth companions.' That was before doulas came into

27

fashion."

"Yeah," Betsy added. "Now we get you coming and going. And at this point in my life, I think I need a menopause doula."

After their shared laugh Lil spoke next. She pushed her empty plate aside, placed her clasped hands upon the table, and leaned in toward Betsy. "So how does all this work?"

Now we are down to business, Betsy noted to herself. She adopted a more clinical tone as she described the essential details: *You must make an oral request to your physician followed by a written request and a second oral request after a 15-day waiting period . . . your own doctor, as well as a second consulting physician, must certify you have a terminal illness with six months or fewer to live . . . your doc will then prepare the prescription and we will provide you with a list of pharmacies willing to fill the script . . . It costs about $3,700 for the Seconal and $750 for the DDMP2 . . . Neither is covered by Medicare . . .Typically, the process from the time you meet with the docs until you receive the meds takes one to two months . . . You must be able to swallow and absorb the medication . . . You have to administer it yourself . . . The first med is an anti-nausea/anti-anxiety. It helps you keep down the other meds . . . Since the law was enacted about 69 individuals qualified to use Act 39. Some of these took their terminal meds, and others passed without using medical aid in dying.*

Even as she was speaking, Betsy was studying Lil, looking for a reaction that might suggest a particular concern or some confusing detail. Lil offered nothing—no twitch, no gasps, no questions—a silent sphinx. She had already made up her mind, Betsy concluded to herself.

"Now, Lil, of all the people I have met throughout the years, I've never had a client with no questions," Betsy remarked.

Lil nodded.

"Most folks wonder if it hurts," Betsy ventured.

"Living is filled with its share of pain," Lil replied. "I don't suppose dying is much different," she added with a twist of her head.

"My question, and it's more for me than for you," Lil mused, "is how I tell my family."

The Second Decision

When she awoke early the next morning, Lil found herself revisiting a familiar theme, a rationalization she had told herself many times: We all have secrets, and those thoughts and events we prefer to bury and hope remain hidden. In her forty-five years of marriage, she fancied herself a direct and open partner. But in her heart Lil recognized that was less than half the truth. She was well-versed in the unspoken. However, some truths she knew she had to share. Russell would be first.

Though she infrequently showcased her skills, Lil was an excellent cook. This Friday evening, Russell intended to be home early. Several weeks ago he told his team about Lil's condition. They were very supportive. But tax season was unforgiving, and he was running late. He opened the front door hurriedly, ready to apologize and anxious to see how Lil was feeling. Within two steps he recognized the delicate aroma of sauteed veal with lemon and capers. Turning the corner to the kitchen, he saw the table was set with the fine china inherited from Lil's grandmother, which had been used no more than a handful of times over the past decade. The flickering light from two candles cast elusive shadows dancing across the already-plated food. He noted the side of risotto and smiled in spite of his suspicion.

Lil, dressed casually in jeans and her favorite shirt, stood in marked contrast to the elegant meal on the table. She kissed Russell on the forehead and invited him to one of the two seats placed next to each other at the small round kitchen table. She poured him a glass of Savoie Blanc and settled into the chair next to him.

"To us," Lil toasted, raising her glass.

"To us," Russell rejoined, a tear already drifting down his face.

He returned his cup to the table and embraced Lil fully, hugging her in silence.

Russell released Lil. She gently wiped away his tears with her index fingers. After taking a sip of the wine he broke the baguette by hand, as Lil had taught him, and presented her with a generous portion. While cautious with many dietary habits, Lil was a fiend for bread and cheese. She sliced the reblochon and passed some to Russell. They set to enjoy their meal together.

When dinner was over and the table was clear, Lil poured a second glass of wine, moved toward the couch, and patted the cushion next to her.

Russell joined her. She placed her glass on the side table, took both his hands into hers and looked him gently in the eyes.

"Russell," Lil began. "There is one thing I cannot, I will not, do."

He knew what she was about to say. It was a topic they had danced around in the past. But he also knew she was sincere in her belief. And that he now had no choice in the matter.

"I refuse to be a burden . . ."

For as long as they had been together, whenever they would discuss the prospect of growing infirm, Lil would always say, jokingly but not, "When the time comes, just push me out on an ice flow or leave me on the side of a mountain."

When they planned for retirement, Lil steadfastly refused long-term disability insurance, telling their financial advisor, "I assure you that is something I will not need."

"Russell, I will not abide some slow, debilitating descent with other people spooning food in my mouth. I will not die in some sterile hospital tethered to tubes with beeping lights and buzzing alarms, interrupted every two hours by someone taking a level or giving me a med or cleaning a catheter, the smell of disinfectant in my nostrils as if we can sanitize death. Even if I was clueless then, I know it now. And I won't do it." She handed him the brochure Betsy had provided.

He looked at it silently, the words screaming inside his head – *End-of-Life*

Choice, Death with Dignity, six months. Finally, Russell simply said, "I know." He had always known. Yet he had quietly thought he would not need to face this moment. He was older. He was a male. The actuarial tables that he worshiped on a daily basis predicted he would precede her by 5.27 years. He knew now he was not to be so lucky. And he accepted it much like he had come to accept this unexpected relationship with a woman, he had regularly told himself since the start, who was clearly out of his league.

Relief washed over Lil. She had told him, at least given him the brochure. The relief flowed from her face down her shoulders, through her relaxed hands, and into him. It was the relief of sharing an unspoken truth and having it embraced when we feared it would not be.

Lil looked into those dependable eyes. It felt good to have some of the truth out there. But after a pause she added, "Well, you could have argued with me, just a little bit."

Russell saw the same twinkle in her eye that had attracted him and so many others to her. He again pulled her close.

Over the next few days, Lil shared her ideas for how she wanted to spend her final months. She compiled a short list of her favorite restaurants, bought tickets for a Broadway show, and selected the half-year subscription option to the Book of the Month Club. Each evening, when Russell returned from work, she would sit down with him and review the plans she had devised during the day. It was on the third night that she floated the idea.

"I would like to embark on a final adventure, a grand tour," Lil introduced.

Choosing to ignore the word final, Russell nodded. His first thought was a cruise to Alaska. "Yes, a grand adventure," he said.

"Europe," Lil said.

Russell's mind immediately flew from Juneau to Paris. "Europe would be very nice," he replied. They had never been to Europe together. He imagined himself on a river boat, taking coffee on the private veranda as they floated from one city to the next.

"The mountains," Lil continued spreading her hand before her as if envisioning the scene.

"Yes, the mountains," Russell reacted, pivoting once again. The Rhine will take you from Basel to Amsterdam.

"Hiking in the Alps!" Lil went on to describe the Tour du Mont Blanc. She excitedly detailed all the towns they would visit, the paths they would take, and the vistas they would see. It was as if she knew the route already.

"Hiking?" was the best he could muster.

Comfort Kit

Debbie's visits were both routine and special. First were some basic vitals, including weight, blood pressure, heart rate, and oxygen levels. Then Debbie would review Lil's diet and sleep log, always paying extra attention to how much water she was drinking. "Water is the Mother's best medicine," she remarked with such frequency that by now Lil had begun to complete the sentence for her – exactly what Debbie had wanted.

After reciting the scripted questions – What has changed since the last visit? How would you rate your pain on a 1–10 scale? How many days have you had little interest or pleasure in doing things? – it was time for the part of the visit Lil looked forward to most: Just sitting and talking.

At the first home visit, Lil made tea. It had since become part of the routine. The ritual had now grown to include some homemade soda bread or a treat from Rene. A spot of tea with bread and jam makes for good conversation, Lil told herself, repeating a favorite phrase from her grandmother.

Lil appreciated Debbie's gift for being both direct and compassionate. Her caregiver's straightforward manner mirrored Lil's approach to her condition. With Debbie, Lil felt free to ask questions—no fear, no hesitation. With each successive visit, Lil increasingly accompanied her questions with more personal reflections. Debbie became the confidante Lil had never had before, and Lil became a communicator she had never been. These two changes were liberating.

"Once you tell them, people forget how to smile," Lil observed. "Like the world has already ended, or they're the ones who are checking out," she added between sips of raspberry zinger. "I finally told Lois after last week's book club. She breaks down. Starts crying. I'm the one who had to hug her to get her settled."

Debbie nodded. "That's the curse of being the strong one, Ms. Lil."

"And then I saw her two days ago at the Fresh Market. She's chatting with another woman, all happy. She sees me and her face falls down. Eyes get watery. Here we go again, I thought," Lil said with a shake of her head. "I just walked by and told her I would see her next week."

"People are funny. And death talk makes 'em funnier. Some'll get all blubbery like Ms. Lois, and others will smother you with sunshine," Debbie counseled with a chuckle.

"That was Sandy. I told her after yoga class," Lil began. "She grabbed my hand. Started patting it. Told me everything will be alright. And then asked if I wanted to go to the flower show next month."

"So what did you tell her?" Debbie inquired with a wry smile.

"Said I would get back to her." Lil laughed. "Thought about saying how it would be a good chance to pick out a floral arrangement for the funeral. But I resisted the temptation."

"That's the thing about death. Sometimes people don't know what to say. Or they want to do something. You know, to fix it or make it better. But there ain't no fix for dying." Debbie offered. "And sometimes they are just plain old afraid. Afraid for you, maybe a little, but mostly afraid for themselves. Those are hard truths to face. Most folks spend their lives running from them, but our path will take us there anyway," Debbie concluded.

Lil took another sip of tea before speaking. "Promise," Lil began solemnly. "You'll be honest with me? No premature clouds or fake sunshine."

"As real as we can be," Debbie replied, looking squarely into Lil's eyes.

So, their compact was set: genuine, honest, and real. Later, as she was walking the Tour, Lil would look back and recognize that Debbie did a better job living up to the terms of their agreement.

It was on this fourth visit that Lil shared her plans for the TMB. "Now that is one crazy-ass idea. You would never catch this woman walking over rocks up the side of a mountain when I could take the bus and see the view just the same," Debbie responded. "Sleeping in a dormitory? I am mighty particular about who I allow in my bedroom, at least most nights," she laughed. "But it sounds like a great idea for you. Knock yourself out, sister. I'll see you when you get back, and you can tell me all about your blisters and snoring strangers."

* * *

Debbie had requested that Russell join them for her next visit. "Though it is early, with your adventure plans coming up, I should go over the E-Kit with you – with both of you."

Though Russell was typically at home during the visits, he told Lil he preferred to "give the girls their space." Lil wondered if there was more to it. But as Debbie had asked, Russell joined the two women for the April appointment.

After the initial routine, Debbie quickly shifted to the primary topic. "Dr. Hsu has prescribed a comfort kit to help manage some of the common symptoms that may occur. As of now, beyond some back pain, occasional nausea, a little weight loss, and some fatigue, Ms. Lil hasn't had many symptoms," – Debbie paused for a quick glance to the heavens – "But it is good to be prepared."

"Let's see what we have in our pharmacy." Debbie spread the contents of the kit onto the kitchen table. "You've got all the meds to help with the big five: Pain, nerves, nausea, plumbing, and juices. Not everybody has all these, and there is no exact time schedule," Debbie instructed, looking over the top of her glasses. "But these five are pretty common. So you have what you need in case a new symptom pops up or a current one gets worse."

Debbie then went over each item individually. "Let's go through the plumbing and nausea first. You've got Compazine to help with nausea. This one is a suppository, so you'll need a little help," she winked at Russell. "Dulcolax is for constipation. Also a suppository. You win again, Russell. And there is a tube of lubricant.

"There are a few options for nerves. You have some Ativan. That'll settle you down. And if you feel yourself getting feisty and anxious, this Haldol is your ticket. They are all clearly labeled and color-coded, so you don't go mixing them up.

"Sometimes your lips may get too dry, so there are sponges and swabs. Just dip 'em in water and swipe it on like your favorite lipstick, or you can dab 'em if you like." Debbie modeled both techniques as she spoke.

"Sometimes your body can't decide between being too dry or too wet. If you get extra secretions in the throat and airway and you feel like you're rattling – that's usually much later on – then you can use the Atropine under the tongue.

"Now for the good stuff. Low-level pain, like a four or a five, you have some super Acetaminophen. Another suppository. And when the pain gets more intense, Mr. Morphine will help you out. That you give orally using this syringe. The usual dose is point two five mils." She handed Russell a syringe and had him practice using a vial of water.

"Keep all these together in the fridge – some are temperature sensitive. And Mr. Russell, sweetheart, remember these are for Ms. Lil," she commented with another wink in his direction.

Debbie then turned her cautious eye toward Lil: "And you should not take these solo. The nausea and plumbing meds you can decide about on your own, but always let Mr. Russell know what you're taking. For the anxiety or pain meds, before you start with those, reach out and call me or the hospice. Russell, you keep a detailed record of what Ms. Lil is taking and when."

"He'll be very good at that," Lil joked.

"And for heaven's sake," she added with a slight wag of her finger, "There are no prizes for being a hero. Don't let the pain get ahead of you. So use them when you need to. Quality of life, remember. The whole idea is to make Ms. Lil as comfortable as possible. Any questions?"

"How do we know when it is time to move to the more serious meds, like the morphine?" Russell asked.

Debbie paused and thought before responding. Her tone changed subtly. "The body has a way of telling you, of preparing you. But the best approach is to reach out to your hospice team. Tell them what is going on, and they will be there to help. Remember, you are not alone. I can also come over. Just make certain you follow their directions. A few drops of morphine may help you sleep easy. The point two five will smooth out the pain. But you do not go to the full syringe."

After a moment of hesitation, Russell added, "How will we know when we are near the end?"

"I'll tell you that," Lil replied.

Debbie smiled lightly, her eyes vacant for a moment. "There are signs. And again, everyone is different. A month or so before, the person may stop their usual activities, eat less and sleep more. And it can be strange, even though they are not eating that doesn't seem to cause any suffering. Me? I miss a meal and I'll be fussing within the hour. Don't eat for a day and I'll be gnawing on your fingers. But for people on the final journey, it's different. It is just the body's way. You don't have to tell a body how to be born; the body knows how to die, too."

Debbie looked at the couple, holding one another's hands. Though they said nothing, their faces told Debbie they wanted to hear more. So she continued.

"For some they may begin to withdraw and not want to see anyone. Others want nothing more than to see all their loved ones. To say goodbye. To tell them how much they love them. And those can be beautiful moments.

"One to two weeks out, often they'll start to sleep more. The blood pressure goes down, temperature drops, breathing gets erratic, they may wet themselves. The skin starts to look paler, even a little blue. Sometimes, arms and legs will twitch, and it can be tough to get comfortable, so they may pick at their sheets or take off their clothes. I had one love, he went full Monty. Didn't matter who was around. Wife said he was always a bit of a show-off, anyway. Took the family a little getting used to, but eventually it was 'Oh well.' Friends and neighbors would come to visit, and it was the oldest child's job to prepare them, just a little bit." Debbie stared into the far corner of the room as if reconstructing the scene and chuckled.

Debbie then refocused on Lil and Russell. "And every once in a while, there is this momentary spurt – like they've been re-energized. I had this one man, Mickey. He looked like he was right at the doorstep. All day long, he was on the couch, not responding too much. His breath was shallow. His wife and kids and grandkids were all in the room together with him. They took turns sitting next to him, rubbing his shoulders, telling him how much they loved him. I had gotten to know them real well and they had called me over. One of the kids had put together a playlist of some of his favorite songs. They had that going in the background. And then all of a sudden, out of nowhere, he sits up, and he starts singing 'Take Me Home Country Roads' by John Denver. It wasn't even on the playlist. Just starts singing acapella. And his family, they start singing along with him. It was beautiful. His wife said, 'Damn, I didn't even know he liked that song.' And the tough part about that? They start thinking he is gonna get better, but when you get this spurt, that's usually a sign we are getting closer. And that is what it was for Mickey. He went back to sleeping and passed the next day at 12:01. The family was with him. And at 12:02 they start singing John Denver again."

"Am I talking too much?" Debbie asked.

"Not at all. This is helpful," Russell replied.

"In the final days and hours the body is actively working on dying. The skin becomes more blotchy, first in the arms and legs and then into the middle. Looks like little rings of color. Lips may start to droop, and eyes stay open. The breathing may even stop for a period of time. You may think the person has passed, only to have them begin breathing again. I had one family, the husband Marco – I think he had a little coochie-coo on the side – his wife, Lily, was the sick one. She looked like she stopped breathing. He went to close her eyelids, you know, the way they do in the movies. Out of nowhere, she goes and swipes his hand away. Scared the bejesus out of him. Gave him the stink eye, too. Now she hung on for another week, just to spite him, I think . . . When all this is happening, not much you can do but be there. And keep talking to them. Let them know they are loved. They say hearing is the last sense to go. I don't know about that. But I do know those words of love can be comforting to those who are staying around."

The three of them sat together for a few moments in silence, each with their own private thoughts.

"Well, I hope that helped a bit. But we have a good bit of time before we sing our final song together," Debbie added. "We can go over all this again when you come back."

"Yes, it is good to be prepared," Russell said.

"Yes, to prepare," Lil added distractedly.

"Amen to that," Debbie responded instinctively. "And when you are ready, it would be good to bring in the rest of the family for some of this conversation. Preparing is good for everyone." Debbie held a steady gaze on Lil even after she had finished her sentence.

"I'll let you know about that," Lil added a few seconds later.

"Yes, right. I'll bring some pamphlets and information you can share to get started. You just let me know if you need me." Debbie said as she exited the home.

Preparations

Russell

After Sophie agreed to join them and confirmed that Luke would also attend, Russell warmed to the idea of the Tour. While not his first choice of location, the prospect made Lil happy, which made Russell happy. She was clearly more excited about the trip than her other plans. And so, as he had for much of their married life, he chose to follow her lead.

Though he and Lil had completed many day hikes, vacationed at some mountain lakes, and even camped in the Presidential Range, he had never gone on a backpacking trek. Prepared, methodical, and precise – those qualities that made him successful in his work, Russell now applied to this trip. He read *The Complete Walker*, some chapters twice, and befriended the Outdoor Adventures associate who had encyclopedic knowledge on the art of tying hiking boot laces. "Who knew it was so complicated?" he confided to her. But YouTube videos had become his go-to resource. And today, with the enthusiasm only found among the newly converted, he was sharing his know-how with Lil.

"Did you know you should put your sleeping bag on the bottom?" Russell shared pointing to an animated graphic he found online.

"Aha," Lil replied flatly, focused on a computer screen of her own.

"It is bulky but can be stuffed in snugly, so it gives your pack a good base," he explained, parroting back the words he had just heard. "The gear you need during the day should be at the top or in the outer pocket so it is easy to get to."

"Makes sense," Lil filled the pause absently.

"The heaviest items should be in the middle of the pack and close to your back. And the lightest stuff at the top. That helps to keep your balance so you don't fall and get hurt."

Lil heard that portion. "No, I wouldn't want to fall and break my neck, now would I," she muttered curtly.

Russell winced, immediately apologizing, "I didn't mean it that way." His apology came out more annoyed than he intended.

"Don't get all knickered. I know you didn't mean it," she said more sympathetically this time. Without taking her eyes off her site, she added, "You keep learning about the zen of packing, and then later this afternoon we can load up and go for a practice walk through the neighborhood," she offered, regretting her bad temper.

Russell knew when he was being placated and accepted it. He clicked on the next video, "How to Check a Backpack for a Flight."

Lil returned to her screen for an answer to her current dilemma: How am I going to keep my morphine below 25 degrees Celsius?

Sophie

The faculty room was empty except for Sophie and Anita. Few teachers had off period 5, and those that did tended to congregate in the social studies office, nicknamed The Fun House, as opposed to Bleak House, the home of the English department.

"So, how's your training going?" Anita asked.

Sophie lifted her eyes from the essay. Anita heard the pen grow silent. Typically, they would simply chat away while continuing to chase down run-on sentences or reconcile subject-verb agreement. Anita looked up to see Sophie smiling. She pushed aside her own pile of term papers and leaned forward, raising her eyebrow and inviting Sophie to say more.

Her friend's patience was one of the many qualities Sophie admired in Anita. She didn't intrude. She would inquire or invite. Sophie felt safe with Anita.

"Pretty well, actually," Sophie said in that tone midway between self-satisfied and embarrassed. With anyone else, she would have said 'not bad' or 'Okay, I guess' and shifted the focus quickly. However, over the years, Anita had transitioned from being a colleague to being a confidante. They discussed all the topics friends do - children and husbands, vacation and money, books and movies, politics, and co-workers. And with Anita, Sophie could also share some of the real she kept hidden from the rest of the world – her resentments after Luke's birth, her irritation with her mother, and all her many inadequacies as a teacher, a spouse, and a parent. Anita was the single friend Sophie had confided in about Rick's addiction.

"I am up to thirty minutes on Jacob's Ladder," Sophie announced. "And my legs aren't nearly as sore," she added proudly.

"Way to go, missy," Anita replied, genuinely impressed. "Remember when you had to stop after three? And you came in here the next day hobbling around like someone had beat you with a bat."

"Yeah, but thirty minutes isn't the same as walking eight hours," Sophie said, reflexively dismissing the praise.

Anita responded with encouragement. "That's true, but you also won't be climbing uphill on all fours the whole day." Anita had a gift for helping people reframe the story in their heads. "Remind me again. What's your target?"

"Forty-five minutes by the end of May. Not there yet," Sophie said, using the magic word she often employed with her students.

"Have I told you how much I admire your determination?" Anita said.

"Enough to start coming to the gym with me?"

"I might have to," Anita replied, pushing her wheelchair away from the table and toward the sink. "You're starting to look all muscly." She returned with a fresh cup of water and a wide grin. "Did you see the way that new math teacher was eyeing you? Looked like he was doing some private calculations."

Sophie smirked back. She had lost five pounds over the past two months.

She did notice she was more toned. In fact, she felt better about her body now than she had in many years. "Too young," she demurred. "But I did catch a Silver Sneakers man at the gym watching me. All sly-like, through the reflection in the mirror," Sophie added. "I smiled at him. He blushed and turned away."

Anita joined her friend's laughter. She took another sip of water before asking, "So, how is Luke doing with all this?"

Luke

It was a warm evening, a rarity in March. Sean sat on an Adirondack chair, caressing the Martin D-35 his aunt had given him in middle school. He had asked Luke to take some shots for his Instagram.

Nobody took better pics than Luke. Luke didn't post much himself, usually five or six a month, but each one quality. His profile had its own aesthetic: a single focus, lots of low light, not much color, and hardly ever any faces. Around school it was known as "the Luke look."

Kids would ask how he got such "wicked good pictures." Luke would shrug it off as "just lucky." It was anything but. He had been playing with ISO and aperture settings as long as he could remember. Though his phone had a dope camera, he would only use that with Stories. For anything in his Feed, he always used his A7S3. Always edited in Lightroom. And always uploaded at max res. Recently, people started asking him to take pictures that they would add to their own Feeds. Occasionally, he agreed. If it were a good friend like Sean, he would do it for free. Sean was his only good friend. For others, he would charge fifty bucks an image. It was a pretty good side gig. He was banking the money for an even better camera.

"Have you talked to Nikki yet? Or at least texted her," Sean asked.

"Move the chair over here," Luke replied, ignoring his friend's question. The backyard sloped down away from the house. Luke was pointing to a level spot about ten feet from the bottom of the hill. Sean threw him a look and clawed a diminished chord. He then placed his guitar back in its case and obediently moved the chair.

With the camera in hand, Luke lay on the ground to check the composition. The chair was cupped in the negative space between the distant mountains to the left and the rising slope of the backyard on the right. Perfect, he thought to himself. Wearing a satisfied smile, he stood up again. "Now we wait," he said, still ignoring the question.

Sean accepted the delay. He had heard his friend's lectures about the "golden hour" many times before. He retrieved his guitar, placed it next to the chair, and sat down again. He pulled out a joint from his harmonica case and lit up. He knew his friend wouldn't take a hit, so he didn't ask. Luke knew Sean wouldn't stop, so he didn't press.

Sean had been smoking since middle school. His parents considered themselves enlightened and didn't object. Besides, they smoked more often than Sean did. Their only rules were "No Using Before School. No Buzzed Driving. Know your Source. Don't Disrespect the High."

Luke had tried pot several times in eighth grade, but the habit never took. "Luke's too much in love with his body," Marley, Sean's sister, teased. She was partly correct. He did obsess over his body and liked the way it looked and felt. But more truthfully, he was afraid. His dad's experience had frightened him. Instead, Luke found distraction, however fleeting, elsewhere.

"So, things better with Momma Sophie?" Sean asked after a few inhales.

"What do you think?" Luke replied. Sean was about to answer when Luke continued. "She keeps asking me to go on hikes. 'Good practice,'" he said, mocking her tone. "I keep blowing her off. Last weekend she asked again for like the tenth time. Pissed me off. I told her, 'You don't listen. I don't want to go on any of your effin hikes.' She hasn't said anything since then." Luke's mouth twisted into a broken smile.

Sean was nodding slowly. Thinking.

"What?" Luke said quickly.

"You gotta chill more. Cut Sophie a break. She's been through a lot." He paused. "You too." Another pause. "You need each other." Sean spoke with the freedom he had earned from staying at his friend's side forever.

Luke listened, shaking his head. "I want your mother," Luke said eventually.

"Hey, I told you before. Stop jonesin' on Momma Robin, you pervert," Sean replied.

Luke laughed and lifted his head. His mellow friend had once again pulled Luke out of his deepening funk. "The light," Luke announced. "We got fifteen good minutes – max."

Sean put down the joint and picked up the Martin. He adjusted his trilby to sit lower on his forehead and started playing. Once Sean closed his eyes, Luke knew it was time.

He started with a low angle, lying on the ground the way he had initially composed the shot. A few F-stops down, Sean became layers of shadow against the fading light of the sky. A money shot, for sure! Luke took a dozen other wide angles, as Sean had requested before he changed lenses. He much preferred a shallow depth of field. The story is in the details, Luke told himself, repeating a favorite mantra from *The Essence of Photography.* He maxed the shutter speed to freeze the vibration of the strings. He blew open the iris to highlight the tension in Sean's fingers on the fretboard. Sixty more images over the next ten minutes, some shot from the hip, others carefully calculated. He was about to wrap when his eye jumped wide: The night sky reflected off the lacquered finish on the guitar's body. Luke framed the shot through the guitar strings. It looked like all the colors of the world were imprisoned. Click. One shot. He was done.

Sean kept playing. It was another three minutes before he realized Luke was no longer shooting. "All finished?" he asked, slightly embarrassed at not having noticed sooner.

"Talent doesn't take long," Luke replied smugly.

Sensing his friend was in a better mood, Sean risked the topic again. "So, are you going to talk to Nikki?" Pause. "Don't do another Katie, dude."

Medicinal, Of Course

On several occasions during the two weeks since Debbie's last visit, Russell had woken in the middle of the night only to find Lil down in the kitchen. "Just can't get back to sleep, that's all," she would tell him.

At their May visit with Dr. Hsu, three weeks before their trip, Russell raised the topic. To his surprise, Lil did not deny it. She spoke about her trouble getting and staying asleep, as well as a growing feeling of anxiety. The insomnia left her tired during the day, and she was worried about the Tour. Lil knew that a good night's sleep would be essential. Walking for hours each day would be tiring enough. Dr. Hsu mentioned the Ativan but Lil was reluctant to move to the meds.

"Too soon," Lil said.

"Chapter 86 gives us another option," Dr. Hsu offered.

* * *

Debbie brought the stash to the next home visit. "Honey, as the great spiritual teachers have taught us, it is all about the mind-body connection. The belly starts to roll, and we can't get comfortable no matter how we curl up. Soon, our mind takes us to a million places, and none of them are good. That's why the good doc prescribes you these," Debbie added.

Beyond some occasional weed while in college, Lil had never been inclined toward recreational drugs. Over the recent decades, her mind-altering experiences were limited to wine with a meal and Advil laced with codeine when she broke her ankle.

Debbie proved a capable teacher. "Nowadays, you have a choice. You can smoke it or eat it. Hell, you can even vaporize it or dab it on your skin like some happy perfume. Whatever rings your bell, sister Lil."

"I'm going old school on this one. Let's light it up," Lil smiled.

"You go, girl," Debbie replied with a high-five. She set to breaking the bud and rolling the joint. "Remember, short breath to start, hold it and exhale slowly. You gotta walk before you fly."

After a few gasps, Lil was off. She offered the joint to Debbie.

With a squinty eye and a downturned brow, Debbie waved a hand. "No can do. I am a professional, and I am on duty. But I will stay here and model deep breathing for you."

Their laughter caught Russell's attention. He wandered by the open door, saw the bluish haze, recognized the smell, and moved on to the kitchen. As he drew his own deep breath, he thought about how good it was to hear Lil laugh. The feeling soon faded as he caught himself wondering how many more times he would hear that sound.

"Now you get whatever kind you want. A lot of patients with cancer like Cinderella Ninety-Nine. Sometimes it goes by C99," Debbie shared.

Lil appreciated how Debbie didn't avoid the word. Cancer. It is what she had. You can't hide. You can't duck. You just have to face it.

"Dutch Haze is another good one for nausea. Me, I am partial to Purple Kush. It makes me think of Prince," she added with a wink. She started singing, "Little Red Corvette." She was surprised when Lil joined her for the chorus, "Baby, you're much too fast."

Lil gave her a hug and held the squeeze for a moment longer. Lil had grown fond of her in the short time she had known Debbie. It is not uncommon for the client to grow attached to their palliative provider. Dying gives birth to a complicated web of emotions. The journey has moments of intimacy found in few other life events. However, the connection between these two women was more than caregiving and information. Despite their differences in age and circumstances there was a bond, a genuine sisterhood.

"Oh, let me breathe now, mother. It is time for me to go," Debbie joked as she grasped the hands that had just released her shoulders. "I've gotta go feed Ms. Bellyache her soup and change her diaper." As she stood up, Debbie said, "We have two more visits before you wander off on your foolishness and leave me all alone with Bellyaches and Boneyhands." Debbie never used the real names of her clients, relying instead on pseudonyms that belied her affection. "Is there anything you want to cover before you leave?"

Lil was prepared. "Well, yes," she began. "I was just wondering how I could keep my meds at the right temperature. With all the changes in elevation, some places will be quite warm, and other spots will be below freezing. And not all the huts have electricity. I just wouldn't want the meds to go bad."

"Oh, honey, don't worry about that. You won't need the whole kit. You ain't that close," Debbie added with a nod. "You can leave most of it at home. If you take your favorite flavor here and carry that prescription, you'll live the high life in those mountains."

"Still, I would just feel better if I had it with me," Lil replied with a steely smile.

Debbie's right eye narrowed. With a short intake of breath she added, "Well, I'll think on that." She released Lil's hand. After a quick final hug, she walked toward the door. As she turned the handle, Debbie also turned toward Lil and asked a prepared question of her own. "Any decisions on how you are going to tell the rest of the family?"

Lil shook her head. And for the second time in two minutes, Debbie's eyes narrowed. Debbie added, "I am here for you. You let me know how I can help." With that, she closed the door and moved on to her next client.

Goodbyes

Sophie

It was Anita who had suggested a therapist. "Helped me out with my adjustment to the chair," she had confided when she had handed Sophie the sheet with a dozen names and numbers. "The secret is to find a good match and to give it some time."

Initially, Sophie held on to the list and did nothing. It was after another ugly blow-up with Luke, the night she said, "I can't take this anymore," or maybe it was, "I can't take you anymore." She wasn't sure. But she saw the anger, the hurt, the fear behind his eyes. And she was sure she didn't know what to do. That was three months after the funeral.

She had clicked with Christi from the start. And just in time. The first two she tried – no spark. She was about to give up but then the school called. The teachers had noticed some changes and wanted to schedule a meeting, an intervention, with the Student Assistance Team. Sophie had panicked. God, I can't lose him too, she remembered thinking. She called the last name on the list, Christi, and was able to schedule an appointment for the following day. They had been meeting for more than a year. Every week at first. Now, every other week. I am making progress, Sophie told herself. And unlike when she first tried that on, she now believed it.

"Well, your trip is a week away. I admire all the work you've put into preparing. And not just physically but emotionally, too," Christi said about midway through the hour.

49

"I am proud of myself, too," Sophie responded after a brief hesitation. Positive self-affirmation still did not come easily.

"Let's try some more role plays," Christi suggested. "For the first one, you provide the trigger, and I will practice the mindful response. Then we can switch it up. Ready?"

Sophie took two relaxing breaths and began.

Sophie-as-Lil: *You're late.*

Christi-as-Sophie: *I know I am late, and I am also disappointed. The conductor said there was some unexpected trackwork.*

Sophie-as-Lil: *Always an excuse (mumble, mumble). This wouldn't have happened if you had taken the earlier train like I suggested.*

Christi-as-Sophie: *Well, I am glad I am here now. And I am looking forward to spending some time with you.*

"That was good," Christi said with a clap. "A Golden Globe for each of us! Now, let's unpack it."

Sophie offered her quick analysis. "Typical micro-aggression from Lil," she began.

Christi nodded and whispered, "A micro-aggression from your mom."

Sophie smiled at the subtle coaching and continued. "You-as-me Acknowledge the Facts and Identify the Emotion. You don't take the bait and instead focus on a Positive Future."

"Well done!" Christi said. "I like how you named the techniques. That's a sign you are making them your own."

"Specific Praise," Sophie teased her therapist.

Christi smiled and patted her heart. "Now let's switch and do another. You be you, and I'll be Luke."

Christi-as-Luke: *I don't want to be here. I never wanted to take this trip.*

Sophie-as-Sophie: *I know you didn't want to. But I am so very grateful that you are here with me. I do feel guilty forcing you to come along.*

Christi-as-Luke: *Then why did you make me?*

Sophie-as-Sophie: *Well, your grandmother isn't going to be around forever. I thought it would be good . . . wait, that's not it . . . I was. No, I am afraid. The idea of being alone with my mom for the whole week . . . I get panicky . . . And I am afraid for us . . . to lose you.*

Christi-as-Luke: *You can't make me like it.*

Sophie-as-Sophie: *I know. (long pause) I love you.*

Christi rubbed Sophie's upper arm. "Unpack," she said softly.

"Luke Repeated his Script. I used a Gratitude Response and then took an Emotional Risk," Sophie began. "You know, to try and Break the Pattern," she explained.

Her therapist nodded encouragingly. "I noticed you changed direction in the middle. What was your thinking?" Christi asked.

Sophie smiled sheepishly. "That line about Lil not being around forever. Too much like emotional blackmail. Definitely not compassionate communication. Besides, it was a distractor, not the real issue."

"What were you most proud of in your simulation?" Christi asked.

"That I told him . . . that I loved him," Sophie said with a pained look stretching across her face.

Christi grabbed two tissues and gave one to Sophie. "I think you are ready to embark on this journey. That is both my professional judgment and my personal opinion. And before we finish for tonight, I want to challenge you with one final thought."

Sophie shifted in her chair, sitting up straighter. Christi would often end with homework – a specific skill to practice or task to complete over the next two weeks. But there was something in the therapist's tone that sounded different.

"Over the past few months, when talking about your mother, you have used the word 'anchor.' It has come up over and over. How she is a weight pulling you down. How she keeps you tethered. Unable to move on. You've connected this to your dreams of drowning, of being swallowed. That is all good work and important insights. My challenge to you is to explore this symbol a little more."

Sophie started to sweat. She lifted her arms away from her side and pushed back in her chair. "What do you mean?" she said as both a question and a delay.

"Words we use over and over, those are important words. Often with layers of meaning. This time together with your mother may give you a chance to consider some other facets to an anchor. May be worthwhile. May not. You'll decide. We can talk about it when you return," Christi shrugged.

Luke

Luke pulled on his board shorts and tied the laces at his waist. Nikki was still on the blanket in the grass.

"I am glad you called," Nikki said with a cautious look up. "Anyway, it is good to be back together now," she added when Luke said nothing.

She stood up, approached Luke, and draped her arms across his shoulders. "Two weeks is a long time. I wish you didn't have to go."

"Me too," he said.

"I will miss you," Nikki said expectantly.

Luke nodded. It was an acknowledgment, he told himself. Not a lie.

He reached down to pick up the blanket, and his mind stuck on the similarities between this evening and two nights ago with Katie. I'm such a dick, he told himself.

Lil

June was to be Debbie's final visit with Lil before the trip. The flight to Geneva would depart in a few days, and the return was scheduled for two weeks after that.

Debbie and Lil proceeded through the usual checks. Though she was down another two pounds, her vital signs—blood pressure, heart rate, temperature, and respirations—were generally good.

"Not bad for a dying lady, huh?" Lil added.

"I'll give you five of my pounds if you'll give me your blood pressure," Debbie replied.

After reviewing her food log, Debbie commented, "Damn woman. That's an awful lot of pasta and cheese."

"Just getting in shape. All that walking will eat up those calories."

"Well, you can still afford to drink a little more water. That'll help keep everything moving and soft." They laughed together.

"Oh, I brought you something, Ms. Lil." She reached into her bag and removed the gift. "Now, this is usually for insulin, but it should work fine. It has a little digital reading here, so you can always tell what the temperature is. S'posed to keep things cool for up to thirty hours. And then you have to refreeze these," Debbie added, pointing to the removable gel packs. "Ms. Blue Toes swears by this and says it never let her down. I also got you a couple of these cold packs if you get lost for a few days and can't find a fridge – just crack 'em open and pop 'em in."

Lil smiled broadly and cradled the gift with both hands. "You are precious, my friend. And it is purple!"

"Purple is the color of strong women, my gram always said," Debbie explained with a wistful look.

Lil looked into her friend's eyes, inviting her to say more.

"She's how I got into caregiving, you know," Debbie ventured. "We were always close. She had lupus for as long as I had known her. But she never complained. Then, in her final year, when the cancer bit her, she came to live with us. You wouldn't know to look at her that she was dying – she kept busy, cleaning, going to church, ministering to others. I was named after her, you know: Big Debbie and Little Debbie. I would go along with her, keep her company, help her out, watch over her.

"That final year, the only time she would get testy is when people would say to her, 'Mother Johnson, slow down! Mother Johnson, you can't do that! Mother Johnson, why don't you relax and rest?' She would flash them the cold eye and say, 'I got plenty of time for dying, it is the living hours that are in short supply.' And she would tell me, 'Snack Cake, if they try to stop me, you best get out of my way, 'cause I will bring them down.' She was a powerful little woman. And I always remember her in purple.

"The last thing I remember her saying to me was 'thank you for walking the final miles with me. You have been a gift.' That's when I knew my calling: to accompany souls on their final miles."

Lil nodded and raised her cup of water: "Here's to strong women."

Debbie joined the toast.

Lil lowered the glass to the table and placed the purple cooler case on her lap. The two women shared the silence.

Lil spoke first, reaching out her hands. "You've been good for me, my friend. I will miss you."

Hearing the meaning behind the words, Debbie clasped Lil's outstretched hands. When the first tear escaped, she pulled Lil close and held her tightly.

"I am not going to see you again, am I, Ms. Lil?" she whispered.

"The living hours are in short supply," Lil replied. "Thank you for walking the final miles with me."

They released one another and looked into the face of a friend. At the same moment, the tight line across their lips relaxed into a warm smile. Without another word, Debbie packed her equipment and passed through the door for the last time.

II

Part Two

The Tour

Day 1

L il rose from bed at 5:32 AM. The wooden planks creaked as she walked to the east-facing window and quietly opened the shade. The early rays from the still-hidden sun snuck into their room. Lil cast her eyes upward. Faint traces of the brightest stars were visible in the cloudless sky. It would be a gorgeous day for hiking! Russell scratched his head and rolled over.

Ten minutes later, seated at the small wooden table and fully dressed, she heard Russell climb out of bed and shuffle to the bathroom, his feet sounding as if they never left the floor.

Lil placed her hands on her knees to stop the tapping of her own feet. She closed her eyes and took her morning inventory. There were her usual companions. An ache in her back – "That's the tumors pressing against your spine," Dr. Hsu had told her. Some low-level nausea – "background noise," Lil called it. Her muscles and breath felt encouragingly strong. Her body was not the source of her anxiety this morning.

She and Russell had flown into Geneva two days earlier. They spent the time exploring the city on foot, enjoying the cobblestone streets and the long walks along the lake. Their bus ride from Geneva to Les Houches was uneventful, and they arrived in the village by midmorning yesterday, rested and ready. The worry arrived later with Sophie and Luke.

Lil had repeatedly suggested to Sophie that she and Luke should arrive two days before the start of the hike. "No," Sophie was steadfast, "graduation and in-service." The day before was the best she could do. First, the flight to Paris was delayed. Then, they missed the morning train to St. Gervais les

Bains. It was 9:25 PM before mother and son finally arrived at the hotel. Lil's plans for a relaxing dinner to celebrate the start of their adventure turned into a curt exchange. Sophie began with a preemptive parry. "I know. We should have left earlier." Luke mumbled a hello while pressing past his mother. He added something about "getting to bed" and "a big day" before he disappeared into an adjacent room.

Lil had determined not to say anything about Sophie's poor flight planning – it reminded her too much of past conversations with her daughter. Yes, she had thought about it and repeatedly mentioned it to Russell. But she desperately wanted this trip to be different from the past. Yet last night it was like her daughter could read her mind. "That's because," Russell had told her before going to bed, "it was written on your face."

Russell emerged from the bathroom, his hair still damp with tufts pointing in a dozen different directions. It was just after six. Lil was eager to put last night's awkward start behind her and get to the trail. "Do you think they are up yet?" she asked, rising from her chair.

The squint in Russell's eye told her the truth she already knew. "I wouldn't count on it," he said diplomatically. "I know you are ready, pumpkin. But I wouldn't expect them until seven or well after."

Lil sat back down, folded her hands in her lap, and exhaled slowly.

"And you know that boy will want to eat," Russell said, playing on his wife's sympathy for her grandson. "Why don't we walk to the market? We can come back here and make them breakfast. That will save some time not having to go to the restaurant."

Lil nodded and tossed her half-dressed husband his jacket. Five minutes later, they were walking east along l'Avenue des Alpages toward the Super-U. Even at this early hour, they passed a few dozen hikers heading in the opposite direction toward the trailhead in La Fouilly.

Lil's first thought was that everyone else was starting, and here we were heading in the wrong direction. Then she caught herself. Instead, she imagined Sophie and Luke sitting down to their surprise breakfast, with Luke enjoying a second helping of bacon. "Can't go wishing away the minutes," she said aloud. She wasn't certain if Russell heard her. But he was smiling.

They arrived at the market ten minutes before it opened. Russell feared he might have to talk her off the ledge. But to his surprise, Lil took the delay in stride. They sat down together on a bench. Lil wrapped her arm beneath her husband's and pressed his hand into her lap.

"Fourteen miles, huh?" Russell said, referring to the distance to the first hut in Les Contamines.

"Yup, but it is the elevation gain that'll really get you," Lil added with a twinkle. "Four thousand five hundred feet." She had meticulously planned the route and even included some alternative transportation options should her body start to flag. While the Tour was a hiking adventure, on most of the paths, you were never too far from a town or village where a quick hop on a bus, taxi, train, or gondola might save you several arduous hours. This was her backup plan. Lil hoped not to use them, but she had thoroughly prepared.

"I was really hoping we were going on a riverboat cruise," Russell mused, kissing her lightly on her cheek.

At 6:59, a middle-aged woman opened the door with an enthusiastic "Bonjour." The small crowd that had gathered entered the village market.

Lil dispatched Russell to get a warm baguette. She sped through the produce aisle, grabbing eggs, mushrooms, an onion, and a pepper. Even with adding three-quarters of a pound of thick-sliced bacon and a half-stick of butter, she still managed to be first in line at the check-out. They left the market at 7:05, were back at the hotel at 7:20, and the bacon was sizzling at 7:35. Strategically, Lil had left their door partially open.

Within five minutes, there was a light knock. Lil saw a sliver of her grandson in the gap between the door and the frame. Russell waved him in.

"I smell bacon," Luke said, smiling. He ran his hands through his mop of brown hair as he entered the room. He was barefoot, wearing black joggers and a t-shirt from swimming sectionals. A light scruff dotted his face, too sparse to call a beard but still noticeable. He kissed his grandmother on the top of her head and had to bend slightly at the waist to do so.

Lil thought he had gotten taller since she had last seen him and paused to think how long ago that had been. Three months, or was it four or perhaps more? "Sit down," Lil said in a jovial tone. "But save some bacon for your mother."

"She doesn't eat bacon," Luke said. "She would want me to have hers," he added, placing six strips on his plate before reaching for the eggs and bread.

"Save some for me then," Russell added.

"Better hurry," Luke replied. "That pig is flying off the table, and it is survival of the fastest."

Gone was the sullen teen from last night. Seated before her now was the grandson she remembered. Whether a good night's sleep or the crisp bacon was responsible, she did not know. Either way, she was grateful. For the time being, Lil forgot about the late start.

Sophie entered the room 15 minutes later wearing a blank expression with a trace of caution. For a brief moment, Luke and Sophie locked eyes, a wordless exchange Lil did not know quite how to interpret. Russell caught the shadow of pleading eyes flicker across Luke's face.

"Good morning," Sophie managed in a neutral tone as she entered the room. She squeezed her father's hand warmly and sat beside Luke.

"Sorry, Mom, Russell ate all the bacon," Luke lied with a broad smile as he passed his mother a largely empty plate with bacon crumbs and a piece of bread. Luke mimed his mother's response as she replied, "I don't like bacon anyway."

Lil, who was stationed near the stove, added a small omelet to Sophie's plate. It was perfectly crafted with the slices of pepper and mushrooms distributed expertly across the top.

Though Lil felt the minutes ticking away, she savored this moment. The silent truce, fortified by the morning breakfast, held. No one mentioned the late flight, the missed dinner, or the testy emotions—these events were added to the mountain of the unspoken past as if, for the time being, they had never happened.

It was Russell who ended the feast. "Enough of this lollygagging, we've got some hiking to do. Lil's been ready to go for four hours," he said with only slight exaggeration. "Meet you outside in fifteen minutes."

"We'll be there in ten," Sophie responded with a nod at her mom. She stood, grabbed Luke by his upper arm, and headed to the door. Luke reached back to swipe the last piece of bread.

Lil and Russell quickly cleaned the dishes, grabbed their packs, and made it outside in fifteen minutes. To their surprise, Luke and Sophie were waiting for them, their packs already hoisted on their backs.

As his grandparents approached, Luke dipped his head, cast his eyes over the top of his Rayban sunglasses, and pointed to his watch. Russell reached for the object hanging from the strap across his neck and put on the identical pair of sunglasses. "Nice shades," Russell remarked as he walked by his grandson.

On this first day, they took their first steps at 9:05. According to the guidebook, they would arrive at Les Contamines eight hours later.

The route followed a road, Le Rue D'Essert, for the first mile. Lil and Russell were in front, walking side-by-side with Sophie and Luke in line behind them. Compared to the steady stream Lil and Russell had observed two hours earlier, the flow of trekkers was down to a trickle. They encountered more cars than people.

Russell had his phone in his hand. He had downloaded the route into AllTrails, an app he purchased a few weeks ago and had used during some of their recent training hikes. It displayed the entire Tour as a red line superimposed over a topographical map, along with dozens of side trails designated by dashes.

Russell held the screen in front of Lil as they walked. "See, there we are," Russell said, pointing to the blue dot that traced their location using the cell phone's GPS signal. "Right on the red line!"

Lil tugged on his left arm to prevent him from walking into a telephone pole. "You'll be a red line when you walk out in traffic, my intrepid navigator."

"Just wait until we get in the mountains and arrive at a fork in the path with no sign to guide you. We'll see who's laughing then," Russell replied with a good-natured wag of his finger. "We are going to keep that blue dot happily dancing on the red line."

Luke scanned the occasional storefronts. He wasn't exactly sure what to expect but this wasn't it. He hadn't done any research. The guidebook his grandmother sent him sat unopened in his bedroom back home. By the end of the first mile he was already bored. This is overrated, he thought to himself. This town is lame. Nothing's open. It doesn't even have traffic lights. He reached for his phone. No signal. He was only able to see the photos he had already viewed twice earlier today: a party at the lake. Sean playing his guitar in front of a bonfire. Nikki blowing a kiss. The swim team posing at the edge of the pool. Only this time he didn't smile or laugh. He couldn't comment or post back. He shifted the weight of his pack on his back. The straps were digging into his shoulders. This truly sucks, he concluded barely fifteen minutes in on the first day.

Sophie walked in silence. Despite the six-hour time difference she wasn't tired. She was excited. As she placed one foot in front of the other, a realization slowly emerged. At first, it was faint. Just a hint of something she had slowly lost, something that, in her darkest moments, she feared she might never find again or, worse, didn't deserve. Walking this street, thousands of miles from the familiar, uncertain about what was around the bend, the feeling announced itself. She felt confident. She felt good. I can do this, she told herself. She laughed aloud at the irony: It was her mother's invitation that brought her to this moment.

They passed a sign welcoming them to Le Fouilly. Russell announced, "The blue dot says we should be heading left soon."

"Like where that sign says," Sophie replied, pointing at a directional arrow with the engraved TMB symbol affixed to a large wooden post.

Luke let loose of his sour mood long enough to laugh at his grandfather.

"We start going up from here," Lil said. So far the grade had been largely flat. She knew that the climb over the next six miles would take them just shy of 6000 feet, about the same distance from the bottom to the rim of the Grand Canyon, but Lil didn't mention that. "This would be a good time to take out your sticks and tighten up."

What is she talking about? Luke wondered. He then watched his grandmother remove her hiking poles from the strap on the side of her backpack. Flipping two latches, she extended the three telescoping sections and locked them in place. Hunching her shoulders, her pack rose slightly, and she cinched the waist strap so it sat tight on her hips. She then pulled down on the straps that lay along the front of her shoulder pads, drawing the body of the pack closer to her back. Finally, she reached over the top of her pack, found the small straps, and pulled them forward, bringing the top of the bag closer to her. This reduced any backward sway that might cause her to lose her balance.

Russell and Sophie followed suit and completed the same sequence of adjustments. Luke just stood there.

Lil approached her grandson. "Didn't you read any of the articles I sent you?"

"Been busy," he said with a smile and a flick of his hair.

Lil smiled back before adjusting his straps herself. He rolled his eyes, but when she was done he did admit to himself that the pack felt better. With the weight sitting more on his hips, his shoulders weren't so sore.

"Are you gonna use your poles?" Lil asked.

"Don't need no canes. I'm not an old man," he said, nodding toward Russell and starting up the path to his left.

Luke's return to good humor was short-lived. The path cut through a residential neighborhood, much of it on paved roads. All of it was uphill. The macadam carved a series of curves into the hillside as they passed houses and yards and then open fields. Behind him, Luke could hear the incessant tap-tap-tap of the hiking poles striking the road. After fifteen minutes, the fields gave way to a band of trees that marked the edge of the village. Luke stopped in the shade cast by a tall oak. His shoulders were starting to get sore again. With a shrug, he shifted his pack and tightened his straps. Tap, tap, tap. Lil and Russell continued past with just a nod. As Sophie neared, his mother reached out to touch his shoulder. The look on her face silently asked the question mothers have been asking for millennia: Are you okay? Luke's wordless response was equally clear. Sophie withdrew her hand and moved on.

Russell could feel the beads of sweat dripping down his face. His shirt was already soaked. He didn't remember this from his YouTube videos. Sophie felt the thumping of her heart beating in her chest. She checked the app on her watch: 135 bps – the rate she typically hit when running. She had removed her puffer jacket when they had begun the climb in La Fouilly. She stopped again to now unzip and remove the lower portion of her pants. Lil didn't notice her perspiration or her heart. Her mind was in another place.

For the next mile, the footpath alternated between fields and trees. What didn't change was the ascent – an average 20 percent grade with an elevation gain of 1000 feet. It was not technically difficult – they would encounter far more challenging terrain later in the Tour. It was more the timing. These were the first miles on the first day before their legs were accustomed to walking for hours, before their lungs adjusted to the thinner air, and, most importantly, before their minds knew what to expect. The start of the Tour has a way of humbling the ill-prepared or inexperienced. While the TMB has many surprises and pleasures, they must be earned.

There was also a noticeable absence of distractions. Once leaving La Fouilly, they had been on the trail for more than an hour before they encountered any other hikers. A young couple had stopped at a turn in the path. They were propped against a large boulder, their packs at their feet, and they shared a look of distress on their faces.

They seem so sad, Russell thought to himself. "Good morning," he said with a warm smile. "Nice day for a walk; just wish some of it was downhill."

The woman managed a light laugh between her labored breaths. "Got that right," she replied. After a pause, she added, "We didn't think it would be this tough."

"First days are the worst," Lil added. "It will get easier after you get your hiking legs."

"How long does that take?" the young man asked.

"Two or three days," Lil replied as she headed back up the path.

The man let out an audible gasp.

Russell sought to comfort the distraught hiker and showed them the AllTrails map on his cell phone. "Look, we are right here," he said, pointing to the blue dot. "La Chalette is about a mile further. It's a snack bar. That'll be a good place to rest and get something to eat."

As Luke, who had been a hundred yards behind, overheard the conversation, two thoughts jumped to his mind: That guy looks worse than I feel, and, more importantly, did Russell just say food? With a rush of energy, he passed by his grandfather and his mother and caught up with Lil.

"Russell said there is a restaurant just ahead," Luke said.

"That's true," Lil replied.

And after she offered no further comment, Luke asked, "Well, are we gonna stop?"

"If you want to," she said.

Damn right, I want to, he thought. It came out as "HeYa," and with a newfound motivation, Luke picked up his pace and put some distance between himself and his grandmother. After four additional switchbacks and what seemed like more than a mile, Luke began to doubt Russell and the blue dot.

For much of the morning, Luke had been hearing the clang of bells. At first, he thought of church. But as they climbed higher and the number of buildings grew fewer, that didn't make sense. Now, there was a virtual chorus, some ringing sharp and crisp at a steady cadence, others providing a dull thunk at erratic intervals. As he rounded the fourth switchback, he found the source. Spread across the hillside to his left were a dozen or more cows, each with a bell strapped along its neck. And low on the slope, just beyond the three-stranded wire fence, stood a massive black bull. The collar around its neck was easily eight inches wide, made of tooled leather, and embroidered with strands of edelweiss. The thick bell draped beneath his neck was the size of a pumpkin. What struck Luke the most were the short curved horns protruding from the stoic head. A mottled black at the base of the horn gave way to a cloudy white along the curve before switching back to black at the tip.

Luke looked into the face of the animal. "You are one massive creature, Ferdinand," he said aloud while he fumbled for his cell phone. He stepped toward the fence turning the camera back and forth from landscape to portrait to better fill the frame. The flicker of the sunlight off the glass screen startled the bull. The animal snorted, squared to face Luke, and, with unexpected quickness, charged to the edge of the fence. The bell around its neck clanged furiously. Now, it was Luke who was frightened. As the face of the bull filled the screen of the phone, Luke fell backward, and the phone flew from his hand.

When Lil, Russell, and Sophie rounded the turn, they saw Luke seated in the field about five feet off the path. His legs were spread out in front of him, and he was leaning against his pack. The bull's head was pressed between two wire strands of the fence. It could have easily pushed its 2000-pound body through the barrier, but the beast seemed satisfied with the outcome. As the others approached, the bull slowly withdrew its head and sauntered up the hillslope.

"That thing almost ate me," Luke stammered as Lil and Sophie approached.

"What did you do to upset the peace?" his grandmother asked.

"Nothing. I was just taking its picture," Luke replied. "And then it got all pissed off and went John Wick on me."

His mother and grandmother each took hold of one arm and helped pull him to his feet.

"Did anyone see my . . ." Luke started to ask as Russell approached, holding out Luke's phone, which he had found in the nearby grass.

"Well, let's see what you got, Mr. Halsman," Russell teased, encouraging Luke to show them the picture. At the start of the three-second live photo, the bull stands motionless. It then turns quickly and bursts forward. At that point, the sky moves, the ground bounces, and the image comes to rest on a clump of green grass. The audio was even better: "Look here, pretty" – snorting bull – clanking bell – 'Ah fuck.'

Luke's face turned bright red. Around his friends, he was no stranger to foul language. In fact, he had a reputation as a creative curser. However, he tried not to swear in front of adults, especially his family.

"Now that is precious," Russell concluded with a laugh. "Send it to me so I can post it on my Instagramp."

"No can do. I'm deleting that one," Luke lied, planning to post it to his own account should he ever be able to connect to the internet.

"Let's get going," Lil interrupted. "I'm hungry, and if I am not mistaken, I smell food. And no more upsetting large animals," she added.

They set off, Russell and Lil in front. Sophie walked protectively next to Luke and occasionally glanced back toward the fenced pasture to ensure they were not being followed by a bull with a grudge. They turned the first corner. They did not see any buildings, yet the teasing smells announced they were close.

With each step, they inhaled deeply, this time not from fatigue. Each person focused on a different scent.

"Do you smell that bread?" Sophie asked.

"I smell chocolate," Russell offered.

Luke registered grilled meat and, in an urge that was part hunger and part retribution, announced, "I want a bullburger dripping with cheese."

"Just get me to the coffee," Lil said.

After the next bend, they spied the source of their delight. In front of them was a one-level wood and stone building. A curl of smoke drifted from a chimney in its center. A dozen picnic tables, each with a blue umbrella, were scattered across a terrace. Though they had encountered less than a handful of hikers up to this point, the cafe was bustling. Most of the tables were taken. They made their way to a corner of the terrace, set their backpacks next to the chairs, and joined the queue stretching out the front door.

It was 11:30. They had been on the trail for about two and a half hours. In that time they had covered three miles and gained 3300 feet in elevation, about the height of two World Trade Centers. Though they had not reached the midpoint of the day's hike and were still three miles away from Col de Tricot, the highest elevation for today, they wordlessly agreed now was a good time for lunch and a rest.

Despite his initial instinct for a burger, Luke noticed several other patrons with an oversized plate of spaghetti swimming in a light sauce abundantly decorated with grated cheese. Suddenly, all he could think of was the pasta parties with the swim team. "I'm loading with the carbs," he said as he ordered the pasta carbonara with chicken. Russell chose the ham sandwich on a croissant by enthusiastically pointing at the plate of the person in front of him. Sophie selected carrot, avocado, and *reblochon salad à l'orange*, only partly because she thought she could pronounce it; it also looked good. Lil requested *le soupe aux cailloux*.

They returned to the table and quickly set upon their food. "This is really good," Sophie proclaimed. "I wasn't sure what to expect, being up in the mountains away from the villages. Will all the places be this good?" she ventured to ask.

"Mostly," Lil offered with a confident nod. "You are in France, love. Say what you want, but the French know how to cook."

Luke hadn't said much. His concentration was focused on ensuring none of the noodles slipped off his fork. His ears perked up when he heard a jumble of enthusiastic voices. Lifting his eyes, he saw a group approach the terrace, a mix of boys and girls who looked about his age. Each carried the same pack with a "World Quest" logo embroidered on the back.

Luke looked around the rest of the tables. He did a quick tally: Four couples in their twenties or thirties; he couldn't exactly tell. A group of three guys, two with beards and the third desperately trying. One family with two younger kids. And a bunch of assorted gray hairs. He was the only teenage sad sack out walking with his parent and grands. Suddenly, he felt very embarrassed. Pushing down the lid of his cap and sliding deeper into his chair, he refocused on his plate, hoping not to be noticed.

Luke needn't have worried. The arriving entourage was oblivious to anyone outside their tribe. He turned his head slightly, surveying them from beneath the rim of his hat. They were laughing and showing each other something on their phones. Several of the boys pushed each other good-naturedly. Another had his arms draped over the shoulders of two girls. A few couples were holding hands. Luke exhaled heavily. As the last of his breath left his chest, he shook his head, closed his eyes, and muttered to himself: "What the fuck am I doing here?"

There were some adults with the tour group. Luke guessed they were guides or teachers, maybe in their twenties, maybe thirties. Once you got past nineteen, he couldn't really tell. One of the adults, a young guy with a square face and neatly trimmed scruff, started to address the group. Luke noticed several of the girls point at him and start to giggle. Even a few of the boys were giving the thirsty eye. "This is a quick stop, so get something to run," the young leader said. "We meet in fifteen. Chum your mate to the station over there," pointing down the slope, "and don't be late."

Sophie, Lil, and Russell had all noticed the change in Luke's demeanor. Russell attempted to engage him in conversation, but Luke responded with a shrug of his shoulders.

When the last of the students had entered the cafe, Luke said to his mom flatly, "I'm going to get a dessert and wander a little bit."

"Okay," Sophie replied. "We should be ready to go in about ten minutes."

Russell excused himself. "A quick visit to the bathroom before we set off. And the lad has a good idea about dessert, I think."

When they were alone, Lil turned to Sophie. "That boy runs hot and cold, and the temperature changes quickly."

The comment surprised Sophie. She was not used to Lil offering a critical word about her fair-haired grandchild. The criticism was usually reserved for Sophie or Rick. She paused for a few seconds and then replied, "Tell me about it. Sometimes, I don't know what to say or do for fear of doing the wrong thing and setting him off on one of his moods."

Lil nodded.

They saw Luke exit the cafe. He was now smiling and talking to one of the World Quest girls. He followed her as she left the terrace and walked down toward the low hill.

Sophie continued, "The therapist said it's a common response to trauma. Mood swings, overreacting, withdrawing." She searched her mother's face.

Lil scanned her daughter's face in return. She noticed the faint lines nesting in the corners of her eyes. Her lips seemed slightly thinner. It was strange for Lil to think of Sophie as aging; she always saw her as her Young Miss. But the passing of time weighs heavy on every body. And the events of the past eighteen months only brought additional weight. "I didn't know Luke was seeing a therapist," Lil said, quickly adding with a nod of her head, "That's good." She thought about it but did not ask Why didn't you tell me sooner?

Sophie replied, "We both are, actually. Separately, of course. But they are

69

with the same practice."

Lil arched her left eyebrow and repeated, "That's good."

At that moment, Russell returned carrying four bags. "I bought something for each of you, but you can't open it until our next stop."

The two women were still seated, their eyes focused on one another. Neither immediately responded to Russell's announcement. He remained still, holding the unclaimed bags in outstretched arms.

And then, as if a silent signal had passed between them, they stood up simultaneously. They shouldered their packs and plucked a bag from Russell.

He wasn't sure what had occurred while he was gone, but as they weren't arguing, he took it as a positive sign. "Thank goodness," he said. "My arms were getting tired."

"You are a dear, Russell," Lil said. "Grab Luke's pack and come along."

They walked in the direction Luke had gone and stood at the top of a rise. From their location, they could see the small train station tucked at the bottom of the short slope. Luke was standing at the edge of the platform still chatting with the girl from the cafe.

"Did you send me that invite yet?" Luke asked the girl while looking at his phone. The lone bar on his signal icon flickered intermittently.

"Just a sec," the girl replied.

A tall boy with skin the color of the afternoon clouds approached the girl. "Em, we gotta go, NOW," he declared impatiently. And, with a nod up the hill, he added to Luke, "Best be on your bike, mate. Looks like Mummy wants you." The boy then laughed as the girl stifled a giggle.

Luke glanced toward the hill, where Sophie, Lil, and Russell were still standing. His embarrassment flamed to anger. He turned back to face the tall boy and yelled, "Piss off, Casper!"

The outburst caught the attention of the rest of the tour group. Several stepped toward Emily and the pale young man.

Luke tilted his head slightly and pursed his lips. His raised eyebrow invited a response. The other boys were initially silent, but their bodies stiffened and leaned in. With his eyes locked on the first boy, Luke counted to himself

– one, two, three, shit. He felt his face starting to flush and his heart rush. Through tight lips, he delivered a final "pfft," turned away, and trudged up the hill. When he reached the top, he snatched his bag from Russell and said, "Let's go."

The path rose steadily from the cafe through open fields and toward a forested hillside. It was a quiet walk. Luke remained in front, his head down, placing each step angrily onto the earth. Sophie had tried to catch up to him, but as soon as she neared, Luke increased his pace to keep the distance. Even as she felt for her son, a part of her was relieved. As had frequently been the case over the past eighteen months, and if she were truthful to herself even before that, she wasn't certain what to say.

Lil had matched her steps with Sophie. Seeing Luke's silent rebuke, she reached out her arm and placed it on Sophie's shoulder. "Leave it for a bit. He'll come back around."

Reflexively, Sophie felt a flush of anger and the urge to shrug away her mother's hand. The familiar script from her childhood raced in her mind. Stop telling me what to do, she silently thought.

And then Lil added, "You're a good mom, Sophie."

The rising tension in her face ebbed. With sagging shoulders and a quivering jaw, Sophie managed. "I don't feel like it."

Lil's response was quick and matter-of-fact. "Well, I wouldn't say it if it wasn't true."

Sophie laughed at the truth of the comment. The mother she knew might not tell you everything, but everything she would tell you was true, at least true to Lil. Sophie also knew her mother to be tight with praise. Coddling is the death of independence, she remembered her mother instructing Russell. Sophie couldn't recall what exactly they were arguing over. But for the teenage Sophie, rather than confidence and independence, her mother's approach had sown doubt and anger and distance.

As Sophie pondered, Lil ventured a bit further. After all, leaving the past behind was part of the reason for the trip. "He is a good boy. He may be a little lost right now. But I know this," Lil said and turned to her daughter,

"He will find himself. And he is damn lucky to have you. You might not know all the answers, and sometimes there aren't any, at least no good ones. But you have been there with him every step, and you still are. That makes you a very good mother." Lil stopped talking and was surprised to find she was pointing her finger at her daughter's chest. Lil lowered her hand awkwardly and noticed that it was now her jaw that was quivering.

Sophie couldn't help but laugh. She reached out and grabbed hold of her mother's lowered hand, squeezing it tight. "Yes, commander," she replied. She had last spoken the words as a frustrated adolescent storming out of the house. But now, as they stood facing each other on a French hillside thousands of miles and decades away from that past, the tone was appreciation, not disdain.

Their moment was interrupted by the wail of the train whistle. The two crimson red cabs of *Jeanne*, one of three trains servicing the Mont Blanc Tramway, was approaching. The line began in Saint Gervais and ended eight miles later at the Nid d'Aigle. It was popular with skiers, hikers, and sightseers who were eager to access the views of the southeastern slopes of the massif without the fatigue of walking uphill for hours. Though it was powered by overhead electric cable, in a nod to nostalgia, the tramway continued to use a steam whistle when approaching stations or crossways.

Five minutes earlier, shortly after Luke had left, *Jeanne* had stopped at the Bellevue station adjacent to the cafe. The second cab was now filled almost entirely with the World Quest tour group. With about a hundred yards separating the hiking path from the railway, as Luke turned his head toward the train, he could easily see several boys hanging out the window. The clang of the wheels made it difficult to hear what they were yelling, but their gestures were clear enough. The tall, pale boy was blowing kisses while several others were more explicit.

Sensing the potential for trouble, Russell had quickened his stride to close the gap separating him from his grandson. He saw Luke clench his fists and tighten his body. Russell positioned himself between his grandson and the train. Without looking back, the old man gave the World Quest passengers the universal finger, holding it high while continuing to walk next to Luke.

When he saw his grandfather, Luke's face lightened. He couldn't remember Russell ever cursing, not even a hell or a damn, let alone flipping someone the bird. Luke joined Russell and flashed a double. He then placed his left arm around his grandfather's shoulder, and the two men followed the path as it turned away from the rail line and onto the wooded slope ahead. What neither saw behind them, but was plain to everyone on *Jeanne*, was Sophie and Lil joining in the salute.

When the two women caught up to Russell and Luke, all four were smiling.

"Russell, what has come over you," Lil said with mock indignation.

"Ah, that felt good. I hadn't done that in a while," he replied.

"I've never seen you do that, ever," Sophie added.

"Well, back in the day . . ." Russell continued rubbing his chin. He left the sentence unfinished.

"You could have started a scene," Lil chided.

"Little miscreants deserved it," Russell said. "Besides, what are they going to do? Jump off the train and chase us down."

"This is a ten-day hike that goes in a circle. You may very well run into them some other day in some other place," Lil cautioned.

Russell offered no response. It was Luke who replied. "I liked it. And don't worry, Nan. I got Russell's back. Let's go," he said for the second time in half an hour, only this time without a scowl.

They continued along the well-marked trail, tucking in and among a copse of trees and then emerging onto a dirt path only to pass into another forested stand as the pattern repeated itself again and again and again. Much like the morning, this midday segment was arduous. While most of the time was spent in silence, this quiet felt different from earlier in the day. Their bodies talked to them less. When a thigh or foot or shoulder announced its displeasure, their mind regarded the discomfort as a mere passerby, to be momentarily acknowledged and then bid adieu.

As they walked, they stepped outside of time. A footfall transporting them to places real or imagined. One moment, Luke was running on the pool deck, grabbing hold of some reluctant friends before jumping into the water, and then in a flicker, he was pressed against a nameless body temporarily embraced by their warmth . . . Russell was seated at an outdoor cafe with Lil. They were younger then and yet to be married. Lil was almost laughing at what he didn't recall. She looked at him with those sparkling eyes. When he blinked, he was sitting alone at Cathedral Rock, sobbing and afraid... Sophie was back with the before-Rick. They had rented a cabin near the lake. It was October, and they weren't expecting an early snow, but they had each other and plenty of firewood. They swore that Luke was conceived in that cabin, and that's why they had to buy a vacation house there. "That damn lake house," she said, the anger starting to swell.

Even while lost in their thoughts, their feet propelled them forward. When they returned to the present, their eyes were more attuned to the now around them. They noticed the scales of grey-green lichen on the rock, the blanket of color from the delicate blooms on the hillside, or the light dancing across the backpack of the person in front of them. They heard the chirp of the marmot, felt the light breeze cool their face, and smelled the calming scent of spruce. After one particular turn, Lil put up her hand to stop the group. She needn't have. They were all transfixed by the scene before them. Up to this point, they were able to see a few modest peaks, a view down the valley, or an occasional chamois bound in the distance. But this view was unlike any of those. Here, they stood witness to the entire southern panorama of the massif. A jagged cascade of granite ridges capped with the whitest snow. The mountain flanks carved with mottled grey ice melting into green valleys. All against a backdrop of the bluest sky dotted with the first puffs of clouds heralded by a westerly wind: the majesty of the Alps. The sight deserved its reputation as one of the finest views of the whole Tour, aptly stationed on the afternoon of the first day when weary hikers began to doubt the wisdom of undertaking such an adventure. Even Luke stood motionless before taking out his phone and framing some shots.

Lil narrated the scene without turning her head away from the natural beauty before her. "Those two are the Dômes de Miage," pointing to the lesser caps on the right. "That's the general direction we will head, but well beyond Les Contamines where we will stay tonight." Turning her arm to the left, "That is le Glacier du Bionnassay tucked in between le Dôme de Goûter and Aiguille de Bionnassay." She shook her head. "If you were here forty years ago, that glacier would be another two to three hundred meters further downslope almost to the foot of the valley. Damn climate change." And bringing her hand back slightly to the right and upward, a smile returned to her face. "That," she said, pointing at the single peak that towered above all others, "is Mont Blanc herself." At 15,700 feet, the highest mountain in the Alps, a full thousand feet higher than Mount Rosa, the next highest peak in western Europe, or the more famous Matterhorn. Luke took a picture of his grandmother. She was staring into the distance, wiping her eyes as if she were greeting a long-lost friend.

Lil broke the silence. "We best be going. The clouds are building behind us," she said, pointing to the wisps of grey battling to overtop the ridge line on the far western horizon.

They walked through woods, across stone, and atop an occasional snow-field hiding in a shadowed nook of the mountainside. Thirty minutes later, they heard it before they saw it. What had begun as a faint rumbling was now a steady thunder. A final scramble down a short boulder field, using hands and poles to aid with balance, led them to the source: Le Torrent de Bionassay. The water was milky grey, any other colors scrubbed away by the relentless grind of water across stone and time. The roar spoke to its power. It crashed down a boulder chute rushing to escape from under the snout of the glacier whose name it shared.

"How are we getting across that?" Sophie asked again. Her initial request was lost in the din.

Russell, who had been faithfully tracking the blue dot, pointed upslope.

"Way cool, full stop," Luke proclaimed, looking in the direction Russell had indicated. About 100 yards upriver, he spied the suspension bridge and rushed towards it.

When Sophie arrived she was relieved by the construction. The handrails were formed of a two-inch cable anchored into stone on both sides of the gorge. They provided the main support for the bridge. A series of three-foot-long suspension cables hung from the handrail at 10-inch intervals. These formed the sides of the bridge while also holding the two lateral lower cables onto which the wood decking was affixed. It looked far sturdier than the frayed rope her mind had first imagined.

Luke was already about halfway across the hundred-foot span when Sophie reached the threshold. He was taking more pictures. He carefully positioned the phone with the lens, looking through the series of metal rings used to connect the suspension cable to the handrail. As his mother stepped upon the decking, the bridge shifted, and Luke lost the shot. He snapped up, initially annoyed. He saw a hesitant look run across her face. As she took her next step, Luke spread his feet wide. He grabbed both handrails. Shifting his weight from side to side, the bridge swayed with him. Sophie squealed like a little child as she grabbed hold of the handrails and then laughed. She started running toward him with her hands gliding along the cable to keep her balance. Luke bolted off for the opposite bank.

Lil and Russell arrived in time to see Sophie chasing Luke over the final few yards before the son embraced his mother, both laughing on the other side. Lil squeezed Russell's hand. Together they walked across the bridge and joined the rest of their family.

The path continued to zig and zag uphill, with occasional level stretches providing some respite. They continued at a steady pace without much conversation. Luke started singing songs in his head the way he would when he had to swim a 1500. Russell was counting his steps and restarting when he reached 1000. Sophie listened to the clack-clack of the poles against the ground. Lil was savoring each breath. After another hour, they reached the Col de Tricot, a grassy saddle pass separating the valley of Bionnassay and Miage to the south.

"Seven thousand feet," Lil announced. "This is the highest point on this stage of the Tour."

"We made it!" Luke exclaimed. "All downhill from here."

"Not quite," Russell interrupted, showing Luke the elevation profile from the map. "We go down a ways and then up a bit before a steady run down into town."

The wisps of clouds they had observed behind them a few hours earlier had knitted into a thick gauze. Though the sun still filtered through, it was noticeably cooler.

"Let's make it a brief stop," Lil advised. "We still have about two more hours to go. I would recommend taking out your waterproof and throwing on the pack cover. I am not certain the rains will wait for us."

Ten minutes later, they were back on their feet. While this section of the trail was not as extreme as the earlier miles, their bodies were spent from the first six hours of walking. The blanketing clouds dampened their spirits. And then it started. What began as an ominous burst with droplets the size of pomegranate seeds quickly settled down and alternated between a drizzle and a light rain. Though their waterproofs kept them dry, they slowed their pace to avoid slipping on the wet stones or losing their footing in a patch of mud. After an hour in the rain, they all wanted the day to be over.

Club Alpine de Francaise

A light rain was still falling by the time they arrived at Le Club Alpine de Francaise. Following the blue dot, they passed through the center of Les Contamines across the stream and up a small hill to a home on the corner of Route de Nant Fandraz and Le Vieux Chemin. The house was similar to many they had observed walking through the town center: a steeply pitched roof anchored atop whitewashed stone walls. Each window was framed by wide green shutters, one on either side, and a wooden planter below. Even in the haze of the drizzle, the profusion of flowers commanded your eye: Look at me. A series of blue and white umbrellas peeked over the top of a low wooden fence: Come sit down. A large French flag swayed in the breeze: You have arrived.

The group of four stood frozen at the side of the road. The prospect of not having to walk any more gave way to a collective, "Now what do we do?" This was their first hut. They were uncertain as to the procedure.

Lil stepped forward, "Let's move people. I am starving, and something smells good." Clicking her poles on the asphalt, she marched toward the flag in the final 30 yards. Luke quickly followed, leaving Russell and Sophie to catch up.

A young woman in a tank top and hiking shorts stood at the threshold of what looked like the back of the house. Pressing her pack against the middle of the door, she held it open for Lil and waved her in. "Merci," Lil responded.

Luke looked over the young woman. His adolescent mind did the calculus that now came automatically to him. He stepped behind his grandmother and grabbed the edge of the opened door with his left hand. He reflexively swallowed and gestured with his right. "After you," he said.

She turned her head ever so slightly, tightened her mouth, and, with four quick waves of her fingers, directed him forward without a word.

Shut down, boy, Luke thought to himself. He lowered his eyes toward the floor. Mumbling a "thank you," he released the door and sheepishly followed Lil. In the corner of his eye, he saw the young woman shake her head as if she knew what he was thinking.

Lil walked up the steps to the main floor. The hall opened to a small kitchen directly in front of her – the source of the enticing smells. A larger common dining area was located on the right, and to her left she could see three open doors and another set of stairs leading down.

In the kitchen, a man was busy sautéing vegetables over the stove, and a woman was slicing some bread. A small child danced around their feet, trying to catch an elusive dog who seemed all too familiar and none too thrilled with this game.

"*Bonjour, nous cherchons les wardens de le refuge,*' Lil said with a smile.

"*Bonjour, et bienvenue. Je suis Michel.*" The man said releasing the pan and wiping his hand on a towel. "*Je suis l'attendant. Ceci est ma femme, Ronique, et notre fille, JoJo.*"

Sophie and Russell had joined Luke as Lil spoke with Michel and reviewed the details for the hut. Sophie whispered to Russell, "I didn't know her French was so good?"

Russell laughed, "Neither did I. But you and I both know your mother is a mystery."

Lil turned to the group. "Okay, we already broke one of the cardinal rules: Poles and shoes stay downstairs," she said, gesturing to the stairway on the left. "Showers are also downstairs along with a wash basin."

Her traveling companions listened closely as if she were sharing the secrets of life.

"Dinner is served at seven – that's about an hour from now," Lil continued.

Luke's shoulders sagged as his stomach reminded him of every calorie he burned. He noticed Russell doing the same. Lil shot them an eye.

"You must shower before dinner. Our room is the first one on the right.

There are twelve beds. Most folks are already here. You may take any bunk that is open." Now, it was Sophie's turn to lower her shoulders. Lil chose to ignore her.

The troop made their way to the stairway leading to the lower level. The dog followed them, happy to escape from JoJo.

The hallway was dimly lit. The final three steps turned a blind corner into the basement. It was the series of wooden racks that first caught Luke's eye. Half the racks were filled with hiking boots while the remaining pegs held an assortment of Crocs sandals in the most gaudy colors Luke had ever seen.

"Okay, these are cool," Luke said, trading in his size 12 Keens for some large pink crocs. "A definite upgrade."

Seeing Luke smile lifted Sophie's spirits. Sophie, Russell, and Lil happily removed their boots and selected their footwear, everyone but Lil choosing a separate color. She chose pink and gave Luke a wink.

Two large basins were located to the immediate right, with some line strung between the walls. A series of socks, shirts, and underwear occupied almost every available inch of the drying line. Hiking poles were hung neatly on a separate series of pegs built into the wall behind them. No backpacks were stored here—those were to be kept in your room.

Past the wash basins, a narrow hallway about half the room's width led to five doors from which they could hear running water. Sophie, who had harbored unwelcome thoughts of communal showers, was relieved to find they were private stalls with doors. After removing a towel, soap, and change of clothes, they tucked their packs temporarily beneath a long wooden table and moved closer to the showers.

Outside the furthest door, a moderately overweight man, just shy of middle age, leaned against the wall. His eyes were closed, and a towel hung from his hand.

He looks beat, Luke thought silently.

Three of the doors opened almost simultaneously. The inert man slowly lumbered toward the first shower, placing his hand against the door frame for support. Russell and Lil claimed the remaining two. It was an unwritten rule on the TMB that, all things being equal, seniority had its perks. This applied especially with regard to bathroom privileges—showers included. Sophie did not need to wait long before the fourth shower was available, leaving Luke to wait a little longer for the fifth.

Sophie let the warm water wash over her tired muscles longer than she would at home. This might be one of the nicest showers I have ever had, she thought to herself. Hiking had that power, the ability to amplify the pleasure of the ordinary.

In the small dressing area adjacent to her shower, Sophie changed into light grey yoga pants, a sports bra, and a loose shirt – the same outfit, minus the sports bra, would serve as her sleeping clothes. When she re-entered the hallway, she saw that only her backpack and Luke's remained. Lil and Russell had already moved upstairs. The young woman she met when first entering the hut was washing some clothes in the tub. Sophie could hear Luke lathering vigorously in his stall. The young woman looked at Sophie and smirked. "Ah, boys," Sophie remarked.

"Not much different than men," the woman replied.

They shared a knowing laugh together. Choosing not to wait for Luke, Sophie grabbed her backpack and headed up the stairs to the first dorm room on the right.

The door was slightly ajar. When she pushed it open, she was immediately struck by two observations: First, this is a lot of beds crammed into a single room, and second, that is one monumental butt crack.

The shower did little to refresh the big man they had earlier encountered downstairs. If Sophie had not seen his hands move, she would have thought he was dead at the foot of his bed. He was on all fours, slowly fumbling through his backpack. His body bent at such an angle that his shirt rode north while his shorts sank south. Either he did not notice or he was too tired to care.

With a short glimpse more than sufficient, her eye quickly explored the rest of the room. A man and a woman – Sophie couldn't tell if he was her father or her boyfriend – were discussing who would get the bottom bunk. Neither seemed inclined toward compromise.

In what Sophie took to be the norm, you claimed your space by placing your sleeping bag liner or your backpack on the bunk. Later, she would learn that using the backpack, given the accumulated sweat and dirt, was bad form, and all you really needed was to turn down the top blanket. But to her novice eye, on this first night on the trail, it looked like only three bunks remained open, and all of them were uppers.

Luke now entered the room and was met by the same revealing view of their roommate. He offered a less restrained response, scrunching his face in mock horror. Sophie shot him a shushing glance and said, "Looks like these two are open?"

Continuing to feign horror, Luke tiptoed around the prone body and tossed his bag onto an upper bunk. He lifted his mom's gear into the adjacent bed. "Let's eat," he said.

"Good idea," agreed the new roommate, who, with the assistance of the bed frame, slowly stood up. "My name is Juergen," he introduced himself.

Dinner 1

The dining hall consisted of four long tables located in what was originally the living room in the chalet's previous life. While not fancy, it was inviting. Large timbers, hand-sawn by all appearance, framed a square in the middle of the space and formed four separate alcoves with a long table in each. On one side of the table, a built-in bench provided seating for five or six; on the opposite side sat an unmatched set of separate wooden chairs. On the walls hung various pictures and posters, most featuring black and white photos from the area. An enormous three-dimensional topographical map, Le Massif du Mont Blanc, commanded attention from behind a waist-height serving cupboard.

At this hut, randonneurs were assigned to tables. You found your seat by looking for your group name on a slip of paper at a table. Michel would later explain to Lil that Ronique did the assignments. "*Elle a un talent pour ça,*" he said. "*Elle melange les ages et les genres mait sais qui doit s'asseoiur avec un autre. Non?*" By the end of the trail Lil would send Ronique a small card thanking her for the introduction to such wonderful *compagnons de voyage*.

Lil and Russell were already seated next to one another on the back bench when Sophie arrived with Luke and Juergen. Sophie noticed her parents' fingers were interlaced, lightly bridging the space between them. She didn't remember them holding hands so often in the past. Juergen, moving with a measure of energy that surprised Sophie, took a chair opposite two men seated at the near end of the table. Sophie sat next to him and across from her mom and dad.

Luke spied a chair in the far corner next to Lil. Homerun! he thought.

83

I can eat quietly, nod a little to Nan, and not have to talk to these other people. However, as he moved toward the space, he was disappointed to find a quarter zip already placed on the empty seat. Lil seemed to know what he was thinking. She shrugged her shoulder and gestured to the chair opposite her. "Here, have some bread," she said, pushing a baguette and plate of cheese in his direction. Even while chewing energetically, Luke managed to look sullen.

The woman to Luke's right was turned around, chatting with a couple at the table across the room. Her skin was baked brown with the crepey texture of someone who lived outdoors but didn't believe in the protective powers of sunscreen. Luke guessed she was somewhere between 35 and 70. She was talking more loudly than the distance between the tables required. The near-empty wine glass next to the empty bread plate probably had something to do with it, thought Lil.

The young woman who had earlier held the door open was the final dinner guest to arrive. She approached the table, lifted her quarter zip from the chair, placed her cell phone near her plate, and sat next to Lil.

"*Bonjour, je m'appelle Lil,*" said Lil extending her hand.

"I'm sorry, I don't speak French. My name is Malee. I am from the United States by way of Australia."

"So are we," Luke offered too enthusiastically. "I mean the United States part."

Lil and Malee shared a smile. Luke, whose internal voice was telling him yet again, You're so stupid, started to blush. The well-baked table mate broke contact with the other group. "Well, ain't this just like a family reunion then? I must be the favorite aunt, who everyone tries to hide from when I visit. My name is TW but you can call me Tennessee, it'll be easier to remember," she said with an appealing drawl.

The unwelcomed developments of the past two months had propelled Lil toward much reflection. So often, she concluded, we travel through our lives closed to the fresh opportunities surrounding us. We fail to notice the way the light is shining a little differently through the clouds or how the dew drops glisten on the thread of a spider's web. We do not take stock of how our body feels just a little different this morning or the last time we read a good book or called a close friend. We elect not to notice that person next to us in the check-out line or the subway, avoiding their face to see if they are happy or sad, overwhelmed or content. And we certainly do not ask them how they are, or if, in accordance with some perfunctory script, we do ask, we do not truly listen when they answer. For Lil, these omissions were part of why she chose this trip. With her little time left, she did not want to spend it in oblivion – she would be moving there soon enough. The Tour du Mont Blanc is a little like the first week at college. Life throws a bunch of random strangers together. Everyone has their own history and backstory. After a day of each walking their own individual path, the shared evening meal, spiced with conversation and laughter, quickly makes friends of strangers, allowing each to see life with fresh eyes. In this place, Lil strangely felt at home.

At the men's end of the table, the bread and soup were served with silence and awkward pauses. Dependably, it was Russell who started the conversation. "My name is Russell, and I am an accountant in the United States. This is my daughter, Sophie,"

"My name is Juergen, and this is my friend, Max," gesturing to an equally large man seated opposite him. "We are from Germany, Stuttgart actually, and we work with Daimler."

"Ah, the old Daimler Chrysler?" Russell added with a smile.

"Those are words we do not say in Germany," Max added quickly with a wink and a laugh at Juergen.

Juergen explained. "Let's just say it was not a marriage made in heaven. It is like when a good friend says to you," casting an accusing eye toward Max, "'I have someone I want you to meet. She is a nice girl, very attractive and smart too. I think you will like her.' So you agree. Then you meet in the coffee shop, and she looks more like an older cousin or maybe an aunt from your mother's side of the family. It was not a good idea, eh."

Max laughed into his hand and looked ready to protest when Juergen added, "You know what I say is true. *Alles vergeben und vergessen.* We will speak of it no more."

The quiet man at the end caught himself laughing and added, "I am Jakob," and almost as an afterthought, "I am a retired doctor."

Sophie had always been struck by how men introduced themselves. Most often, it began with a name and job. Almost as frequently, the search for connection would quickly lead to sports, a favorite football team, or, worse yet, something they played when they were younger. Sophie was in the middle chair, situated between two different worlds of conversation. When she listened to the men on the left, her ear would perk at some snarky comment from Tennessee on the right. But by the time she turned to the women that moment had passed, seemingly without her. She felt adrift, unable to land on either shore.

After the football conversation, a particularly awkward spell descended on the testosterone group. The men resorted to asking for a second helping to occupy their mouths. Russell then took them down a risky path.

"I just want to put this out there, a confession, if you will." During the dramatic pause that followed, he looked at each of the men. "I just want to apologize . . . for our President. I assure you, no one in our group voted for him."

The three European dinner mates laughed heartily. "Ah, *ja*," Juergen replied. "That is what every American we meet says," Juergen shook his hands and wiped his brow in imitation of the Americans: "'We didn't vote for him . . . No, we didn't vote for him.' But the question I have to ask you my friend, if no one voted for this man, how did he become your President?"

"That is something I ask myself almost every day," Russell replied. "My working hypothesis is anyone who voted for him is not the sort of person visiting Europe and walking through the mountains."

Raising a glass in the air, Juergen said, "Let us drink to Making America Great Again, someday." It was the first of many toasts that evening among the newfound friends.

At the other end of the table, Tennessee needed little encouragement to keep up a spirited conversation. Unlike Sophie, who could sit quietly for hours and, in this regard, was much like her mother, Tennessee seemed a stranger to silence.

During one of those infrequent pauses, Lil asked, "So what is your story?" The prompt provided all the opening Tennessee required. "I came here from the Camino," referring to another of Europe's great walks.

"Now that was a hell of a time. Not nearly as hilly, and they drink a lot more than on the TMB from what I can tell so far," she added, draining her third glass. "I met a lot of nice people from all over. And though I am not religious, I will tell you there is something to it. With all those shrines and churches, even for a heathen like me, I was moved."

"And you went straight from the Camino to here?" Malee asked, quite impressed.

"Hell no, girl." Tennessee corrected. "I stayed in Santiago for two days, and then I walked south to Porto. Then I came here."

Malee's eyes widened. "You are the Tennessee Wonder Woman."

"Ya, I sometimes wonder myself," mused Tennessee.

"Aren't you exhausted?" Sophie asked.

"You get used to it after a while. I am not saying it's not painful. Depending on the day, either my knees, my hips, or my feet will hurt, or sometimes all three. But I just treat it as my body's way of letting me know I am still alive."

"So why do you do it?" Lil asked. "What's your truth? If you want to share it . . ."

Tennessee looked at Lil and trusted the sincerity in the older woman's face. Her lips tightened, and for the briefest moment, her face turned serious.

"So . . ." she began. "While I am walking *to* all these places, it is also true I am walking away from something, from someone. TJ, to be exact."

"Your husband?" Malee asked quietly.

"More like my not-much-of-a-husband," Tennessee replied. "We got married young. I am not certain now what I saw in him then. I was seventeen and he was twenty." She paused. "My poppa, he was not exactly the nurturing type. More the drinking type. So it was a good way to get away."

Sophie reached out her arm and gently touched Tennessee's shoulder.

"TJ was a nice boy, and he was not a drinker, and he did have a job. And, oh yeah, his mom was a drinker, so I guess we had that in common. Marrying TJ was my ticket out of my house."

Tennessee paused for a moment and smiled, the sort of smile you have when you find something you thought you may have lost.

"And ladies, I will tell you this," she said, wagging a finger. "Young man, you turn away and close your ears," she told Luke. "He was not much in the bedroom. And I mean that literally. One moment, his little thing would be pointing to the floor, and the next moment, it would point to the roof, but not much would look different. It was like that little light switch you can't quite find against the wall plate. Quick flick, it's up. And then just as quick, it would turn off."

The three women laughed together. Malee repeatedly made a gesture of a flicking light switch.

"Okay young stud, you can come back now," Tennessee said to Luke, who had never stopped listening.

"So we muddle on for fifteen years, the usual mix of the good and the bad. And then things start to change a little in the conjugal department. It seemed like the light switch was never turning on, if you catch my meaning. So I made him get checked out and get some of those special blue pills—still not much changes. I start counting the pills. I notice there are more pills missing than visits to the honeypot."

Malee began shaking her head.

"So I pulled him aside one night, and I said to him, Timothy James, let me say this to you in the clearest way possible. If I catch you cheating on me with another woman, I will cut that little man clean off, if I can find a pair of scissors small enough."

Luke winced.

"So two years ago, I come home early. I was supposed to work my monthly overnight, but I got god-awful sick from some unforgiving chicken. And don't I catch him in the act all tangled up bobbin for the worm with his fishing buddy and best friend from childhood, Roy Wilson.

"I was madder than a wet sittin' hen. I said, 'Roy, I hope you like that little popsicle 'cause it didn't do much for me. You get your asses out of here before I kill you both and say you died of unnatural causes.' I packed TJ's clothes in a green trash bag and chucked it on Roy's front lawn. I haven't talked to him since.

"For about a year I went around all angry, feeling sorry for myself. Working but bored something fierce. Then, six months ago my auntie died, real sudden. Well, she didn't have any kids, and she left me a little money stash. Not much, but more than I had in my savings account. I remember watching this film – *The Way*. A father was supposed to go on this long walk – the Camino – with his son. But his son dies. The man goes on the walk anyway. It was like his way of making sense. I said to myself, 'That's exactly what I need to do.' So I put in for a half-year sabbatical, and here I am."

"I admire you, Tennessee," Lil declared, reaching out to hold Tennessee's hands.

"You are a warrior," Malee added.

"You are a courageous woman," Sophie shared.

Tennessee looked briefly at each woman and lightly wiped an eye. "I am not courageous. Some days I am scared shitless, and other days, I'm just lost. But being out here with my sore feet and aches and pains beats sitting around feeling sorry for myself at home."

"And that is exactly why it is courageous," Lil added, agreeing with Sophie. "Facing the fear. Moving forward. When you get to my age, sweet child, we call that living."

"Amen," Malee added.

"Your turn," Lil said, turning to Malee. "Why are you here?"

Tennessee had broken the ice. Malee dove right in.

"I've been in Australia for the past two years, working in VivActive. It's like a boutique fitness center. Very small, and expensive, too," she began.

That explains why she is in such good shape, Luke said to himself, scanning her body yet again.

"I was in Australia for junior year abroad and loved it. So after I graduated – my degree was in exercise physiology – I moved there. I didn't have a job, but I figured I could find something."

"How did your parents like that plan?" Sophie asked.

"They were pissed," Malee initially smiled and looked Sophie square in the face before turning her eyes down.

For a moment, Sophie imagined herself as Malee's parents. She recognized the look. Part challenge, part independence, part spite. She saw shadows of it when Luke spoke with her, and she vaguely remembered it when she was a teen arguing with her mother.

"But I made it work. I found a job at Anytime Fitness. It's like a chain," she explained. "And a roommate, Carolyn. Later, she hooked me up with VivActive – a definite upgrade over Anytime. I was making good money and having fun."

Tennessee interrupted, "Okay, girlie, you went from happy land down under to walking the mountain tops by yourself. I smell a boy somewhere in here, and I am not talking about you, puppy," she said, glancing at Luke.

Malee smiled. "I have, or had, or maybe still have, a boyfriend. Christian. I met him at VivA. He is from Australia. And he looks it. And he doesn't have TJ's problem," she added with a smile. The ladies laughed. Luke blushed.

"Oooh, I knew it. I am starting to get hot flashes here. Tell more," Tennessee encouraged.

"Things were good, are good. They were really good early on for the first six months. We had a great group of friends. Lots of fun. We would go out to the clubs, nice restaurants, and tons of outdoor activities. I was starting to think maybe this was something serious."

No one interrupted her during her pause this time.

"But I wasn't certain. You know, there is always something in the back of my head wondering. And that's the way it's been with almost all my boyfriends," Malee said, her eyes searching around the table.

"What was in the back of your head with him?" Sophie asked.

Malee pursed her lips. "He never seemed to want to introduce me to his family. I get that sometimes. I don't always want to introduce my boyfriends to my parents either. No offense," she said apologetically, looking at the older women at the table. Luke nodded his agreement.

"And sometimes, when we would be out somewhere or doing something, he would be looking around. And I am not certain he always heard what I was saying. But he was always interested in sex. Don't get me wrong, I like sex, but not every night. Sometimes you just want to go to sleep, you know."

Sophie and Lil nodded. Luke squirmed. "Sounds like I may need to take this Australian hottie off your problem list," Tennessee joked.

"And then last month – poof – VivActive goes out of business. I go from seeing Christian every day to a few times a week. Carolyn and I don't have jobs, but we have the rent to pay. My parents are bugging me, 'When are you going to come home? Isn't it time to come home now?'" Malee swallows a muffled laugh.

"That is a lot to juggle," Sophie offered sympathetically.

"Tell me about it," Malee added. "So Carolyn and I were sitting around one night. We were talking about the things we are talking about now, and how I was uncertain about what I should do. Her situation is not much different, you know. And she has the brainstorm. 'Fuck it,' she said. 'We are young, we've got no responsibilities, nothing to tie us down, we can get a job anywhere. This is a time to be living. We should take the money we have in the bank and travel the world for a month. Have an adventure. Figure out what we want to do with the rest of our life, and do it.'" After a pause, Malee added, "So here I am."

"Where is Carolyn?" Lil asked cautiously.

"Oh, she is spending her first week in Spain. She had an old boyfriend who was there, and she wanted to 'try things out' again. I had heard about the TMB. I thought it would be fun, and it is very different from Australia. Besides I was thinking I might get a job with a travel company, leading adventure tours with REI, that sort of thing, so I could put this on the resume. We are going to meet up in Zadar in ten days."

Tennessee stood up, raised her arms, and bowed toward Malee. "You go, girl. I wish I had your kind of balls when I was younger!"

The man-conversation at the other end of the table had dried up. Russell tapped Lil on the arm. "Madame translator, might you be available to help me pay our bill?" The norm in the huts is for travelers to reconcile their bill immediately after dinner. In this way hikers are free to get an early start the next morning.

Lil pushed back from the table and stood up, preparing to leave.

"Whoa there, sweet Nellie. You can't just get up and leave us after the Aboriginal child and I have spilled our hearts on the table. I suspect there is a juicy story behind that Mother Teresa smile of yours," Tennessee said, tugging lightly on Lil's sleeve.

"It is a ten-day hike, my friends. We can't tell all the good stories on the first night. All will be revealed in good time," Lil confided before exiting the table.

Day 2

Sophie thought the sheer exhaustion of the day would draw her quickly into sleep. She was mistaken. Thirteen people sharing a room is not conducive to a good night's rest. For the first hour, as her anonymous roommates shifted to get comfortable, the wooden beds creaked like a chorus of bullfrogs after the first spring rain – the croaking punctured by an occasional burst of flatulence she was convinced was from Juergen. The father/boyfriend argued in low tones with his daughter/girlfriend, something about "not wanting to go on this trip in the first place." Just as she started to drift away she was jolted alert as one of the roommates banged into the door on the first of many nocturnal bathroom visits. It was after midnight when she finally fell asleep. She awoke groggy and unrested.

Russell had fared only slightly better. The mattress was thin, a foam pad, really, and his sleeping bag offered little extra cushioning. No matter which way he lay, some part of him ached. Turning from side to side only succeeded in identifying another pain.

The noise did not bother Lil much, and her muscles felt surprisingly good. Of the four travelers, she was the most prepared. She had been walking daily, often for distance and frequently in the mountains close to home. She also benefited by knowing what to expect. No, what interrupted her sleep were her regular companions of late: the discomfort in her stomach that wavered between slight nausea and an indecisive cramp, along with the dull back pain that breathed with each beat of her heart.

Luke had the easiest time falling asleep. He had managed to post a few pictures and read some messages before losing his signal again. As it often did, his struggle came in the deepest part of the night. He shot up. Eyes wide. Breath quick and shallow. His shirt was soaking. Thankfully, he had not screamed the way he had for the first few months. It was the same dream, more or less. Talking to his dad, or somebody like his dad. At first, it was definitely Dad, but recently he looked less and less like him. "Did you ever?" his dream self asked. His dream dad just smiled, and then he didn't. And then it wasn't his dad, but something twisted and grotesque, and then it was laughing or yelling or crying or something – Luke couldn't tell. He put his hand just below his sternum and tried to control his breath – deep in through the nose, slow out through the mouth. He couldn't bring himself to close his eyes, not just yet. After ten minutes his heart slowed a bit – still fast but enough that he didn't feel he would explode. He pulled off his wet shirt and tucked it deep toward his feet. He had not thought to bring a second shirt into bed but he would remember to do that for the rest of the trip. Instead, he lay on his back and wrapped his arms in front of him, rubbing his shoulders with his hands, trying to warm himself in his own embrace. He returned to sleep just before waking up.

This hut, like most accommodations along the trail, was demi-pension. In addition to the room for the night, your fee included dinner and breakfast. Breakfast was much simpler than dinner the night before. A sideboard in the dining area contained several cereals – each one a variation on granola – some juice, fruit, pastries, bread and cheese. The food was out by 6:00 and put away at 9:00. Guests could grab and go as their schedules demanded.

It was no surprise that Lil was first dressed. Sophie and Russell found her already seated at a corner table, chatting with a man who seemed to know everyone in the room.

Lil provided the introductions. "Lyndon, this is my daughter and my husband. Sophie and Russell meet Lyndon."

"The pleasure is all mine," Lyndon replied in the manner of someone with a gift for making people feel at ease. He added, "You two are trekking with a remarkable woman," nodding toward Lil.

"Lyndon runs a tour operation. Corporate team building or some such scam," Lil explained.

"A little outfit," Lyndon replied. "Get some businessers out of their posh life and challenge them for a spot. Well, best be going. I have to roust a few out of their bunks." Turning back to Lil, he added, "Thanks for the good breakfast company, Lil. I will keep my eye out for Luke."

Russell kissed Lil atop her head. He slowly lowered himself into his chair with two hands on the table. He landed with an audible "ooh." "Is it possible for bones to be sore?" he asked.

Sophie, who had managed her seat without assistance from the table, laughed and placed her hand on his shoulder. Russell gasped in mock pain.

"Stay seated and rest those bones, old man," Sophie teased. "I will get you something to eat."

Watching their daughter make her way to the breakfast, Russell asked his wife in a conspiratorial whisper, "How are you doing?"

Lil did not mention her back or stomach. She had come to view them as ordinary and expected. Background noise not worthy of further attention. She smiled contentedly, placed her hand on Russell's, and by way of an answer, she said, "I'll manage."

Sophie returned, balancing two bowls in one hand and two plates in another. She made a second run for juice and coffee before taking a seat next to her father. Despite the aches and pains, the mood around the breakfast table was lighthearted. They were swapping stories about their struggles to sleep in a room full of strangers when Luke approached, cereal and fruit already in hand. He wore a blank look on his face and greeted them with a barely perceptible nod. When they tried to engage him in conversation, his response was limited to single-word answers. He seemed neither happy nor angry but flat, as if preoccupied with some private thought. They did not press him.

"Yesterday was the hardest day of the whole Tour," Lil said, stretching the truth just slightly. "Today, there are fewer mountain passes, and the last four miles are almost entirely level as we walk alongside the Torrent de Glaciers. About five miles in we should hit the le Cafe des Ciels. That would be a good place to stop to eat."

While she spoke, Russell opened the app and looked at the trail preview.

Yes, he saw the single high crossing, and the final miles did indeed follow the river. But his eyebrow involuntarily twitched when he glanced at the elevation for Col des Fours: 8700 feet—a full 1700 feet more than the highest point yesterday. Silently, he swallowed his words.

"We should arrive at Le Chalet de Mottets by five," Lil concluded.

They were dressed and on the trail by 8:00. A good hour earlier than the first day.

The initial steps were painful. After thirty minutes Russell had warmed up and the ache in his muscles seemed to fade. The path was a steady incline but not so steep as the previous day.

The four travelers fell into a rhythm. Step-click, step-click, as boot then pole made contact with the earth.

For the first hour Luke lingered silently in the rear. His mind still wrestled with the images from his dream. He repeated the same words over and over to himself – stupid, stupid, stupid. Finally, he stopped and stabbed both poles into the ground. "Fuck it," he said both aloud and to himself. With a deep breath, he gripped his poles tightly and pushed away from this spot. His attention focused on his legs as they propelled him forward. He tightened and then relaxed his forearms. He flexed the muscles in his upper arms, shoulders, and chest. Exercise, his therapist said, was one of his coping mechanisms. It made him feel better, at least for a while.

As Luke passed them, Lil thought she detected the slightest smile on his face. "Let him go," Lil suggested to Sophie. "He is in his own zone. There is only the one path to the cafe."

For the next hour they kept a good pace. Luke separate and ahead. Sophie, Lil, and Russell behind but keeping him within eyeshot. They weren't the fastest on the trail that morning, nor were they the slowest. They passed a number of hikers, including the couple they had encountered resting under the tree the day before. A short time later, they were humbled when a family of six strode crisply past them. The unit hiked in a single line, two teenage girls in the front, followed by the mother and two smaller children – one boy and a girl – with the father at the back. Each one was smiling, and the youngest one whistled while he walked.

For a time, Sophie's eye followed the happy family. She noticed that every ten minutes or so the person in the back would proceed to the front of the line before being replaced ten minutes later by a sibling or a parent. She imagined what lay behind this order, this smoothly functioning family system. She weighed the possible backstories. Were the parents taskmasters? Commanding the children to stay in line. Nagging them to keep their room neat. Put away their clothes. Get their homework done before dinner. Had the children surrendered to the inevitable, grudgingly accepting that compliance was the best short-term strategy, at least until they could escape to college or work or drugs? Or were the parents nurturers? Expressing boundless faith in their children. Encouraging them to explore their interests and seek out new challenges. Had the children flourished and grown to see themselves as capable, strong, and worthy? Sophie was about to settle on the latter when her voice of experience reigned her back: There are no fairy tales, she chided herself.

Luke was a good ten minutes ahead of his mother when the happy family reached him. His mind had remained focused on his body, finding both distraction and satisfaction in the exercise. The whistling of the young boy caught his attention, and he glanced to the right. He saw the dad, two little kids, and a mom but his eye was drawn to the two teenage girls. He smiled and nodded as they walked by. He was sure the second girl had seen him and lifted her head in acknowledgment.

As the family passed by, Luke sped up. He didn't quite join the line. He stayed slightly back, but his mind quickly filled the space between himself and the girl at the end. Luke found himself drifting into another fantasy – a different coping strategy, according to his therapist. He imagined reaching toward the girl and pulling her close. Luke closed his eyes and could almost feel her soft hands sliding down his back when he tripped on an unseen rock and tumbled to the ground.

He wasn't hurt, and no one seemed to notice. The family line had kept on walking. The girl did not look back. Luke wiped the dirt off his knees and started walking again. He didn't close the gap and let the family walk into the distance. Stupid, stupid, stupid, he told himself again.

Le Refuge des Ciels

Ten minutes later, Luke arrived at le Refuge des Ciels. It appeared different from most of the other refuges along the trail. There were no dorms. The cafe building was set apart from what looked like a family home. He could see a barn and stable a little farther behind the house. This seemed more like a working farm than a mountain hut. While it might not welcome overnight guests, a trail of inviting scents – baked bread, bacon, cinnamon, coffee, and chocolate – drew a large crowd even at this early hour.

A stone and rail boundary protected the grass courtyard. A tribe of wandering goats nibbled at the tufts of grass sprouting at the wire fencing strung along the railed sections of the enclosure. Most of the dozen tables that dotted the courtyard were already filled. The clientele was distinctly mixed. There was the usual hiking crowd with their backpacks and sticks. But the travelers were outnumbered by what looked like locals, the tradespeople, farmers, and families of the area. Though Luke had lost track of the days, it was a Saturday morning. And the cafe was the social hub of La Ville des Glaciers.

Luke bid a silent adieu to the marching family and the girl who paid him no heed and turned his attention to food. Lifting the latch on the wooden gate, he swiftly crossed the courtyard and entered the building. It was more of a kitchen than a cafe. Three generations of women busied themselves mixing and baking, stirring and pouring. The older women prepared the products, following recipes long etched in their memory. The younger women fed baking trays into stone ovens and tended an army of frying pans set atop stoves that looked twice their age. Four children, three girls, and a boy, sorted the goods with ungloved hands onto four wooden displays. The only nod to technology in the whole operation was a chip-enabled credit card reader staffed by an amiable matron who could do sums faster than any calculator. She kept the line moving and the cash flowing in.

Luke did not immediately join the ordering queue. He stood beside two men he vaguely recognized from Le Club Alpine and considered his options. The men in front of him started joking with one another. "That one there looks like a little Oliver Twist," said the wider of the two, pointing at the boy sorting out the fruit tarts. He then held out his phone and was about to take a picture when the boy stopped, looked him square in the face and shook his finger. Still wearing a stern look, the lad then pointed to one of several signs placed above the food display: a red circle with a diagonal slash superimposed over the image of a camera and cell phone.

The wide man raised his hands in mock surrender, but as the boy returned to work, he took the picture anyway.

No sooner had the flash faded then the boy let out a piercing cry, "Papa!"

Initially surprised, the phone man presented a self-satisfied smile and was about to joke with his mate when three large men appeared from a corner of the room. They grabbed the phone man, his friend, and Luke by the front of their jackets and shoved them out of the cafe and into the courtyard. Neither Luke, the photographer, nor his mate offered any resistance, nor would it have been effective if they had. Their escorts had spent a lifetime working the fields and were used to moving much larger packages.

Once outside, a group of similarly dressed local men rose up from the picnic tables and stood behind the escorts. Luke stepped backward, trying to slink away from the confrontation, when an unyielding arm pushed him toward the phone man.

The older of the escorts started energetically berating the photographer in French while the other residents nodded their agreement. The photographer felt his heart race and his mouth run dry. He struggled to swallow. He hung his head and looked down at the ground.

When the escort finished his juicy tirade, he lowered his pointed finger out of the photographer's face, turned his palm upward, and said in heavily accented English, "Give me the phone."

The photographer's chin shot up. He pressed his phone to his heart and was about to speak when another voice interrupted him.

"Gaspard, what is the problem?" Lyndon asked, stepping in front of the photographer and standing at an angle toward the older man.

"*Monsieur Lyndon*," Gaspard said. "*Celui ci*," he continued, pointing to the photographer, "*Est un connard.*" And switching to English, he added, "He tried to take a picture of my grandson even after the boy told him 'non.'"

The tour leader shook his head sympathetically. "Yes," Lyndon replied. "He is an ass." And switching to French he added, "*Je m'excuse pour son comportement.*"

Turning to the photographer, Lyndon said, "Give him the phone."

As the photographer was about to object, Lyndon rolled his eyes and leaned towards his client. "If you want to leave here without bodily injury, give him the phone. If you don't . . . well, there is not much I can do to help you."

The photographer considered his options. And without looking at the older man handed Gaspard his phone.

Gaspard nodded. Smiling, he showed the phone to the crowd. There was a gasp of satisfaction. Some shoulders relaxed, and people began to return to their seats.

"Open the pictures," Gaspard directed. His English was suddenly much improved.

The photographer entered his password, opened his phone app, and returned the device to Gaspard. Gaspard selected the picture of his grandson and, with a satisfied swipe of his finger, deleted the image. He then returned the phone.

"*Merci*," Lyndon said.

"*D'accord*," Gaspard replied.

"*Vous devez vraiment obtenir des clients plus agréables*," Gaspard added with a laugh.

After Gaspard and Lyndon embraced, Lyndon turned to the photographer and his friend. "You two best be off. I don't think you will be getting any fruit tarts here. I'll meet you by the first signpost just a little farther up the path. Try not to piss off anyone on the way there."

"How you doing, Luke?" Lyndon asked, turning to the boy.

"That was crazy," Luke said with an anxious laugh. "I almost pissed my pants."

"I'm glad you didn't," Lyndon replied.

"And I didn't even do anything. I was just standing there next to the guy." Luke felt he needed to explain.

Lyndon nodded in agreement. "Luck of the draw, Luke. But now you've got a good story to tell your family."

"Hey, how do you know my name?" Luke asked, suddenly concerned that this man he had never met knew him by name.

"I met your grandmother this morning. She told me how proud she was of you and how appreciative she was of you taking this trip with your family. She said you were an athlete and good at photography," Lyndon explained. "I told her I looked forward to meeting you. I didn't know it would be at your first mountain brawl."

Luke wondered what else his grandmother might have mentioned, but he didn't ask. Instead, he turned to the question that had confused him: "Why were they so angry over a picture? The guy probably would have just posted it, and it would have been like free advertising," Luke asked.

"That's a bit complicated," Lyndon began. "The longtime locals, the ones who have been here for generations, they can harbor a real ambivalence. You know, the way things have changed. They like the money for sure, but they get nostalgic for the way things were – a simpler life of hard work connected to the land and the comfort of family, friends, and community. They fear losing what they love." Lyndon paused. He glanced at Luke. Luke returned the glance before looking away.

Lyndon tightened his lips and contemplated for a moment. He did not see that Luke, who was looking down at the ground, wore a similar expression. Lyndon continued, "So yes, Gaspard sells to the tourists, and makes a pretty penny," Lyndon added, "but he serves the community. And he does things the old way. Food prepared from scratch. Cooked in ovens that his grandfather built. The locals, they appreciate how he honors the traditions. Plus, he charges them only half of what the tourists pay, so they feel like they are in on the game." Lyndon turned to face Luke directly. "And most importantly, he is very protective of his family. He doesn't want them or their work treated as if they exist for the amusement of the tourists. So be polite when you order, smile and say thank you, and like the sign says, no pictures," he added with a wag of his finger. "The little dance you just witnessed," Lyndon confided, "that happens once or twice a month. It's all well choreographed. It is a rare trip that someone in my group doesn't run afoul of Gaspard. When it's over, the locals have protected their values, the tourists have a bit of excitement, and no one gets hurt – usually," Lyndon concluded with a slap to Luke's shoulder.

Lil, Russell, and Sophie arrived at the cafe just as Lyndon was finished speaking with Luke. Sophie saw Lyndon slap Luke on the back. They both seemed happy. She was relieved to see that the boy's mood had shifted. She hoped it would last.

Lyndon saw them approach. "You got a fine boy here," he said, first looking at Lil and then toward Sophie. "He helped me get out of a bit of a squeeze."

Luke blushed lightly. "Doing what needs to be done to help the clients," Luke said automatically. It was a phrase his father had often used. The left side of Sophie's face twitched involuntarily. Luke quickly changed the subject. "They got the best stuff in there. But you better mind your manners, or you'll end up with more trouble than treats."

Luke grabbed hold of Lil's arm and headed toward the door. Russell quickly joined them. Luke waved to his mom to accompany them.

Sophie replied, "I'll grab a table. Just get me a plain croissant."

Lyndon gestured toward an open table by the gate. He remained standing while Sophie sat. "You've got a good family there," he observed. "Your mother is a tough biscuit, but sweet inside, I think." Lyndon noticed a dubious turn to Sophie's smile. He chose not to comment. He then recounted the exchange between Gaspard and the photographer. "Your boy's a good egg. He stayed calm. He has a right head on him." Lyndon paused and considered asking about Luke's dad but thought better of it.

"Well, thank you for your help," Sophie replied.

"The pleasure was all mine," Lyndon said, extending his hand. As Sophie reached out, she noticed the absurd dialog in her head. How should I shake his hand? A firm grasp around his whole hand, a light touch with my fingers pressed in his palm? In the end, it was just a handshake.

"I hope to see you again," Lyndon concluded. To Sophie, it sounded like he meant it.

As she sat alone for those few moments waiting for her family to return, Sophie's mind revisited a familiar series of images: Rick standing on the pool deck cheering for Luke, Luke and Rick laughing as they tried to set up a tent in a rainstorm, Rick lying motionless with the pipe still next to him, and Luke standing dry-eyed and hands clenched at the cemetery. She shook her head in an effort to dislodge the images, as if denying them a foothold could change what was.

As Lil, Russell, and Luke approached the table, Sophie's eyes focused on her son. "Fake it until you make it," her counselor had coached her. "A smile can actually release the neurotransmitters associated with joy." Sophie forced a smile onto her lips.

They savored their treats while Luke excitedly told his version of the photographer's tale. Sophie felt her shoulders drop. When Luke got to the part about trying to slip away, she reached out and grabbed his hand, and he let her.

"Well, your friends can't beat that story," Russell said before he thought better of it. At the mention of his friends, Luke's enthusiasm dimmed.

Lil quickly added, "Best be going. We're burning daylight."

The Descent to Le Chalet

Throughout the day the weather remained perfect for hiking. At mile eight, just after 1:00, they reached le Col de Fours and took lunch before beginning the winding descent into the valley. Luke sat next to a boulder with his back to his family and his phone in the shadow of the stone. The previous evening, he had sent several messages to Sean and posted some pictures to his feed - the video of the bull, the cable bridge, and the mountain vistas. Since mid-morning he had been trying, without success, to see the comments. Even now, at an elevation of nearly 3,500 feet, all he got was a red undeliverable.

While they continued to make steady progress throughout the early afternoon, Luke's mood darkened. In the quiet rhythm of his steps, as his feet moved forward his mind wandered, cycling through images from his dream, his father, his friends, his unread messages. His father was joking, smiling, breathing – then not. His friends were laughing and he was with them – and then he wasn't. They were talking about him – and then they forgot him. He revisited all his shouldn'ts and should haves: I shouldn't have said that, I should've told someone, I should've been nicer, I shouldn't be so moody, I should've stayed home. I shouldn't have so many fucking shoulds . . .

Several times during the descent, the others tried to engage with him. But Luke was now mired in his unhappy place. He communicated his displeasure by dragging his feet, muttering about blisters, and distancing himself. By mid-afternoon, self-absorption grew into sullen annoyance followed by mental insurrection. When Russell tried to draw him out a second time, Luke snapped back: "I never wanted to do this trip."

Russell inhaled sharply. He raised his eyebrows and eventually nodded his head. "OK." Pause. "We'll meet you at the Chalet." He resisted the urge to say more and moved forward to rejoin Lil and Sophie, leaving Luke to walk the remaining three miles alone with his thoughts.

This last leg of walking alone was the cap to an inglorious afternoon for Luke. Day two of ten days in mountain hell, he told himself. Twenty minutes ago the sign read "*Chalet des Mottets – Quinze Minutes.*" The growling of his empty stomach mixed with the grinding of the stones beneath his feet churned the anger in his head. Finally, he saw the red flag of the refuge peeking above the hollow in the pasture to his right. He quickened his pace, excited that his torture, at least for today, would finally be over. And just when he allowed himself a flicker of joy, a cowherder's daughter appeared, as if from nowhere, and pulled the rope across the hiking path. She ushered the cows from the pasture on the left to the field on the right, the traffic jam leaving Luke imprisoned at the intersection.

"Are you fucking kidding me!" He threw down his poles, kicked at the mud, and raised his fists to the sky. The cows lolled their heads as they crossed the path. The bells around their neck clanged loudly as if celebrating his misery.

He watched the slow parade, observing that cows had a remarkable ability to walk and shit at the same time. It seemed as if each step pumped out a never-ending trail of liquidy crap. As Luke pondered this talent, a flapping tail of a particularly prodigious cow swatted some of the brown crap onto his pant legs. "You are fucking disgusting!" he yelled at his bovine tormentors. The girl laughed. At 17, Luke hadn't cried in three years. He felt like crying now. Instead, he let loose his own stream of verbal bile.

Luke arrived 15 minutes before dinner. The rest of his family had already showered and changed. He ran into them as they were walking down the stairs to the dining hall.

Luke thought about just heading to dinner without showering. But he could smell his own stink and cow shit on his leg. Besides, hut etiquette was clear: Shower first then eat. He checked his phone. The messages were still undelivered. He stripped to his shorts, threw a towel around his waist, and headed to the co-ed shower room.

Even at this late hour, so close to dinner, there were more people than stalls. Taking a seat on the wooden bench, he waited his turn for an open shower. He was fourth in the queue behind two older men and a fit middle-aged woman. He remembered the woman. She had passed him earlier in the day during a particularly steep ascent. Her whistling and chipper greeting annoyed him then. She still seemed happy which made him angry all over again.

A young twenty-something with the lean body of a climber entered the shower room trailed by two younger women. The young women seemed to know one another and they chatted softly in what Luke took to be Italian. He watched the two friends. They were clearly studying the young climber who took off his shirt, undid his manbun and began washing at the sink. Luke recognized the look. It was the same attention he would often receive from girls, and even some of the guys, at the pool back home.

The two friends noticed Luke staring at them. Luke quickly turned away but could still hear them laughing softly. He felt himself blushing.

The taller of the two girls approached and sat next to him on the bench. He turned his head slightly in her direction, not making eye contact. "You were looking at us," she said in accented English.

Luke's initial instinct was to deny. "No, I was just . . ."

She raised an eyebrow. "It is okay. You are cute, too," she said as she stood up and headed to an open shower.

Luke shifted on the bench, placed his hand on his knees, and leaned forward. His eyes followed her as she and her friend walked. Though it was his turn for the shower, Luke waved the next person through while he remained seated for a few more minutes.

Dinner 2

Le Chalet de Mottets was a much larger hut than the first night. Like most of the other refuges along the route, it was a repurposed structure. Formerly an animal barn, the left quarter had been converted into a kitchen where the meals were prepared for the hikers. Twenty rows of tables easily accommodated up to 120 travelers. An array of farm tools – halters, sieves, baskets, and hundreds of bells – hung on the walls. The display was like a museum of medieval husbandry; it also included an equally impressive collection of climbing gear.

Unlike Le Club Alpine there were no assigned seats. Lil, Russell and Sophie had arrived five minutes prior to serving and chose a table near the kitchen, saving a seat for Luke. They were soon joined by two other groups: the young couple they had encountered on both days and the family of six who had marched past them earlier in the morning.

Lil greeted the couple with a warm smile. Hands tightly entwined, the pair moved as one to the two empty chairs opposite her. They briefly released their grasp as the man pulled out the seat for the woman, only to reclasp her hand once seated, as if afraid the other might float away. Young love, Lil thought to herself, sometimes just a little too clingy. In that flash of an instant, she thought of Russell. Of how they managed to be both together and apart. Her independence and privacy comforted her, especially now, adding to her confidence that he could go on without her.

As often occurred, the conversation between the tablemates started with an annotated biography and some anecdotes from the day. And, when the trail magic works well, as it did this night, the exchange moves beyond pleasantries. The boyfriend, not husband, as Lil had learned before finishing the bread and cheese, took the initial risk.

"May I ask you something?" he said sheepishly, shoulders and head leaning toward Lil as if requesting a secret. Lil didn't answer and the boyfriend did not wait for one. "How do you do it? You are some bad-ass hiker," he said. "You are like three times our age. We saw you this morning at breakfast. You had, maybe, a ten-minute head start. We were joking – 'We'll catch her in the first half hour.' But we were in your dust the whole way."

He paused for a moment, and Lil was about to answer. But the boyfriend continued, "We passed your grandson toward the very end, but we never caught you up to you. How do you do it? I mean . . ."

The girlfriend hit him on the shoulder. "Quit talking, so maybe she can answer?" He stopped abruptly, teetering between anger and embarrassment. He turned to his girlfriend and found comfort in the look on her face.

"What Mr. Sometimes-Annoying-Doesn't-Know-When-To-Stop-Talking means to say is that we really admire you," she shared.

"Yeah, what she said, that's true. All of it," the boyfriend added after the briefest of pauses, "So what's your secret? Tai chi, organic vegetables, good genes?"

Lil chortled in what Russell would describe as the classic Lil laugh. It was a low rumble on the exhale that continued for one or two more waves longer than you thought it would.

Lil liked these two young ones. A part of her laugh was quietly chiding herself for being so judgmental when they first arrived. They were clearly in love. It was an early love for sure but beyond mere infatuation. With time, perhaps this love would be tempered by an acceptance of each other's faults. Lil found the promise of freedom in that kind of love.

"When I was a young woman, a long time ago, I learned," Lil began, "the secret, if there is one, is to simply keep going. You make a choice. Then there is no choice. One foot in front of the other. Keep going. No use crying or wishing it weren't so. Go where your journey takes you. That's my way."

The couple nodded silently, even the chatty partner.

"Damn, I told you she was bad-ass," the boyfriend finally said.

They all shared a Lil-laugh together. They finished the meal in good spirits, revealing stories and insights that surprised even themselves in the telling. The joy of this moment unclouded by the knowledge that in less than a year, two of them would be dead, including the girlfriend, then wife, perishing in an accident while the young couple honeymooned in Costa Rica. No, tonight was about friendship, the promise of love and continuing on our chosen path, one step at a time.

On the other side of the table, Russell introduced himself to the family, a husband and wife from Devon with the four children: two teenage twins, a young boy, and another daughter. While he had seen them on the trail earlier in the day, it was only now that Russell noticed the girl had Down Syndrome.

With the enthusiasm of a puppy, Connor, the Devon boy, attempted to stab pieces of carrot from his sister's plate. He had no interest in eating them – he hadn't touched the vegetables his mum had optimistically assigned to him. It was just a game. His sister smiled and giggled as she first intercepted his efforts with her own fork and then counterattacked, rescuing her hijacked carrot from her brother's plate.

People trusted Russell. He was a patient listener who communicated his full attention with his animated eyes and dependable smile. Encouraged, the parents joyfully shared stories of their adventures traveling as a family. Russell never raised the subject of the daughter's condition. The parents went there naturally.

"We just treat Angel the way we treat all the other children. At first, when she was born, we were angry and then afraid. Sometimes we still are," the mum confessed. "Then we decided, 'Well, we can't change it. Have to go with it.' And we have been going ever since."

The father continued, "Whenever we have a holiday we plan to go somewhere new. And, whatever we do," he added, "it has to have some challenge to it."

"What was your favorite trip?" the dad asked his son.

"That's easy. That whitewater trip last summer," Connor answered.

"Beats the slog out of all this walking," his mischievous smile tempting his father to respond. "Remember when you fell out of the boat and lost your hat and you almost pulled mum in the water when you tried to climb back in?" Another baiting look, this time met with mock outrage from the father. The boy laughed heartily.

"What was your favorite trip?" the dad now asked Angel.

"This one," she said, neither pausing nor looking up.

"That's what she always says," the mum added. Looking sympathetically at her husband, she reached out and grabbed Angel's hand. "And she is right."

Russell nodded. "That sounds like something my wife always says. 'There's only the now. Don't go wasting it wishing for something else.'"

Unlike Russell and Lil, Sophie sat in relative silence, with a vacant chair between her and the family. She scolded herself for not waiting for Luke, all the while knowing that, given his current mood, her company was neither welcomed nor helpful. Still, her guilt over this imagined abandonment joined the pile of self-anointed offenses crowding her soul. To distract herself from her growing melancholy, Sophie's eyes explored the room. Her attention was captured by a group of women seated three tables over. Judging from their laughter and their faces they were very much enjoying the evening.

From the back of the hall two staff members wheeled out what looked like a giant jack-in-the-box. The women were wearing what Sophie imagined to be traditional Alpine dress, though her knowledge of the subject was primarily informed by multiple viewings of *The Sound of Music* and the logo from a bottle of St. Pauli Girl. Each had a white dirndl blouse tufted on the shoulders, with a black smock over the front and a blue apron that almost reached the floor. Colorful embroidered needlework decorated the waist and straps of the smock.

The women stopped at a small square in the midst of all the tables. They opened the top of the box. To Sophie's disappointment, nothing popped up. Instead, there was a series of tubes that looked like organ pipes. Intricate three-dimensional frescos decorated each side of the box. The carved scenes featured many of the same images as the embroidery. The smaller of the two women opened a hidden compartment built into the base and removed a folded parchment scroll. As if on cue the room grew silent. The woman fed an edge of the scroll into the bottom of the box and nodded to her partner. The larger woman took hold of a wooden crank the size of a tree branch and slowly turned the handle.

A rich melody filled the hall and cheers erupted from all corners of the room. Though the tune was unfamiliar to Sophie, it was apparently well-known to many in the crowd. Multiple voices quickly joined in. Several others clapped and hooted, clanking their mugs on the solid wooden tables, as if they were at a German biergarten. Of all the revelers none matched the enthusiasm of the women's table Sophie had spied earlier.

Sophie studied the women with a mixture of joy and longing. Several of them stood up and started dancing, Flamenco style. Sophie thought of her own circle of friends. She had difficulty imagining them ever matching the enthusiasm she now witnessed before her. Whether inspired by the alcohol in the wine, the friendship at the table, the fatigue of the hike, or the power of Duende, she could not truly tell. But Sophie knew that neither she nor her friends possessed this spirit of abandon. She was both inspired and saddened. One of the singers caught her eye and raised her glass in Sophie's direction. Sophie lifted her glass slightly in return.

Though she wasn't certain, she thought she saw the woman gesture with her hand, the slightest of movements, perhaps inviting Sophie to join this sisterhood.

Sophie thought for a moment. She wondered what it would feel like to join this tribe, even for one evening. To be filled with such joy, to unleash the song in your heart, careless about what others might think or say. Sophie thought, and at that moment found she could not imagine it. She pressed her feet into the ground. She did not move. Instead, she turned her eyes away from the woman and into that empty space separating her from her mother. Sophie remained anchored where she was.

Luke arrived 15 minutes in. Sophie raised a hand and motioned to the empty seat. He joined her without objection. She tousled his hair, greeting him, "You finally made it, I thought we had lost you."

He shook off her touch with a practiced twitch of his head. "No thanks to those cows," he said in a not-unpleasant voice. The prospect of food had helped lighten his mood, but it was the compliment from the Italian girl and his imagined fantasy that had raised his spirit.

Luke took out his phone and scrolled to his still unreadable messages. He frowned and shook his head. Sophie noticed the look. She leaned in and said quietly, "I heard someone say they turn on the Wi-Fi at midnight. But only for half an hour."

Luke's eyes widened momentarily. He then checked his phone again – 7:20. With a shrug of his shoulder, he turned his attention to the bread and cheese already at the table. He spent the next ten minutes joking with Angel and Connor. He largely ignored the older twins, embarrassed by his earlier fall. Besides, they seemed more interested in one another. Occasionally, Luke would scan around the room looking for the Italian girls. He never saw them.

They smelled the next course well before its arrival – that most delicious odor of braised meat surrendering its flavor. As the staff walked the giant crocks to the tables, Sophie noticed Russell gently lifting his hands, ushering the scents to his widened nostrils. The Devon boy sat at the ready. A fork in one hand and a spoon in the other standing sentry at either side of his empty white plate. As the servers walked past the table for the third time, bringing food first to the patrons in the back, the impatient boy said, just a little too loudly, "Well, ain't that a load of tosh." Luke unsuccessfully stifled a laugh while Connor's mum smacked the lad two ticks more than gently on the back of his head. As the boy squinted his eyes and rubbed his noggin, Angel stole another piece of bread from his plate.

Finally, their patience was rewarded. The servers delivered three giant casserole dishes, one at each end and a third in the middle. Lil, the Devon dad and Sophie did the honors of dishing out the stew. The dad seemed to take particular pleasure in passing the plates over and around his son, who was the last to receive his ration.

With a gusto befitting simple food, well-prepared, and a hunger fueled by eight hours of walking, the stew quickly disappeared as did the next round of cheese and the caramel raspberry torte.

The crank box stopped when the last casserole was delivered. The conversation, in a half-dozen languages and even more entertaining accents, continued: a symphony of community formed by this new and temporary fellowship. As inspiring as the views can be, for many hikers, the meals together are the enduring highlight of the Tour du Mont Blanc.

La Conteuse – Part 1

While the last of the dormers made payment to the hut guardians, La Conteuse took her seat in the back corner of the dining area. A few of the guests migrated over with their espresso or wine and sat around the elderly woman.

Though the network of refuges had grudgingly made concessions to the 21st century – a few had Wi-Fi, and many now accepted credit cards – through a mix of necessity and choice, they steadfastly guarded their character. It was, after all, part of what made the Alpine hut experience unique. One recent change that had become increasingly popular was to hire local storytellers, *les conteurs*, to entertain the guests with tales of the region. After spending a night at one hut, les conteurs would also walk the route and stop at a different refuge the next night. The storytellers often traveled in small groups of five or six, visiting the different huts in the same vicinity. Over the course of several days it was possible that hikers might hear the same *conteur* night after night or another *conteur* with a set of new stories or a different version of the same tale. Tonight, Signora Maria was at the Chalet de Mottets.

Maria's body was a study in contrast. Her arms were as soft as her legs were muscled. Her calves attested to a lifetime spent walking through the mountains. Her black hair peeked beneath a kerchief. Her eyes, the first feature that drew Lil, were as brown as her skin. A slight milky layer of the sort you see in an older person without enough money to remove the cataracts, or perhaps someone who had seen enough in her lifetime and welcomed a little shadow, clouded her left eye. She could have been fifty or a hundred. It was impossible to tell. But she belonged to these mountains, of that you were sure. To Lil, her eyes had a familiar look.

Maria started softly in a voice that invited your attention. It was an unhurried voice. Her hands gestured slowly as she told stories of the old alpinists. Of how, in 1786, Jacques Balmat claimed the prize money offered by de Saussure for the first man to summit Mont Blanc. "They did not have ropes, or axes, or puffy jackets," wagging her finger as if scolding everyone in the room. "There was no map. No pretty refuges to spend the night. They walked where no one else dared. Everyone said in their little voices, 'Oh, it can't be done, *c'est impossible.*' But Balmat, he had the courage and *cajones.*" Her audience laughed, though uncertain if they should. A slight smile flickered across Maria's face. It was a well-practiced tale. She knew where her laughs were. Buoyed by the attention, her voice grew slightly more animated and she pushed forward in her chair. "Yes, that bastard Paccard was there but it was Balmat who knew the mountains. Paccard loved his flowers and his science. But Balmat loved the mountain. He knew, yes, it was he who knew when to leave a serac alone and go another route. Balmat could read a crevasse the way you read a textie message. He loved the mountain. The mountain let him enter and loved him back."

"What happened to Balmat?" someone asked.

"Same that happens to many great climbers and to a lot of not-so-good ones, too. Fell off a cliff and died," Maria said with a dismissive lift of her head. "But he lived to seventy-one, which is better than most." She paused and then added with a quick glance to her husband, Luigi, seated behind her, "The mountain, she is a fickle lover."

Maria then shared the history of several others. She told of Henriette d'Angeville, la Dame du Mont Blanc, and of Michel Croz ("he died at 35"), Albert Mummery ("he died at 40"), Paul Preuss ("he died at 27"), Louis Lachenal ("at 34"). Her stories bounced through time and location, not following a chronology but, as stories are for us all, each with some meaning and connection to the teller. Maria paused to catch her breath.

"Tell them about Bonatti," Luigi interjected during this pause to her death tally.

"Ah, he lived to eighty-one," she nodded. "Bonatti, now there was a beautiful man." She looked up as if speaking to him personally. "Some of you will be staying at the Refugio de Walter Bonatti. I will be there in a few days, too. It is one of the most beautiful huts in the mountains. Right at the Grande Jourasses. You wake in the morning and the light shines upon the *geants*. There is no more beautiful sight in all of the Haute Savoie. And Walter Bonatti, he is one of the best men who has ever climbed . . ."

She was about to continue when Luigi interrupted, "Blah, blah, blah, you always worshiped him. Not Walter, tell them the story of his brother!"

She moved more quickly than she had all evening. Her head snapped, and she glared at her husband. Maria turned back around, crossed her arms, and shook her head. Her eyes moistened as her silence grew loud. He pressed forward and put his arms gently on her shoulders. "Maria, it is a love story," he implored.

"It is a *tragedy*," Maria said with the edge of pain in her face.

"All love stories are tragedies," Lil spoke up. "It is just a matter of time . . ."

In the long moment that followed, Maria studied Lil's face, and a tear fell to the floor. During its descent, Maria decided: "This is the story of Frederico Bonatti and La Belle Elizabetta," she began.

"Walter Bonatti is the famous one, a legend in these mountains. A man everyone knows, and many pretend to have met. But he had a brother, Frederico. You will not find him in any books. There are no huts, no monuments, no routes named after him. But I knew him, and I remember him still.

"Frederico was the younger Bonatti—a winter baby, born fourteen years after his brother and two years before his sister. Like many young boys, he worshipped his older brother. When he spoke, it was always 'Walter did this' and 'Walter did that.' But after Walter's climb to the Aiguille du Dru in nineteen fifty-five – a climb that remains a legend even today – it was then that Frederico's worship became his obsession. 'Walter didn't start climbing until he was eighteen. Think how good I would be if I started now,' he told us. It was then that Frederico devoted his life to climbing.

"By the time he was seventeen, Frederico had already climbed the Grand Capucin, a feat his brother did not accomplish until his twenties. He was the youngest to summit Aiguille Noire de Peuterey. Here in Mont Blanc, people started talking about The New Bonatti. More handsome than his brother – and Walter was a handsome man. Frederico drew the eye from dozens of the young ladies in the valley. And he enjoyed many short-lived romances. None, however, captured his devotion. In his hometown it was said that the mountain owned his heart – first loves are unforgiving.

"But, in the summer of nineteen seventy-two, he met a beautiful American woman. She was visiting Savoie, teaching English to the children. She taught in three villages, spending two days in each before moving on to the next and then starting all over again the following week. She was traveling from Contamines to Courmayeur when Frederico first met her. It was a cold and rainy day. Frederico was coming down from a training climb. She was the only other person he met on the trail. Mistaking her for one of the boys from the village, his first thought was 'another stupid young goat out on a day like this.' When he caught up to this trail partner, he was surprised. His stupid goat was a stunning young woman. After an awkward stare, he said, 'Mio bella, what is a beautiful young woman doing out on a miserable day like this.' 'Walking, same as you,' came a reply as cool as the rain. The young woman kept moving. Frederico started walking backward in front of her. He smiled his best smile, a smile that had warmed the hearts of many young women. 'What is your name?' he asked. 'What is your name?' came the curt reply. 'I am Frederico,' he quickly answered. And after a considerably longer pause, the young woman finally said, 'My name is Elizabetta.' 'Here, let me carry your bag, la belle Elizabetta,' Frederico offered, stepping beside her. As he bowed slightly, he slipped on a wet stone. He caught himself before his gallant ass landed in the mud. 'Perhaps I should carry your bag, my ragazzino,' she said to him." Maria laughed to herself as she imagined the scene.

"From that moment, Frederico was in love. He was smitten with Elizabetta's spirit as much as her beauty.

"Over the next few weeks, it seemed that whenever Elizabetta would

118

travel from village to village, Frederico would happen to be on the same path. Initially, she was only flattered – what young woman does not enjoy the attention of a handsome man? She enjoyed the company and the conversation.

"After one month of these fortuitous meetings and the long walks that followed, Frederico invited her to have dinner with his family, something he had never done with any other girl. The family was as taken with Elizabetta as was Frederico. 'Finally, someone who could take his mind off of the mountains,' his mother said.

"And in the weeks that followed, Elizabetta would spend her free day in his village. That was where I first met her. And in their time together and on the meadows in the shadow of the great mountains, they enjoyed the many pleasures of young love.

"Elizabetta knew, as only a woman knows, that she had a hold on his heart. And over the course of the summer, she gave her heart to him.

"As August drew to a close, and the date for her return to America approached, a sense of melancholy clouded her days. No, she had not come to Italy to find a husband. Now, though, she wrestled with the idea that she had found her soulmate. Bonatti harbored no such doubt. He knew. He had found the woman he wanted to marry. What had begun as a second love had surpassed his first.

"Two weeks before she was to leave, Bonatti determined that he would propose to Elizabetta. After a picnic dinner with a bouquet of mountain roses, the most beautiful of Alpine flowers that can only be found in the highest cols, Bonatti asked Elizabetta to be his wife.

"Though in love, the young woman reacted with hesitation. This was not the path she had chosen. She froze. She did not reply. When she did speak, she said she needed some time to think. Bonatti was embarrassed and heartbroken. The pain clear on his face, he quickly gathered the remains of the meal and returned silently to the village, leaving Elizabetta alone in the meadow.

"That evening, Elizabetta decided she had been foolish. She knew she loved Bonatti. She decided that in the morning she would find him, embrace him, and tell him yes."

Maria, whose voice had grown softer, started to sob. Feeling the sorrow of *la counteuse*, many eyes in the room also grew moist. "I can tell you no more tonight," Maria managed through the tears. Luigi embraced her from behind and gently kissed her cheek. She turned her face toward him and whispered a message.

Luigi addressed the crowd. "That is all for tonight. I am sorry. If you want to hear the rest of the story, Maria will be at the Rifugio Bonatti in two days. Then she will tell you how the tale ends, perhaps."

Juergen

In a nod to her age, Lil always had a bottom bunk in every one of the huts. Even if she were to arrive late and all the beds were taken, invariably, someone would offer her the space. Normally a proud woman, she accepted the gift with grace. She did not relish the idea of climbing the ladder and crawling over unfamiliar bodies to squeeze into the final bed, especially knowing that she may need to exit once or twice during the restless night.

Many nights she had trouble falling asleep. But tonight it wasn't the disease that denied her that respite. Her head was alive with the events from the dining hall.

Lil slipped from her bunk, grabbed her purple kit from the front pocket of her backpack, and tiptoed out the door. She walked the narrow hallway, down the stairs, and quietly exited to the earthen terrace on the east side of the hut.

It was a gorgeous summer night in the Alps, the sort usually found only in dreams. The full moon was cresting just over the outline of the ridge. This craggy silhouette fell upon the side of the hut, lending a somber hue to the flowers that had so colorfully greeted the travelers earlier in the day. She sat atop the picnic table, enjoyed the view, and replayed Maria's story over and over.

Lil took out the joint she had carefully rolled the previous evening and lit the jagged end. For her, the first inhale was always the best. Once, Debbie had teased her, "Baby, you smoke pot like you're doing yoga. All slow and easy with that zen face of yours." She exhaled slowly and watched the blue vapor swirl into the mountain sky. "Namaste, sister," Lil said.

With each inhale, the command of the full moon quieted. The field of stars slowly blossomed. Her relaxing mind started to name the patterns she observed, some recalled from her past and others born in her current whimsy.

She heard a voice rise from behind her. "That looks like a good idea. May I have some?"

Lil smiled, the universal happy smile of a kind soul slightly stoned, and handed Juergen the joint. He took a seat on the bench to her right.

"*Danke*," he replied. "Oh, that is *sehr gut!*"

"Medicinal grade – powerful and clean," Lil added with a swirl of her hand.

Juergen nodded. A slow loll of a nod that could be either interpreted as contentment or contemplation. After a pause, he turned his head toward her and, through a half-opened eye, risked the question: "What do you have?"

Lil hesitated, uncertain of which path to take. She chose the truth. "Pancreatic cancer." Pause. "Metastasized to my liver." Pause. "Inoperable." Pause. "This will be my final tour, I'm afraid."

Juergen nodded. "I am honored to be here with you, my *tapferer freund*." He took another hit and, with a gesture that looked like half a salute, handed her back the joint.

Relief swept through her as she told her truth to Juergen. Beyond Russell, Debbie, and Betsy, she had not truly spoken her story fully to another, and with them, never had she been so free, especially with that last part. Whether it was the invitation of the pot, the infinite evening sky, or the company of Juergen, she was not sure. But she went on to voice feelings and thoughts she had not said aloud before, not even to herself. She spoke of her pain and her fear, of all she would miss in a future she would never see. She also spoke of her love and her joys and even a few regrets.

Juergen proved a wonderful listener. Every bit as patient as Russell but without the burden of knowing that you will be spending the rest of your life, however long that may or may not be, with this person.

When she finished, she felt liberated. She reached out and took hold of Juergen's hands and kissed them gently. "Thank you, dear Juergen. I needed that, even more than the smoke."

He chuckled, squeezed her hands, and said, "We shall have to do this again, dear friend. And next time, I will bring the stash." He hobbled back to the hut, leaving her to temporarily enjoy the peace among the stars.

Lil returned her supplies to the purple kit. She lingered a moment longer. Inhaling deeply, she savored the night air and this moment of life before stepping off the table. As she neared the side door, Lil noticed someone else approaching the hut. His head was down with his arms folded across his waist. Even in the dark, she recognized Luke. She remained still and watched as her grandson slowly shuffled down the path, carefully opened the back door, and quietly headed into the building. She waited for five minutes before following him in.

Luke's Lesson

L uke left the dining hall with his family when la conteuse finished her tale.

"Do you want to play some cards with us before going to bed?" his mother asked hopefully.

"No," Luke replied distractedly, looking past his mother and among the crowd of people heading toward the dormitories. "It's still nice out. I'm going to wander around a bit first."

His mother nodded silently before adding, "Be careful."

Luke's face wrinkled. Be careful. What did she mean by that, he wondered, his shoulders tightening. He turned and walked away from his mother. After a few steps he noticed he was still clenching his fists. He stopped, drew a deep breath, and exhaled slowly. The way he would before the starting buzzer. The way his therapist had recommended. He released the agitated thought, at least a little bit.

When he opened his eyes, he noticed that many of the younger hikers were heading toward one building in particular. It looked like a long horses' paddock, only with the stall gates closed in and replaced by a wooden wall with a window.

Luke walked toward one of the windows, put his hands to the side of his head, and peered inside. It was neatly lined with dozens of beds and bustling with people. There were no grey hairs or parents with children. While no one looked younger than Luke, at least they weren't old. This'll be the spot, he thought to himself.

He skirted along the outside wall and toward the double doors in the middle of the structure. He pressed by a crowd huddled near the entrance and stepped into the room. It was a single large open space, post and beam construction with a slightly vaulted ceiling that could easily accommodate eighty people. Several of the beds were already occupied. Most of those were only lounging. One seemed truly asleep, his snoring attracting a cluster of mocking onlookers.

Luke started walking around the perimeter scanning the small fluid groups that formed and reformed, all animated by the energy of the young. Across the room, along the far wall, he noticed them, the two young Italian women he had met in the shower room.

His heart quickened. He swallowed several times and stepped forward into the space between two crowds near the door. The girls were looking in his direction. He hesitated for a moment before making his decision. He lifted his arm and waved. The taller girl waved. She then took hold of her friend's arm and moved forward. He lowered his head slightly, wiped his moistening palms across the front of his thighs, and thought of what to say first.

Luke lifted his head and looked at the two approaching women. As he opened his mouth to speak, the two friends walked past him and toward the young climber they had eyed in the shower room. They each took hold of one arm. Luke was close enough to hear their conversation. "Are you ready," the taller one asked. "I hope so," Manbun replied. The three left the dorm together. Luke followed them out. Still hand-in-hand they turned left, following a grass path leading to a field behind the building. Luke turned right and sat alone on a bench near the dining hall, shaking his head and telling himself once again how stupid he was.

Luke looked at his phone. The stark white numbers stared back: 10:10. "Still no Wi-Fi," he muttered aloud. He slammed the phone down on the bench next to him. He then quickly picked up the phone, full of regret. The screen was blank. Panic flooded through him. He cradled the device, fearing he might have broken it. He gently pressed the button on the right and the screen flickered to life.

Suddenly he felt so exhausted. But not for sleep. He was exhausted by his circumstances. By his life. He wanted to talk to his friends – no, to be with

125

them. He wanted to get away. To go home. To go back.

10:12. 10:13 . . . 10:15 . . . 10:19. In those minutes he imagined himself walking to the road. To walk away. Right now. Get on a bus or a train. Go to the airport. Fly home. Sean's parents would surely pick him up. By 10:20 the impracticalities grounded his fantasy.

Luke sat a few minutes longer. If he didn't get back, he knew his mother would come looking for him or at least send Russell. I'll go back, he reasoned. I'll pretend to go to sleep and then come out again at midnight.

Back in the dorm, the moonlight filtered through the heavy paned glass, enough so Luke could find his backpack. Most of the 15 beds were occupied. But his mother's bed, along with those of his grandparents, were still empty.

Good, he thought to himself. At least I won't have to answer any questions.

Reaching into his pack, he removed an extra T-shirt and a pair of slides and climbed into his top bunk. He tucked the extra shirt under his pillow—just in case the dreams returned—and put on the slides, convincing himself they were mostly clean. He pulled the covers up under his chin so no one could see he was still dressed. Holding his phone close to his chest, he turned to face the wall with his back to the room. Then he waited.

Luke was still awake, counting the minutes, when he heard the latch of the door lift, followed by quiet footsteps and some shuffling he suspected was Russell. He stifled a smile, picturing his grandfather picking his way across the wood floor, arms outstretched to avoid any unwanted collision.

"Luke?" he heard his mother's whisper. Luke's jaw tightened but he did not respond. "Luke?" she repeated. After a few moments, the creak of the bed below him suggested his mother had settled in.

Luke hazarded a glance beneath his sheets, careful so as to not move too much. 10:50. Still more than an hour before midnight. He closed his eyes but did not sleep.

Sounds inhabit every silence. At first, Luke listened to the noises around him. The rhythmic breathing of his roommates. The rasp of a blanket being tugged across the bed. The hiss of the air discharged by the radiator. The footsteps of someone quietly leaving the room. And then he listened to the not-silence inside his head. He saw the Italian girls waving and walking past him, the farmer's daughter laughing at him, and the cow shitting on him. He relived the embarrassment of tripping and falling to the ground. He felt the ache in his shoulders, his back, and his feet. He imagined his friends, smiling and laughing at the pool or around a fire. He could almost feel Nikki, or was it Katie? He couldn't tell. And then he saw his father and his not-father behind him. Almost gasping, Luke turned quickly away from the images. Shit, shit, shit, he repeated to himself, worried that he had woken his mother. He held his body still and listened. Nothing.

Get your shit together, asshole, he told himself. As his mind raced, he remembered the box breathing technique his therapist had suggested. "It's what the Navy SEALs do," she had said. After emptying his lungs, he breathed in slowly, counting to four. He held his breath for another four seconds, imagining himself completing the second side of the box. The third step – breathing out slowly – was always the hardest for him. After two seconds he felt like he had nothing more to give. But with effort, he found he could exhale for another two seconds. "You always like to hold something back. Release it," she had teased him when he had practiced during their last session. This final portion was the easiest for him. With nothing left in your lungs, count to four again. Slowly. One . . . Two . . . Three . . . Four. He liked that nothingness. He could get lost there.

Luke completed the cycle several more times. By focusing on the breath inside his lungs, he could escape the torment inside his head. He didn't sleep. But he didn't want to. He just needed to pass the minutes until midnight.

At 11:50, Luke reasoned it was close enough to time. He silently slipped from beneath his covers. Supporting his weight with his arms, he lowered himself from the bed, avoiding the ladder that he feared might creak. Still, his slides clapped lightly when he touched the floor. His stomach flipped and he froze in place. He eyed the body in the bunk below him. Nothing. He allowed himself a small smile as he headed out the same door and down the steps Lil had passed 45 minutes earlier.

After entering into the moonlight he headed toward the path the Italian girls had walked with Manbun. It was on the opposite side of the building where Lil was now speaking with Juergen.

Not sure of how strong the signal would be, Luke stopped about ten yards down the path and waited.

He stared at his phone. No bars for cell signal. But that was to be expected. 85 percent. Plenty of power in the battery – that was good. No Wi-Fi, yet.

The numbers flicked from 11:59 to 12:00. Luke's eyes were wide, his finger poised about the Instagram icon. There were no bars—not for the cell signal, not for the Wi-Fi.

Luke started pacing. His mind raced through the possibilities. *Maybe it is not automated. Maybe someone has to actually turn something on.* He was sweating, even in the cool mountain air. *I'm too far away,* he thought, and ran down the path and into the central courtyard that opened up to all the dormitories. *The signal has to be better here,* he reasoned. Still nothing. Luke turned off his phone and immediately back on, thinking the restart might help him connect. His annoyance turned to anger when the newly refreshed phone still had no signal.

He was on the edge of panic when, from inside the adjacent dorm, Luke could hear the familiar ping of alerts and see the hazy glow of screens reflecting off the window glass. "Yes!" he said triumphantly to the four curved arcs in the corner of his phone.

Luke pressed the icon and started walking back to the path. The connection remained strong. A series of posts and images cascaded across his screen. There were so many, and all at once. He couldn't view them all. But he didn't have to. He suddenly felt sick.

Luke's finger was shaking when he pressed the chat button for Sean. One ring. "Pick up. Pick up. Pick up," Luke said aloud to himself. The two unanswered rings felt like an eternity. Then Sean's face filled the screen.

"Dude, why haven't you messaged? Been trying to reach you, past two days," Sean said with a grim look on his face.

"Tryin'. D-grade signal here, bro," Luke replied. "What's going on?"

"It's blowing up, man. Bad." Sean interrupted. "You seen any of the posts?"

"Just now. Bits and pieces," Luke said, shaking his head and biting his lower lip.

Sean was quiet, shaking his head as well.

"Why all the hate?" Luke managed.

"Started three days ago," Sean explained. "Nikki posted something about her getting back with you . . . Same day Katie posted about you and her hooking up again. She included some pictures."

Luke just stared at his friend's face on the screen.

"First, they are mad at each other. Start passing some angry shit back and forth. Then Mel chimes in and says 'don't be pissin' on each other. Luke's the douche'. . . It catches fire from there. The girls rally. Me Too, stuff. And then some of the boys start turnin'. . . I don't know, man. It's bad. Probably good you're not here," Sean concluded with a weak nod.

Luke was silent. He started scrolling through some of the pictures and reading the messages. It was as ugly as Sean had described, and worse. Someone had commented on the picture with the bull at the fence: "Even the bullshitter knows Luke is a dick."

Luke was numb. He didn't know what to say or to do. Finally, he managed something. "But you've got my six?"

Now it was Sean's turn to be silent. Sean pushed back in his chair. After a long moment, he leaned in toward the screen. "You gotta talk to Nikki. And Katie. And anybody else you need to. Dude, you gotta square up and make this right."

"But you got my back, right? You told 'em..." Luke said pleadingly.

"Tell 'em what?" Sean replied with a shrug. "Last time I told you not to do another Katie. I asked if you talked to Nikki . . ."

"So . . ." was all Luke could manage. It came out more angrily than he intended.

"So, what do you want me to do?" Sean replied.

"Be my friend. Stick up for me," Luke answered, unaware that he was almost yelling.

"Dude, I am your friend . . . But wrong is wrong. You gotta talk to . . ." Sean continued.

"Well, fuck you, Sean," Luke said, regretting the words even before they left his mouth.

129

Luke's chat screen went blank. At first, he thought Sean had closed it. But then he noticed the time: 12:30. The Wi-Fi bars had disappeared. Sean was gone. All that remained were the newly downloaded messages from back home – and the empty feeling inside.

Day 3

The weather for day three was a hiker's dream. From a morning low of thirty-seven, the forecast called for a steady rise into the mid-sixties. The bright sun in the blue-lit sky bathed the land, warmed the air, and lifted the spirits.

To his joyful surprise, Russell found his body acclimating to the rhythm of the trail. Everything seemed just a bit easier now on day three. He shouldered his pack without wobbling. He tied his shoes tight the first time. He knew the proper length to set the sections of his poles. He wasn't certain if his feet and his thighs hurt any less, but at least he had learned to stop listening to them. I think I can do this, he said to himself with some surprise. Sophie was similarly satisfied with her adjustment to the demands of distance hiking.

After her late-night medicinal visit, Lil had found the sleep that had previously eluded her. However, once she lifted her head from her pillow, her mind started racing. The conversation with Juergen. She had never spoken so honestly about her condition to anyone. Not to her friends, not to Dr. Hsu. Yes, she spoke with Russell, but with her husband she held things back – to protect him, she told herself. Her thoughts abruptly turned to Maria. The unexpected story had shaken her. A flood of memories and feelings buffeted the dikes she had so painstakingly constructed. Her spinning head accompanied her as she dressed, nibbled on granola, laced her boots, and set off on the trail. This labyrinth of emotions led her inevitably back to the single question – what to do?

Once on the trail these strands faded to the background and her attention shifted to a more immediate focus: Luke. Even at breakfast he had seemed different. Through much of the morning he neither forged ahead nor lagged behind. Instead, he stayed uncharacteristically close to his family. As the miles passed also absent were the wide mood swings of the previous days. Lil struggled for the right words to capture his disposition. Calm, flat, subdued, somber – she tried them on but none seemed to fit. Finally, she settled on the one that rang true – vulnerable.

She watched the young man, the one she knew and the one she saw now before her. She imagined the swirl of teenage emotions complicated by the tragedy of loss. She recognized a person compelled to put up a good front in the face of trauma. And she sensed in that young man the child he was, the child in some ways we all remain: a soul searching for comfort, for connection, for love. Lil dedicated the day to Luke.

They walked that morning next to each other and often in silence. It was the presence that mattered. When they did speak, at first, it was the small chatter that fills much of our days—the weather, the view, the food. Luke grew excited when he saw two marmots dancing on a nearby moraine. He laughed as Lil whistled, imitating their call, and then watched in delight as the pair stopped, stood on their hind legs, and chirped loudly back before scurrying across the rock debris.

Reflexively, Luke started the celebratory handshake dap he reserved for Sean. When Lil fumbled the first two moves, Luke quickly switched to an awkward high five.

Now it was Lil's turn to laugh. "What was that?" she asked, smiling broadly.

Luke turned his head down, lightly embarrassed. "That was nothing," he dismissed with a flick of his wrist. Lil waited, still smiling. "It's something I do with my friend," he finally added.

Lil stuck out her hand the way Luke had first done. He raised his eyebrows as if to say, "Really?" She nodded. He then took her through an abbreviated sequence: Grab the wrist, raise the forearm, tap the elbows, slide the arm back, wiggle the fingers, move in for the clasp, and touch the foreheads. He omitted the grunts and vulgarities that had become part of his ritual with Sean. By the end, they were both laughing.

"You must miss them," Lil remarked when they started walking again. Luke nodded. He wiped the back of his hand across his forehead, bringing it down just enough to sweep the corner of his eye.

A door had opened, at least a crack. Luke spent the rest of that day with Lil. Lil shared some stories about Sophie as a child, things that surprised Luke. Luke talked a bit about school, his friends, and his activities. Even when the conversation slowed, he remained with her. To Lil, he seemed preoccupied. She chose not to intrude. As the sun edged towards the distant mountain tops, Luke stopped abruptly and surprised Lil. "I am such an idiot, sometimes," he said.

Lil turned to face him. She reached out and took hold of his hands while her eyes searched his face. She debated how to respond. Do I wait? Do I ask? In the end she said plainly, "Sometimes I am such an idiot, too."

Luke continued. "I do things. I say things. I don't know why. It's just dumb. And I tell myself afterward that was so stupid. And it is like I can't shake it out of my head, no matter how I try."

They remained in that spot, together, neither knowing exactly how long. Lil listened, allowing him to go as far as he dared. He spoke as if in code. More generalities than specifics. His language filled with shoulds and shouldn'ts. Lil did not press with questions, but she never retreated from listening. She would nod and rub his arm.

When he seemed to finish all he was ready to say, she held him close and whispered in his ear, "I often feel the same way." After a pause, she continued, "We are each so imperfect, Luke, muddling along as best we can. Suffering and hurt are the price of living, just as love and joy are its rewards. And everything is temporary." She had spoken these words many times to herself of late. There was a relief in speaking them aloud to another.

Luke pushed back and he looked into Lil's face. He saw his own image reflected in his grandmother's eyes.

They returned to the trail. The last few miles to Courmayeur was an easy walk, a gentle slope down through a forested hillside. As they passed a final signpost, Luke asked one of the questions he had been tossing around for the past two months. "Why did you choose this trip?"

Lil had asked herself this same question at the end of her previous life when she first received her diagnosis. While she had many answers, today she offered Luke the one she was ready to share. "I wanted an adventure. Because every adventure is a discovery. And few adventures can equal a long hike in the mountains where, at the end of the journey, you take something with you and you leave a little something behind."

Luke pondered the words. He wasn't certain exactly what she meant, but he liked the sound of it. "So what have you discovered on this adventure?"

"I found you," she replied truthfully.

When he was done smiling, he added, "And what will you leave behind?"

"I'm still working on that one . . ."

Malee's Return

ourmayeur in Italy is much like its French sister town, Chamonix. Together, the communities bookend the seven-mile and twenty-minute drive through the Mont Blanc tunnel. For those wary of having 8,000 feet of rock above them, traveling from one town to another is also possible via two of the most scenic cable car lines in the world, Skyway Mont Blanco on the Italian side and the Aiguille du Midi on the French, which share a connecting station atop the mountain. Choosing neither car nor tram, the trip had taken Lil and her family three days on foot.

After two nights in mountain huts surrounded by gorgeous scenery but not much else, an actual town with a night in a hotel was a welcome treat. Russell volunteered for restaurant reconnaissance while Luke, Sophie, and Lil settled in at the Hotel Edelweiss, a family-owned business in the center of town.

As he wandered, Russell initially categorized Courmayeur as the Italian equivalent of Chamonix. He recognized many of the same high-end designer storefronts interspersed with boutique shops surrounded by countless restaurants, bars, and bistros. But as he walked the cobblestone streets in the old town center, strolled through Museo Alpino in the House of the Alpine Guides, and was routinely greeted with *ciao*, *salve*, and *come stai*, his impression changed. The town had a unique flavor. It seemed friendlier and a little more relaxed than the better-known French neighbor. And the prices – *molto meglio*!

Russell's text alerted his family to his find. "See you at La Terrazza. Reservation at 6. Met some nice people at the bar. Take your time."

Lil laughed. "That man would talk to a tree."

It was 5:00. The prospect of a soak in a warm tub called to Sophie. Luke's stomach growled at him – and Lil came to its rescue.

"Come on, Luke. There is a great place right around the corner. We can grab an appetizer and then find your chattering grandfather." Turning to Sophie, she added, "We will meet you at the restaurant."

After walking up a slight hill, Lil motioned Luke onto the pedestrian-only street that marked the start of the old town. His head swiveled right to left, his nose following the competing scents of chocolate, bread, and tomato sauce. The rumbling in his stomach grew louder. As he turned his head back to the right, his eye caught a familiar face. He waved enthusiastically at a figure one block down the road. "Malee!" he called.

The shadow darted down a side alley.

"That was Malee," he said, turning toward Lil. "The girl we met at the first hut. You know – the one from Australia."

"Yes, I know who Malee is," Lil replied patiently. "And I also know when someone doesn't want to be seen." She let the comment hang in the air. "Come on. This is the place," she said, pushing Luke to the right and under a hand-carved sign: Pan Per Focaccia.

They had entered pizza heaven. The simple glass display case overflowed with a dozen varieties of focaccia, some round, some square, some with sauce, most without. Caramelized onions with walnuts and pear, prosciutto with goat cheese, balsamic glaze with olives and arugula . . . The chalkboard sign also offered a dozen different crepes, savory or sweet. As they stood salivating over the many options, a familiar voice called quietly from behind, "Hello, Ms. Lil. Hello Luke."

Lil turned. There was a sadness on Malee's face. "Dear child," she said instinctively as she embraced the young woman.

Malee wiped her eye. Her lips trembled as the muscles struggled to recall how to smile. "It is good to see a kind face," she managed before her mouth fell again.

"Luke, get three slices and meet us outside," Lil directed as she put her arm around Malee and walked to the small terrace.

136

Luke found them tucked into a corner table nestled in the curve of a stone wall, flowering vines hanging from above. Water bubbled in a small pool bursting with flowers and foliage of its own. Luke placed the slices onto the wood slab table. Lil held Malee's hand, gently massaging the muscle at the base of Malee's thumb. Luke took a seat on the other side of Malee and listened.

"I found out two days ago," Malee stammered. "I got a text," she said, shaking her head. "Bitch couldn't even tell me to my face, or call." She lifted her eyes and looked at Lil. "Said she was back in Australia. Wouldn't make it to Zadar. And was," she paused, glancing at Luke, "with Christian." He reached out for her other hand, and she did not pull away.

"My girl, I am so very sorry for you," Lil said, moving her hand to Malee's wrist and rubbing the point just above her pulse.

"At first, I didn't believe it. Thought she was busting. But I knew, and then I saw the pictures on their feed." She shook her head.

"Guys can be such dicks," Luke said with a touch of anger.

"Got that," Malee said. "Thing is," she continued, "him, I am not surprised at. He always had the eye. But Carolyn, that's the part that burns. We were supposed to be friends, and friends don't do that," she said clenching her fists.

"What do I do now?" Malee said aloud the question she had been asking herself,

Lil took a deep breath.

A half-dozen ideas ricocheted across Luke's brain but he surprised himself when instead he said, "What are you thinking?"

Lil nodded her approval at Luke's tact. He's beginning to sound a bit like Russell, she thought to herself.

"Part of me wants to fly back to Sydney and beat the crap out of both of them. And then I was also thinking about Tennessee's story," she said, making a cutting gesture with her fingers. "But what good would that do? And part of me is so tired," and then, after a pause, "I just want to go home. But . . ."

"But what?" Lil prompted.

Malee looked into the old woman's eyes, "I don't know what to tell them."

"Tell them everything or tell them nothing. Or when you're ready tell them bit by bit – your choice. But whatever, and whenever, make it the truth," Lil offered.

"That's easy for you to say," Malee replied.

"And much tougher to do, I know," Lil added, nodding. "But I suspect that, like most families, they are quietly searching for the same thing you are. Sometimes, you have to take a walk away to find what you lost."

"I wish you were my mother," Malee said.

"It's much easier with other people's children. Believe me. I can be a difficult mother," Lil confessed.

"Got that right," Luke whispered lightly.

Malee laughed and gently pushed Luke on his shoulder. Her mood had lifted slightly. She reached down for the slice with walnuts and pears. Between bites she said, "I am sorry for ducking away at first. I was embarrassed and didn't know what to say."

"I am glad you came back," Lil replied.

"Yeah, you saved me from another dinner date with my grandmother," Luke teased.

Lil glanced at her watch. "Speaking of which, it is almost six—our dinner reservation." Turning to Malee, she added, "Would you like to join us?"

She replied honestly. "Not certain I am ready for that."

Luke frowned and stood up. Malee put out her hand toward him.

Lil didn't see her gesture but did see Luke's expression. "Why don't you stay here," she said to her grandson. "It would be a shame to waste good focaccia."

Luke smiled and glanced down toward Malee, her nod suggesting her agreement. He sat back down, and Lil took her leave.

Luke and Malee spent the next two hours together, first at the Pan Per Focaccia and then wandering the cobblestones of Courmayeur, stopping in shops and sampling some gelato. They talked to one another. They did not hold hands. Luke did not think about her breasts or fantasize about undressing her. Instead, he told her about his friends and the tension with

138

his mom. She talked about her childhood moving from base to base and her hopes for the future. Luke admitted his failings as a boyfriend but kept the deeper pains close. Malee shared her own embarrassments while giving him a short list of qualities young women look for in a relationship. In that one evening they became friends. Their time together ended with a hug, not a kiss.

"If I had a brother, I would want him to be like you," Malee said. "And remember, don't be a dick."

"Right. I'm working on that," Luke replied.

The Rifugio Bonatti

As befitting its famous name, the Rifugio Bonatti commands one of the most magnificent views in all the Tour. At 2025 meters, visitors must complete a steady ascent before arriving at the stone structure. The flat terrace immediately outside the front door slopes quickly down to the Aosta Valley until it meets the Dora Baltea River, only to rise even more precipitously into the stony ridges of the Geants. The Rifugio is so perfectly placed that the light of the morning sun plays across the Geant's face, revealing each day, to those who care to look, a story as fleeting and ever-changing as life itself.

Beyond the remarkable views, many hiking veterans believe the food is tastier, the guests are friendlier and the staff is more welcoming at Bonatti than anywhere else on the route.

Lil felt her heart beat faster as she crossed the threshold and entered the home.

Luke and Russell were ready for dinner well before Lil and Sophie. They joined the other guests lolling around the front terrace waiting for the dining room doors to open. Many were admiring the uninterrupted view down the valley toward Mont Blanc. Some were savoring the teasing smells wafting in from the kitchen. Even more were sipping their wine and enjoying animated conversations with fellow travelers. Luke was silently staring at a bearded man with uncombed hair pressed against the wooden fence, leaning into the void beyond the guardrail. Or, more specifically, he was staring at what the old man held in his hand.

His excitement trumped his hesitation and he approached the stranger. "Is that a Leica M?" Luke blurted out.

The photographer distractedly edged his head in Luke's direction as if hearing a distant memory and said – nothing. Instead, he returned to his camera and focused the M3 rangefinder on the mountain panorama, brushed by the soft light of the near-setting sun.

Russell smiled at Luke's initiative, and chuckled inwardly at the man's response.

Nearby, a woman of similar age to the photographer cast a protective glance in their direction. She excused herself from her conversation with another couple and came to stand by Russell.

"*Bonjour. Je m'appelle Martine.*"

"*Bonjour*," Russell replied. "Unfortunately, I do not speak French."

"*De rien*, English is fine," she replied. "Please apologize to your son and excuse my husband. Pascal is not much of a talker."

"You are too kind," Russell replied with a gentle laugh. "That's my grandson. And he is usually not much of a talker either," he added confidentially.

A bell rang signaling seating was now available.

"After you, *Madame*," Russell gestured.

"*Merci*," Martine replied. She moved toward her husband, who had ignored the dinner bell as much as Luke, and took his arm.

As she walked inside, ushering ahead of her the couple she had been chatting to, Martine turned to Russell and said, "You must sit with us for dinner, *non*?" Russell nodded agreeably. They all claimed a table in the front corner nearest a window overlooking the mountains.

Luke promptly took the chair beside the photographer. Even while seated, Pascal clung to his camera, his attention still focused on the mountainside in the distance.

"This is our first Tour," Martine said to Russell, her French accent adding a lyrical edge to her excellent English. She placed a gentle hand on her husband's shoulder. His focus still did not shift. "Same for Francoise and Nicolas," she added, pointing to the couple across the table.

* * *

Certain the man mustn't speak English, Luke unveiled the high school French he had been casually acquiring – studying would be too strong a word – over the past three years. "*Excusez-moi, est-ce-que cette camera une Leica?*"

With the same caution he exercised after Luke's first question on the terrace, the old man turned his head. His eyes caught the boy's face. A slight raising of the eyebrows, a twitch perhaps, preceded an almost indiscernible nod that Luke took as a reluctant "yes."

* * *

Martine explained, "We met through our children, Jean-Luc and Claudia. Claudia is Francoise's daughter. And we have been friends ever since. We travel together once or twice a year, always someplace new."

Russell asked, "Do Jean-Luc and Claudia ever join you?"

"*Malheureusement, non,*" Martine said, casting her eyes to the floor.

* * *

Encouraged, Luke continued, "*J'adore les photographs de Cartier-Bresson.* I even saw his pictures in the Levy Gallery – the only time I actually liked going to a museum," he added, reverting to English.

The table companion looked back at Luke more quickly now. An unpracticed smile intruded on his stoic face. After a long decisive moment, without a word the old man held out the camera toward the young man.

"No way!" Though shaking his head and pushing his shoulders back, Luke's hands still reached out and accepted the gift.

* * *

Martine and Russell both noticed the exchange between Pascal and Luke. "*Regardez,*" Martine gasped as much to herself as to Russell.

"I hope your husband speaks English because I think Luke has reached the limit of his French," Russell joked.

"Pascal doesn't speak much at all. He has not spoken more than a dozen words in nearly three years," Martine whispered, looking down at the fading swirl in her café noir.

* * *

"God, it feels so solid," Luke gushed, cupping the camera gently in his hands as if it were a newborn child. Pascal pointed to Luke's eye and then to the distant mountains. Luke's face glowed like the rock across the valley.

As a digital native, Luke had little experience with film cameras beyond the pinhole projects from his first photography class. Sensing the boy's confusion, Pascal pointed to the shutter speed dial on the top plate, which Luke adjusted. Then, with a lift of his hand, Pascal impatiently gestured for Luke to bring it to his eye.

It was the brightest viewfinder Luke had ever looked through – no distracting LED lights and numbers, just a clear set of frame lines. Fuck this is gorgeous, he thought to himself. He nervously looked up, worried that in his excitement the words had slipped out. He felt his face turn red and noticed he was sweating. Whether the man had heard him, he didn't know. No words betrayed the photographer.

Stop being a pussy and do it, Luke's inner voice commanded. Luke composed his shot. With a determined press of the smooth shutter release, the moment was captured. When he returned the camera back to its master, both men were smiling. Neither said a word, and neither had to.

* * *

Russell was not certain how to respond to Martine. He noted how she was looking at Luke, her eyes half shut as if to hide her from a sight she deeply wanted to behold and desperately struggled to avoid.

"Our Jean-Luc had the same color hair and joyful smile as your grandson.

Like his father – who he adored – he was a natural photographer. Always with a camera in his hand."

Russell listened attentively, his patient silence inviting Martine to continue.

"With what he learned from Pascal, Jean-Luc was accepted at SPEOS, where he flourished. When he graduated he returned to Annecy filled with hope of working beside Pascal in his studio. His father would have none of it. He recognized the boy's talent and wanted him to create his own destiny in Paris. It was a grand fight, one of the only times I have ever seen them truly argue . . ."

* * *

Pascal reached down into the leather satchel Luke had not noticed before. He took out a folio. Drawing his chair closer to the table, closer to the boy, he opened the folio. Luke was mesmerized. They were some of the most beautiful photographs he had ever seen. As the old man leafed through the images some patterns and themes emerged.

Luke began to narrate some of what he noticed. His first reactions were obvious ones. "They are all landscapes . . . there are no people." Luke continued with his superficial observations. He saw disappointment in the subtle changes to the man's face. "I know, those are stupid comments," Luke grinned at Pascal.

Luke looked harder. "The colors are subdued. And you are messing around with the light. Even with this one – with the sun's position it has to be in the middle of the day, and there is not a cloud in the sky, but the colors are muted. It almost looks like a black-and-white image, but it isn't. The colors are there. Lots of colors are there. It is like you've hidden them." Pascal no longer looked disappointed.

"But I can't figure out what the focal point is. There seem to be so many different ones. Is that because of the rangefinder?" The man shook his head. Reaching across the table Pascal grabbed a rumpled napkin. He lifted the napkin to intercept the fading rays of light. The old man pointed to

Luke's eye, almost touching him. His finger then traced the light through the window to the napkin and onto the table. He directed the boy's focus to that thin boundary separating the light from the dark, as the shadow of the napkin carved a fractured line across the tabletop.

Luke smiled and then leafed back to some of the early images. His eye sought the boundary between the light and the dark, what was shadowed and what was revealed. As he re-examined the fourth photograph, he froze, an idea developing in his mind. "Damn," he said, this time aloud. Along the boundary line, he now saw what had previously escaped him. He leafed urgently through the other pictures. As his mind raced to make sense, he found in each the subtlest hint, a trace of human activity, a ghost of something no longer there. In one case, it was a cairn from a previous traveler. In another, the foundation of a home that had disappeared long ago. While there were no people, along each boundary line there was something clearly left behind. He tested his hypothesis as he looked at the other images in the photographer's folio. That trace of the past – that was the focal point of each scene.

Luke excitedly shared his observation with Pascal, sure the photographer would celebrate his triumph. Instead, a tear slipped from the old man's eye, traveling a jagged path down his wrinkled face. Luke apologized, "I'm sorry, I didn't mean to . . ." Pascal cut him off with a wave of his hand and gestured for Luke to take another picture.

* * *

Martine continued. "Jean-Luc left angry. He packed only one suitcase and did not even take the Leica with him. That Leica," she motioned to the camera Luke now held in his hands. "He went to live with some friends in Paris and quickly found work – talent does not stay hidden. After several weeks right around the holiday he called and invited us to see him at the end of January. On January the seventh, he was at ten, Rue de Nicolas Appert – the same building where *Charlie Hebdo* is published." Martine looked down again.

Russell understood. He remembered the attack from 2015 which killed 12 people and injured a dozen more.

"Pascal blames himself," she continued. "On the days before the funeral, I would hear him talking to himself. 'Why did I say those things? I should have let him stay. I killed my son.' "*Non, non, non, mon amour,*" I would try to comfort him. But it did not help. And after the funeral, he just stopped talking."

Russell reached out to hold Martine's hand.

"After a few months he started back to work, taking photographs. But his images changed, you know. Less color, more mystery, and never any people . . . *Etonnamment,* he sells more images than ever." Martine chuckled ruefully.

"So, we go on these trips together with Francois and Nicolas. Claudia came along at first but then she met another boy . . . *Trop genant, oui?* I don't know if these trips make Pascal happy, but he seems less sad, you know?"

Russell nodded.

Staring at Pascal and Luke, Martine kissed Russell's hand and said, "Thank your grandson for me. He has been a gift tonight." She stepped up from the table, placed her arm around her husband, and kissed him on his cheek.

La Conteuse – Part 2

Before dessert was served Maria arrived. She entered the room slowly as if her predetermined steps were taking her to a destination she preferred not to visit. Her swaying head glanced about the room, measuring the space and its occupants. Maria's gaze paused at Lil's table. Her eyes widened, and then the corners of her mouth sagged as if weighed down by the obligation of a memory.

Maria took a seat on the eastern side of the fireplace, her back to the warming fire. A crowd began to assemble at her feet. The dancing shadow of the flames animated her face even though she had not yet begun to speak. Outside, the receding light left the Geants dark and quiet, better for them to hear the story as well. Stories bring their own light to the darkness.

With no introduction, Maria began. There were none of the warm-ups or theatrics from two days ago. She had come to finish the story. And with any necessary chore, it was best to get on with it.

"To the world, he was strong and confident – a young god who found success in all he chose to pursue. We worshiped him, and because of that, we are partly to blame. Experienced as he was, he was a child to love. When he held out the *rose de montagne*, and proposed to la belle Elizabetta, the young god was trembling.

"When she did not at first answer, his heart quickened—one, two, and three beats each second. As a climber he had experienced this before. The coursing adrenaline as you search for a knob that lies just out of reach, and you must burst beyond the strain in your body to reach the sanctuary of the ledge. In her silence, he found no foothold. This night, kneeling in the

Alpine grass at the foot of his beloved, he felt fear unlike anything he had experienced on the mountain. When she said she needed time to think, his fear turned to shame – and then escape.

"As Bonatti hastily packed up the remains of the picnic and raced back to the village, Elizabetta voiced none of her many thoughts. In their separate silence they unknowingly shared the same reaction: 'I have been a fool.'

"After she had failed to speak and Elizabetta went to her bed, sleep eluded her. The scrambled thoughts crashed against one another: I didn't come here for this . . . what will my parents think? . . . am I being childish? . . . what about my studies? As her frightened mind struggled for her own foothold, her heart told her a truth: I didn't come here for this. But I love him. What will my parents think? But I love him. What about my future? But I love him. And in the steady reassurance of her heart, Elizabetta eventually found sleep.

"That morning, Elizabetta awakened with a start. The questions from the previous night had been put to rest and a single thought now occupied her mind. She dressed quickly, left her room and blew a kiss to me as she passed. She traveled the short distance to the Bonatti home with quick, sure steps. Though her heart was light, her eyes were moist as she approached the door, overwhelmed by the joy she felt and the promise of spending her life with the man she knew she loved.

"The younger Bonatti was not there. She spoke to his older brother, who said he had left before first light, with little gear and even fewer words, toward Dent du Geant. As she turned from the door I saw her face transformed. 'What's wrong?' I asked her. 'I have to find Frederico.'"

Maria paused to look out the front window as the last rays of the setting sun clung to the ridgeline that overshadowed the Rifugio de Bonatti. She pointed at the jagged peak on the westernmost edge. "Le Dent du Geant. It is not the biggest peak in the Rochfort Ridge but with its pitch and slabs, scaling the Giant's Tooth is *molto più formidabile*. A climb – even with ropes and pitons – for the very bold or the very foolish."

Luigi, who had nestled down to her side, took her hand and cradled it.

"I followed after her," Maria continued. "Luigi drove us to the valley. After

148

arriving at the Rifugio Torino, Elizabetta and I used the goat path to the Salle à Manger, which marks the start of the climb. It was almost nine o'clock by then. The sun had retreated behind a veil of clouds, and the gusts of wind rustled the trees. The rain, which had been predicted for later in the day, threatened to arrive early.

"It was not long before we found him at the foot of the Burgener wall. From a distance, you might have thought he was asleep, resting for the steep climb ahead. But the angles were all wrong. He lay alone without any gear at the bottom of the rock face, and in his hand he held a single mountain rose.

"I went back to Torino. Elizabetta remained with Frederico. When I returned with Luigi and several other villagers, Elizabetta was still holding his hand. 'I left him alone,' she said, 'and was not there to stop him.' The men carefully loaded his body onto a stretcher and brought the young Bonatti on his final journey back to his family."

Maria wiped her eyes with a handkerchief Luigi had passed to her.

"In the local villages, they say that when the wind calls your name, that is the day you meet your destiny. The story goes that as Bonatti was climbing the Placche Burgener, the mountain grew angry at Bonatti for forsaking her for another love. She commanded the winds to call Bonatti's name.

"Elizabetta mourned with the Bonatti family. She mourned as if she were Bonatti's true wife. She stayed with the family for a full month before planning her return to America. While none knew then of Bonatti's proposal, all knew of his love for Elizabetta. The family viewed her grief as a sign of her true love, which it was.

"When Elizabetta left, the Bonatti family was as sad as if their daughter were leaving. While they feared they might never see her again, they pledged to forever keep her in their hearts. Over the decades, though she never returned, the legend grew of the fateful love between the young Italian alpinist and the beautiful American woman, who became known as La Bella Elizabetta . . ."

Maria stopped. Her tears were joined by those from more than a few in the audience. Luke noticed his mother among them. He glanced at Lil who sat stoically, her jaw clenched as if to prevent something unwanted from spilling out.

Maria had not told this story in a long time, and the effort had drained her. In her silence, the room began to empty. Some gently touched Maria's shoulder or arm as they passed by en route to their beds. After her eyes had emptied, she raised her head deliberately, her lips stretched tight. With lids barely opened, uncertain they could bear what they might behold, she searched the remaining faces. Her gaze fell on Lil's face. Maria inhaled sharply and clasped her hands as if in a forgotten prayer. Smiling, Lil returned the gesture.

Lil sent her family on ahead, telling them she would catch up with them later. Only then did she approach Maria and Luigi, extending a hand to each. Fresh tears rained to the floor. The three old friends remained together well into the night.

An Unsettled Night

Lil didn't sleep well. The cancer continued to eat away at her body. The previous four days had been physically draining. A storm that had blown in lingered through much of the night, unable or unwilling to crawl over the mountain peaks that encircled the refuge. But more than these minor distractions, it was the unexpected reunion with her past that unsettled Lil.

Yes, Lil had chosen this location intentionally. This was the place she became the person she had been throughout her adult life. She intended to hold that secret close, hers alone to the end. Though she had never mentioned her previous life to her family, the effect was ever-present. Her independence, her strength, and, most importantly, her steadfast commitment to not live in the past. As an adult this is how Lil defined herself. She attributed these qualities to that summer long ago. And since that time she commanded herself to embrace the adventure gifted to us all by every sunrise. In her mind it seemed fitting that she would end her life's tour in the place where it began. Until this night Lil had remained oblivious to the irony that the past she sought to keep hidden had still shaped her every day.

For all these reasons, in her bunk at the Rifugio Bonatti, sleep was elusive. Try as she might to clear her mind, the sound of the thunder jolted her, the fatigue in her body overwhelmed her and the conversation with Maria unsettled her.

Lil felt trapped. The heavy rains made it impossible to sneak outside for her medicinal toke. Her anxiety grew to anger. Her mind found fault with her roommates, none of whom shared Lil's failure to sleep.

Damn, she said to herself. If I do not get some sleep it will be an impossible day tomorrow. Day five was to begin with a long three-hour ascent to the Col de Ferret, marking the intersection between France, Italy, and Switzerland. It promised to be one of the most challenging days of the hike. At that elevation, what was rain here tonight might be snow there even in June.

The room grew warmer. The closed window captured the heat generated by the breathing of her slumbering companions. Lil felt her heart beat faster. She struggled to contain a wave of nausea. She heard herself whimper, just slightly. She was both embarrassed and angered by her reaction.

A hand reached out to her. At first, she thought it was Russell but remembered he was in another row. Besides, his hands were always cold. This hand was smaller and warmer, vaguely familiar but one she had not held in a long time. It stroked Lil's hair gently. After the second pass, Lil clasped and lightly kissed the hand, which then slid sleepily back to the mattress. Rolling round to face her daughter silently in the dark, Lil finally retreated to sleep.

Day 5

The roosters sounded their morning alarm, calling Lil to open her eyes. The sky was still muted by clouds but the rain had stopped. Lil sat up in the chilly air – someone had opened the window – and the cold from the tops of the mountains had descended on the refuge. The puffs of breath from her still-sleeping companions hung in the air like empty thought bubbles waiting to be filled.

"God, my nipples are frozen," she heard Luke mutter as he scrambled from under the covers on the upper bunk searching for another layer to add atop the t-shirt he had worn to bed.

"Mine, too," Lil answered quickly, and not untruthfully.

"Oh, I'm sorry, Nan," Luke replied, his face turning a warm red even in the cool air. "I forgot where I was."

"All good, my boy," she added, tossing him a fleece from his bag by her feet.

Lil smiled at his unguarded moment. She had always loved the boy, that is true. Though through the years, she had grown worried that he often kept things too closed. Adults described him as "a good kid who had it together" – polite in manners, talented at sports, and successful at school. At family gatherings, he would respectfully answer the scripted question with an equally scripted response before turning the conversation to the other person and then excusing himself. Even when the tension between Sophie and Rick was obvious to everyone, and surely Luke would have known too, he didn't act out the way you hear kids sometimes do. Maybe he was more distant, though that happens naturally in adolescence, but never a problem. Lil's concern was most pronounced when Rick died. Luke was somber, but she had never seen him break down or become distraught the way she imagined a child would react to the death of a parent. She remembered the comments at the reception after the funeral: "That boy is strong . . . he is holding up well . . . he will be fine . . . I wish I had a son like that." Lil wondered about the feelings behind the facade and why he felt the need to keep so much hidden. Today, she recognized the trait.

"Let's get some breakfast," Luke suggested, tucking his arm inside hers.

They entered the dining hall and sat at a small corner table near the fireplace. Looking at the breakfast spread, Lil did not hide her disappointment. "Ugh, more granola," she said. "You would think with all these chickens they could scrounge together a few eggs."

"I already decided the first thing I am having when we get back is an omelet, a stack of pancakes, and a half pound of bacon," Luke responded with wide eyes.

Her grandson's mood lifted her spirits as well. "Good, you need to put on some weight," Lil replied, pinching the fatless skin on the side of Luke's waist.

"Ah, now there's the pot calling the kettle black," Luke intoned with an Irish accent. "You're skinnier than most of the girls in my school," he added, tousling her hair with his free hand.

She pinched him again and kissed him on the side of his head. Sophie and Russell joined them a few moments later. Despite the kvetching, Luke enjoyed multiple bowls of cereal. Lil only lightly touched some bread and jam. With her first bite an unsettled feeling rose steadily from her stomach. She avoided her usual coffee and opted for water and some apple juice.

As she stood to rise after her morning nibbles, Lil felt a little lightheaded. Discreetly steadying herself with both hands on the table, she motioned Sophie to carry on ahead while she got another drink. Stability resumed, but walking more slowly than usual, Lil left the breakfast room. Lyndon joined in step behind her and asked in his cheerful manner, "How's the body this morning, luv?"

"Fine," she lied. "How about you," she deflected, uncertain what he had noticed.

"Bit of a rough sleep, a little tired, and didn't feel very hungry this morning," he lied back.

She smiled at his smirk.

"That happens every once in a while. Hazard of being alive," he continued. "That's why I always take some of these with me when I'm hiking."

Lyndon reached into a side pouch attached to his waist and pulled out two bars wrapped in plastic, pressing them into Lil's hand. "Make'm myself. Chopped walnuts, almonds, and pecans, with dates, dried blueberries, and dried bananas. Mix it with brown rice protein powder and some honey. And my secret ingredients which I never told another living soul: cocoa nibs and a dash of sriracha. Now these will keep your body fueled, your soul happy, and lips puckered."

"Thank you, you're an angel, Lyndon," Lil said, accepting his gift.

"Listen, I've got to get back to my group. A few were turning too many last night and one isn't even out of bed. Next trip, I will leave this sorry lot behind and go hiking with your team," he said. "You give a yell if you need anything, and listen to your body!" he cautioned with a change to his tone. "We are all on the same trail, but we each walk our own path, right?"

The refuge warden had advised them they would find some light snow and a steady wind as they made their way up the long initial ascent. Lil and her companions added balaclavas, thicker gloves, and an extra layer beneath their wind jackets. After they shouldered their backpacks, it became difficult to recognize the person beneath the gear.

Lyndon's comment to Lil at breakfast was true. While you may undertake the Tour together, it was an individual journey. The romantic idea of everyone walking along, sharing witty conversation, admiring scenic vistas, all the while bonding with your fellow travelers, was not the full reality of the trail. Everyone walked at a different pace. The small talk eventually ran dry. And one breathtaking view, when it was not shrouded by the clouds, did tend to merge into the next. The methodical rhythm of placing one foot endlessly in front of the other, along with the internal dialog in your mind, filled most of the day. But the bonding, that part was true, and each member would come to it in their own way.

Lil and her family strapped on their gear. This morning, Luke and Russell quickly separated from the group. After a short walk down the path, the same path that led both into and out of the refuge, the duo turned to the left and progressed steadily up the treeless route. As they gained elevation, glancing back they were treated to an ever-widening view of the valley behind. Tracing the trail before them, Luke and Russell could see, against the landscape of mottled greys and whites, an extended series of moving specks – a continuous if erratic line of fellow travelers heading first to the right before shifting to the left and then back again only to repeat the pattern over and over and over. Russell's accountant's mind began to tally the number of switchbacks but then surrendered. Each colored dot was an individual hiker, some of whom had ambitiously begun one or two hours earlier and had considerable distance yet to go. "I liked it better when I couldn't see that far in front of me," Luke commented to his grandfather.

Sophie had hung back while Lil slowly tied her boots, struggled to shoulder her pack, and fumbled for her poles. Lil had spotted Lyndon speaking with Sophie. While she hoped they were sharing a pleasantry, Lil suspected the conversation was more likely about her. This idea angered her. Reflexively, she retreated to her pride of independence. You two busy bodies should worry about yourselves . . . I'll be fine . . . I can do this . . . I walked these mountains before you were even born. In her life's narrative, Lil defined herself as a strong person and a resilient soul, someone who did not require the assistance, let alone the pity, of another. But at that moment, feeling the weight on her back, she sat down and turned her head upward. She closed her eyes and savored the cool breeze washing over her face. She thought of Debbie: "Sometimes the greatest gift is when we find the strength to let them in, just a little bit."

Sophie approached the wooden bench on which Lil rested. Lil extended her right hand toward her daughter; Sophie firmly grabbed hold. Looking into the face of her only surviving child, Lil offered a "thank you." It was a thank you for staying with her this morning, for reaching out to her last night, for joining her on this trip. It was a thank you for that and all the unspoken appreciations Lil had neglected to share while she sought to raise a child as independent, resilient, and strong as she was.

Sophie squeezed her hand silently, much as she had the night before. The two women set out together on the day's journey.

Their first stop came less than two hundred meters from the refuge. Lil leaned against an old farm cart, two wheels broken but brightly painted a stunning blue it had never worn in its younger years, the bright coat created by a sentimental soul who was not yet ready to part with it. The relic, now useless to carry any load, still served as a cherished monument marking a turn from the refuge and forward up the mountain.

In that short distance to the cart, Sophie had noticed Lil's breathing: a quick huff inward, her mouth spread wide, followed by a shallow and equally quick puff out.

"Just a moment, I need to adjust my pack," Lil said.

"No trouble, no rush," Sophie replied.

After a few moments, they were off. Three minutes later, they stopped again. Lil leaned hunched against a stone boulder along the side of the trail. A trickle of other hikers passed by without comment. A few nodded to Sophie. Lil's head was down, eyes cast to the ground. It was not uncommon to see fellow travelers resting along the way. Not everyone started from the same location, so the proximity to the hut was not unusual.

"I'm sorry. Just need to catch my breath," Lil commented without looking up.

"It's okay, I'm with you," Sophie replied.

A similar exchange repeated itself two more times in the next ten minutes. Lil's "I'm sorry" followed by Sophie's "It's okay."

At each stop Sophie considered the options. After the fourth stop, she waved her poles in the air several times, crossing them into a giant X. In half an hour Lil and Sophie had made it no further than Luke and Russell had covered in less than five minutes. The two women glanced up at the snaking path and wondered which of the faint dots were the rest of their family.

157

Lil steeled herself. She inhaled deeply, determined to move forward. After ten steps, she stopped abruptly and folded her shoulders inward. She bent to her knees and placed her hands on the ground, gasping for breath more urgently than ever. Uncertain what to do, Sophie placed her hand on Lil's back trying to comfort her.

As Lil continued gasping for air, a man in a lime Helley Hensen jacket strode quickly toward them. "My sweet Lil," Lyndon said, gently guiding Lil to a seated position upon his backpack. "Deep breath through the nose, then blow out the candles," he repeated while modeling the pattern. He placed his hands lightly on her upper back, unfolding her shoulders from their constricted position and adding the word "relax" to his verbal mantra.

The gasping slowly subsided, and Lil's breathing regained a normal rhythm.

Reaching under his jacket and into a zippered pocket close to his body, Lyndon removed a small metal cylinder. "Now take a hit of this," he added with a sly smile.

Sophie looked at him skeptically. Lil did not hesitate. She depressed the canister housed inside the cylinder and took two deep breaths.

"Don't worry," Lyndon reassured her. "It's just oxygen – a guide's secret. Some of my clients aren't in the best shape, you know. And they don't take much better care of themselves out here than back in the city. Sometimes, I need to give them a little boost to keep them moving."

"Do you have a bandanna?" Lyndon asked Lil.

"No," she replied.

"Here, take this," Lyndon said, passing her one of two bandannas around his neck. "Wrap this loosely around your mouth and nose. That will help warm the air."

Lil placed it on her face while Sophie helped her tie the knot behind her head. It smelled like both a man and a mountain, triggering memories in Lil like only odors can.

"I got a late start this morning," Lyndon explained. "One of my clients had some trouble remembering how to wake up. You did well with her," he said to Sophie. "I could see you stopping on the way up. Once I saw you make the X with the poles, I hurried as quickly as I could."

"Do you think she will be alright?" Sophie asked.

"Her lips and fingernails aren't blue. That's good. Though the air is thinner up here, we are not really high enough for altitude sickness. Most likely just the EIBees, exercise induced bronchospasms. The cold can make the air passages constrict. Plus, I caught her skimping at breakfast," Lyndon was speaking in a voice loud enough for Lil to hear. "I think she'll live," he concluded.

Lil chortled at the hidden irony, adding, "So says you."

"Well, I haven't lost anyone on a trip yet, unless you count my ex-wife," Lyndon responded. "And I am not about to let you be the first."

"I don't think I can continue . . . least not today," Lil confessed. "Even with these 'delicious' power bars," she said through pursed lips, nibbling on one of the homemade treats Lyndon provided earlier in the morning.

"Now, that makes perfect sense to me," Lyndon agreed. "If you head back down to the refuge, the warden can drive you to Lavachey. From there you can take the eleven o'clock bus to Col de Fenetre. You'll arrive a good six hours before the rest of us with plenty of time for a nap and a bite. I suspect with a day off, a good meal or two, and some solid sleep, you'll be ready to go."

Neither Lil nor Sophie objected in the slightest.

A member of Lyndon's crew had just reached them, escorting two red-faced, middle-aged gents with breathing struggles of their own.

"Matteo, be a good lad and carry this backpack down to the hut for my girlfriend," Lyndon said, tossing Lil's backpack to a fit-looking twenty-something with a manbun. "And I'll catch up to your other mates and give them the word," Lyndon said to Sophie and Lil. They'll be jealous they missed the bus trip, for sure."

Lyndon coaxed the two clients to continue up the path while Matteo, Sophie, and Lil headed back down where the mother and daughter would share a ride.

The Bus Ride

They began their ride in silence, each one focused on the imagined thoughts of the other.

Looking out the window, Lil wondered if Sophie knew something was wrong. Really wrong? Had Russell said something? She did not intend to tell her daughter about the cancer. Not until it was all over. Russell had repeatedly tried to convince her, arguing, "She has a right to know." Debbie, in her own way, had encouraged her as well: "The telling is part of the healing, especially for those you leave behind." Even Betsy with Compassionate Choices had called her two weeks ago and offered to facilitate the conversation with the family. But stubborn Lil, independent Lil, secretive Lil had resisted. Was now the time? she wondered.

Sophie wrestled with her own private questions. When she did speak, it was an iteration of her big question—the one she had asked herself hundreds of times, a wonder etched in her memory, as old as any other thought she could recall: "Are you disappointed?" Sophie asked.

Lil turned her head to her daughter. The color ran from her cheeks. Lil repeated the word and held it tight in her mind – *disappointed*. It triggered hundreds of synapses and dozens of possible references. Lil was startled by one: So she knows . . . no she doesn't . . . if she knew she wouldn't say disappointed, she'd have said frightened or pissed-off maybe, but not disappointed.

In the expression that flashed across her mother's face, Sophie thought she saw surprise or perhaps confusion or even fear. Sophie filled the pause. She backtracked and lied. "About, um, not walking the whole way, I mean."

Relieved, Lil laughed. "Hell, no. Four days by foot, and this is our first cheat? I call that a win. Besides, it will give your father something to gloat over."

Sophie laughed and bit her lip.

"Truth is," Lil continued quickly, "What I really feel is grateful." She reached out and grasped her daughter's hand. "I am grateful for you and Luke. For you agreeing to come along. For the chance for us to take this final Tour together." The f-word had slipped out of Lil's mouth. She quickly recovered, "Yup, what I feel is grateful."

Sophie looked into her mother's eyes. Grateful – that word warmed her. She struggled to remember the last time her mother's words had brought her comfort. But today, she recognized the response as heartfelt. It emboldened her. "Disappointed . . . in . . . anything else?"

Sophie's heart was pounding. This was a conversation she had rehearsed dozens of times with her therapist. A topic that had haunted her for much longer than that. An eternal issue at the core of being. Do I matter? Am I good enough? Am I loved?

Lil now recognized this meaning in Sophie's question. She also recognized her responsibility in the need for her daughter even to ask. She let loose of Sophie's hand, pulled her close, and kissed her on the cheek.

"I am not an easy person to live with," she began. "And I was not – am not – always the best mom." Lil took a deep breath. "Disappointed?" she paused. "In you? Never. In myself? Many times."

This confession was the conversation Lil had intended, had hoped, to have. It was also the same hope Sophie harbored deep in her soul, at times so deep as to be unrecognizable. Years of pain and offense, both real and imagined, of missed opportunities left orphaned and unclaimed, had buried the prospect. Over time, both mother and daughter had added layers of dark sentiment until here, now, on a bus riding together up and over an undulating hillside, reconciliation seemed possible.

"I wanted for you . . . from the start . . . what took me so long to find," Lil began haltingly. "I wanted for you to be strong. To be independent, to walk your own path without giving a damn what other people thought. But most of all, to know your own mind and follow your own heart."

As Sophie listened wordlessly, scenes swirled through her mind. The report cards left unpraised. The trophies not displayed. The accomplishments uncelebrated. Sophie thought of the questions she asked as a child – Do you like this? What should I do? Is this good enough? And the responses Lil provided – Does it matter? Do what you want. What do you think? Eventually Sophie had stopped asking. She told herself that she didn't care what her mother thought. It was as impossible a task for Sophie as for any child. And over time, one never-held conversation led to another, and the distance between them grew. The fabric that held them together thinned to breaking.

"I never intended to push you away," Lil said to Sophie as much as to herself. "But I see now that's what I did."

Sophie weighed her choices. She recognized the honesty in Lil's words. She sensed the courage it took to speak so openly, especially for a woman who held her feelings close, for whom privacy was a virtue, and secrets were her stock and trade. I could respond with empathy, she thought, throw my arms around her and tell her all is forgiven. That's what Dad would do. I could tell her I was a difficult child and say I was as much to blame. But that was only partly true, and not how Sophie actually felt. Instead, she listened.

As she listened, her mother told her more and more. Stories about when Sophie was young, and what Lil felt and thought. The joy of cradling her body to her chest, feeling her heart beat for the first time outside of her womb, the thrill of witnessing her first words and her first steps. Lil recalled how Sophie always insisted on reading a good night story to Russell, and how proud that made Lil feel. Her mother's words were like warm water to Sophie's soul. They were the words she longed to hear years ago. Yet the effect was powerful even now. She resisted the urge to ask, to demand an explanation, to scream, "Why didn't you say these things then?" But Sophie knew, even before therapy, that the past is immutable. "We can't change what happened" was an oft-visited theme in counseling. But Sophie learned she can change the meaning she assigns to it.

As she listened now, she realized that though the words were unsaid, there were still signs. She remembered how her friends would complain about their parents never attending their events. Lil never missed a concert or a match. She recalled excitedly telling her mom about a biology lab, and that weekend she found a microscope in her room. Words may have been absent, but there were actions. Listening to her mother on the bus Sophie began to think differently about the space Lil provided in her childhood, to see it not as indifference but as opportunity. And though the thought at first repelled her, Sophie recognized a new truth: Gifted the freedom to be her own person, she had become much like her mother.

When Lil seemed to have said for the moment all she had to say, Sophie responded simply and equally honestly. "I always thought I had disappointed you. That I didn't live up to what you had expected or hoped."

Lil shook her head, and then said, "No. You were you. And I wouldn't have it any other way . . . I was me. And some of *that* I wish I could've changed."

"And what about with Rick?" His death was the third rail, a taboo subject still raw with pain.

Lil felt her body swaying with the motion of the bus as it slowly navigated the winding road. "I loved Rick. I thought he was a good man, a good husband, a good father," Lil began. "And then I hated him for what he did," she said honestly.

Sophie did not interrupt, so Lil continued. "And I was angry that you did not stay with him. He needed you."

"I tried. But I couldn't . . ." Sophie began. Lil opened her mouth to speak, to object. "He was poison for my boy."

Lil clamped her mouth and cocked her head.

"The shoulder surgery didn't go well. He was on the pain meds longer than most. When the prescription ran out and the docs wouldn't renew, he still talked about pain, pain, pain. I told him he would have to just push through. After a week of non-stop complaining, he finally stopped talking about the meds. I thought he was getting better." Sophie paused to shake her head. She continued while looking down at the floor of the bus. "I suspected, even then. He would come home late. There were whispered phone calls. He would spend a Saturday alone at the lake house – 'work,' he said, 'preparing a case.' So I confronted him. I told him I thought he was having an affair.

Thinking that would be the better option. 'No, no, no,' he said. 'I love you. There has only ever been you. It is just work.' And you want to believe, so I did. And then I found some cash missing, and it wasn't a small amount. That's when he admitted it. Said he was getting it from the son of a client. Talked about how he was in chronic pain. So much pain that he thought about killing himself."

Sophie looked at her mother and said, "What do you do when someone says something like that?"

Lil resisted the urge to answer. Instead, she said carefully, "What did you do?"

"I told him we had to get help, that he needed help. He agreed. I wanted him to go residential. I was scared. He said we couldn't afford for him to miss a month of work. He promised he would fix it. Go to meetings. Do a twelve-step, that sort of thing. For a few days, it was better. No late nights. Took ibuprofen in the morning. And then I got a phone call from one of the other lawyers at work, asking if everything was okay with Rick. He said he wasn't certain he should be calling, but he was concerned and shared some things he saw. That night we got into it. I am sure Luke heard us. I told him he had to go into a treatment program. He was dead set against it. Yelling, telling me I didn't understand, didn't love him. Then he started crying and promising, sobbing on his knees . . . Two weeks later, I found some pills and powder hidden in his office. I couldn't believe he was bringing that shit into the house. And then I thought about Luke. I pictured him finding it. Using it. Ending up dead somewhere. I couldn't get the thought out of my head. That was it. That's when I told Rick to get out. That he couldn't come back until he was clean."

Lil wasn't sure how long she held her daughter, gently rocking her in her arms. When she did speak, the first words were simple and true: "I am so very sorry."

"Me too," her daughter replied.

"I should have helped. I should have done something." Lil repeated. "I didn't know the details. But I knew something was wrong." She hesitated and then added, "Why didn't you tell me? Why didn't you say something?"

But Lil already knew the answer and regretted asking.

Sophie contained the flare of anger. She raised her right eyebrow and looked sideways at her mother. "You and I, we didn't have that kind of relationship. Help is not easily accepted in our family."

Lil recognized the truth of the comment. She could clearly see the hundreds of bricks she had placed into the wall that separated her from her daughter.

"I always saw you as the strong one. The independent one. You never needed help from anyone," Sophie explained. "I admired that. A part of me wanted to be like that. I wanted to be strong, too. Not to disappoint you, to burden you . . . Look how it turned out," she mused.

Lil weighed her thoughts. What to say? How much to share? Was this the time? In the end, she chooses to focus not on herself but on her daughter. "I wish I had your strength," she began. "The heartbreak you've endured. The burden you've carried alone. The courage to act, and the choices you needed to make to protect Luke . . . I am ashamed I wasn't there for you. And I am so very much in awe of you."

Healing a great hurt is not possible through words alone. It is a long journey paved by loving acts and shared experiences between trusting souls over time. That bus ride together was a start.

Day 6 - Juergen's Wife

Over the previous night's dinner at the Refuge de Fenetre, the decision was made – for Lil's benefit – to shorten the next day's hike by hopping on a coach to Champex. From there, the route to Forclaz at 9 miles was the shortest segment of their hike. Russell, Sophie, and Luke felt strong. Lil struggled. To her family, she dismissed it as the price to pay for taking a day off.

L'Hotel de Forclaz was quite different from the previous accommodations. It was an actual hotel with private rooms and a sit-down restaurant. After a light meal – she couldn't stomach the veal she had ambitiously ordered – Lil was looking forward to the prospect of a night's rest. She tossed in bed for an hour. Her unrequited fatigue gave way to her urge to smoke. She was beginning to think that her nightly ganja visits were proving just a little too appealing to her body. What does it matter, anyway, she thought to herself. I'll be dead before I'm addicted. Grabbing the antique key, she smiled and left the bedroom.

As she approached the front door, she found Juergen waiting for her. "Ah, if it isn't the beautiful Ms. Lil," he said as if surprised to see her. He leaned heavily against the wooden door, propped it open with his shoulder, and gestured her outside.

Lil brought her hand to her heart and bowed slightly to the big man. As she passed, she touched him gently on the arm – "*Danke, mein freund*" – and they made their way to a table in the middle of a grass terrace.

A parade of silent dark clouds sauntered across the night sky, their silver-grey edges illuminated by a shy moon that would occasionally peek out as if to check on life below.

Juergen was walking heavily. He placed both hands on the edge of the tabletop and lowered himself to the bench, extending his right leg out in front of him. Lil noticed the limp but did not comment.

With a flourish that seemed to Lil more Italian than German, Juergen handed Lil a small case about the size of a clutch purse.

"What is this?" she asked.

"That is a treasure chest," he began, "Made of hand-tooled leather and the finest Cohiba wood from the island paradise, El Cuba. Open it."

Lil ran her hand across the top of the case. Even in the faint light, she could make out the intricate patterns of the carving. She flicked the latch, opened the lid, and was met with the rich, musky smell of six hand-rolled Cuban cigars.

"Oh, Juergen. Very nice," Lil demurred. "But I can't smoke those," she added with a chuckle. "I'm trying to get rid of my nausea."

"Pinch the side and slide out the bottom. You will find a little secret," he replied confidentially.

Lil did as instructed. She ran her finger along the inside of the case and found . . . nothing.

"Good," Juergen said. "If it were that easy, I would have been in much trouble long ago."

He took the case from her. His practiced fingers pressed the two rosettes in the bottom corners, immediately releasing the back of the wooden box. The previously unseen compartment had enough room for his rolling paper, several previously prepared joints, and two ounces of pot.

Juergen winked. "I prefer to hide my stash in plain sight, but with style," he said.

"Juergen, you continue to surprise me," Lil replied. "Aren't you afraid of being caught?"

He waved off her concern. "In Europe, most places don't care. I travel with so little, it isn't even a crime. But it makes me feel like a man of mystery. And where it might be a problem, the smell of the cigars masks any odor. If anyone asks, I look at them with disbelief and say, 'Do you not know what a good Havana cigar smells like?' Once, I had some young security clerk in Iceland tell me he had to confiscate the case because of customs regulations. I started speaking really fast in German with wild eyes and hand gestures. He relented and let me through. I think he just wanted my Cuban cigars."

Juergen rolled a fresh joint, lit it, and passed it to Lil.

"That is a rather large bandage you're wearing tonight," Lil finally said, pointing to the wrapping on his left leg.

"Ach, it is my knee, Ms. Lil. I told you I lost forty kilos, and that is the truth. But I could stand to lose another forty. Also true, eh?" He turned his eye toward her. Her look confirmed she did not disagree.

"Every night my knees have been sore. But I kept telling myself I would get used to it. For the first three nights, I would start out a little stiff in the morning, and then I would warm up, and not too bad . . . Going down is much worse, you know."

Lil nodded in agreement.

"Yesterday was very bad. It hurt the whole time. I started to say to myself, 'Juergen, you can't do this. You are not strong enough.' But then I would say to myself, 'Juergen, you have come this far. You can't stop now.' And I would keep going."

"I have a lot of competing voices in my head, too," Lil confided. "How do you feel tonight?"

"Truly, not good. We started early. I was slow and each step hurt. I made it to the top of the first col. But when I was going down, I was paying attention to what was inside my mind instead of what was under my feet. I fell and twisted my knee. It took me an hour and a half to walk to the ski lift to take me down to the valley. From the bottom, we took a taxi to the hotel."

"I am very sorry to hear this," Lil said sympathetically.

"We are going to rest for a day here. But I am not certain I can continue. My knee is all swollen. I may have torn something."

Lil pressed her shoulder against his and gave him her best maternal hug. She resisted the urge to say, "Everything will be okay." She knew that it was not always the case.

It was Juergen who broke the silence. "Did I ever tell you why I chose to do the Tour?" He asked, knowing full well he had not told her.

"No," she replied unsurprisingly. "But I have been waiting."

"Because I was ashamed," he said.

Lil turned a confused eye.

"By Mila." After a pause he continued. "Five years ago, she had surgery. Breast cancer. It was a surprise. A shock, really. A double mastectomy. Chemo. *Das volle programme*. Thank God the treatment was a success. She has been cancer-free. We still go to the check-ups." He paused.

"That is good news, right?" Lil asked.

"Oh yes, yes. But though the cancer was gone, it left behind the fear. She was strong enough to face the disease. But afterward, after it was banished, she was afraid of everything else. She would not go out. She stopped working. We used to go dancing and drinking," he added with a smile. "I did not know what to do. We went to doctors and psychiatrists, and they diagnosed what you Americans call agoraphobia and depression."

Lil nodded, "That must have been painful for you both."

The big man continued. "Nothing I did helped. I thought, how can you be depressed? You just beat cancer and you have regained your life. And then I would get angry at her. And then I would get angry at myself for getting angry at her, you see?"

He looked at Lil's compassionate eyes.

"Her friend Sonja started to come around. I am not even certain how it began, if Mila called her or I called her or she just showed up. The visits were brief at first, and Sonja didn't say much. She would just sit next to Mila, massage her feet, and talk to her softly. I could tell Mila enjoyed it. She would get excited before Sonja would arrive. She would even bake some treats. And then, after six months, Sonja said, 'Let's go for a walk to the park?' Mila had not been out of the house for almost a year. I had been asking her and asking her. Let's go shopping, let's go to the coffee shop, let's go dancing – nothing. Damn if she doesn't say yes. And they go to the park together." Juergen shook his head. Lil passed him the joint and he took another drag.

"It wasn't long, maybe five minutes. But I remember crying when they

169

left the house. I hugged them both when they came back. Soon they were out more and more for longer and longer. I started to join them. And while Mila would still not go out by herself, it was good to welcome her back to the world of people, even a little bit."

Juergen continued, "And then Sonja said to her, 'Mila, it is time for an adventure, a celebration. Let's go on the Tour du Mont Blanc!' I didn't know what the hell she was talking about. I had never heard of it before. And I am pretty certain Mila had not either. But she said yes."

Lil laughed out loud. This reminded her of Sophie's response, saying yes before knowing what she agreed to.

Juergen looked at Lil uncertainly. "They asked me to go with them. But I said no, no, no. You two go. It will be a good girls' trip." Juergen paused. "But that wasn't the reason. I don't know why I said that. Truth was, I was the one who was afraid. Remember, then there were forty more kilos to this broken-down train. So I said no. But it wasn't just because of the weight, no . . . I am ashamed to say this, but I thought if I said no, then Mila wouldn't go. It was like a part of me," he hesitated, "wanted her to stay the way she was."

In the long pause that followed Lil could see the pain on her friend's face. She patted his shoulder.

"But they went. And they finished it, too. It took them fourteen days, but they finished. I was the one who stayed at home, afraid."

Lil smiled broadly, "That's girl power, Juergen!"

"When she came back, she was happier than I had seen her at any time since the cancer. I won't say she is cured. She still gets anxious sometimes, and things frighten her that did not before. But she gets out and she is happier."

"So eighteen months ago she said to me, 'Juergen you have to do the TMB. And after you do it with a friend, we will do it again together.'" Juergen felt the tears well in his eyes.

"So that is why I am here, dear Lil. I am walking away from home to find my wife again. I am walking to find myself. And when I get home, we will have our life back, together . . . At least that's the story I tell myself."

"That is a powerful story," Lil said genuinely. "I am honored that you shared it with me. Now promise this old lady that when you get home after you kiss your wife and tell her how much you love her, you will one day take this walk together."

"I will, my friend. And when I do, I will carry you with me, in here," he gestured to heart. "And when we get to this very spot, I will tell Mila the story of my good friend, *die schöne* Lil."

He reached out with his right arm, pulled her close, and kissed her at the top of her head.

"I have talked too much tonight," Juergen took another drag and exhaled slowly. "So of all the places you could have chosen, why did you choose this journey?" Juergen asked.

"Dear Juergen, that is a story for another night. I am feeling very tired and must go get some rest," Lil replied. But she would never share that story with Juergen. He would end his hike at Col de Forclaz and return home to Stuttgart. Lil would continue with her final Tour. The two would never meet or speak again.

Day 7 - No Shortcuts

After her conversation and smoke with Juergen, Lil returned to her room and fell into a restful sleep. The next morning, despite some doubt from her traveling companions, she proclaimed herself ready to continue the journey. Her only concession was to allow Luke and Russell to add some of her gear to their packs.

The sky was cloudy as they walked to the trailhead that would take them up to Col de Balme. It was rare to begin the day's hike in an actual town. The majority of the huts were located away from population centers. The last time they had started on pavement was six days ago in Les Houches.

Since the breathing episode two days earlier, Lil's family had conspired to ensure someone would be with her at all times, traveling at a slower pace. If she showed signs of fatigue, their job was to find a bus, train, or chairlift and get her safely to the next hut. Luke had drawn the morning shift.

Sophie and Russell had already passed through the village and entered the wooded trail leading to the first pass. Lil and Luke moved at a more leisurely pace. Lil caught herself looking into windows imagining the events inside this ordinary day. Had the husband kissed his wife good morning, or did he ignore her as he shaved and dressed and sped off to work? Had the mother hustled the children out of bed in a rush to prepare them for school, or did she hug them and relish, at least for a second, the gift of the moment together? Time is not as precious when we fail to recognize it is in short supply. Lil knew she could no longer afford this luxury. She strove to be conscious of the moment, even if only imagining the lives of others.

As his Tour progressed, Luke had also become increasingly attentive to the world beyond himself. Watching Russell, he saw how his grandfather's patient listening sparked happiness. He noticed Lyndon's commitment to looking after others and how everyone seemed to know him, and all who knew him called him friend. He was buoyed by the kindness of silent Pascal. Grudgingly, he had also come to accept the truth in Sean's words and to better see the pain caused by his selfishness. So this morning, his grandmother at his side, Luke also started the day outside his own head. His eye wandered to the streets, the houses, and the landscape around him. Phone in hand, he stopped frequently to compose a shot: a church spire piercing a low-hanging cloud, a row of avalanche barriers at the end of a grass slope, a stone shrine sheltering a chipped statue of the Virgin Mary. He asked the image what story it had to tell. As he changed the angle or adjusted the lighting, he imagined the viewer, inviting them to ask their own question, to create their own story. Was the cloud descending upon the church to erase it from the world or was the spire breaking through the morning fog to bring light to the earth? How did it feel as your tumbling body careened down the hillside and you uncontrollably approached the wooden crosses at the bottom? Who was the old woman who brought the fresh flowers to the shrine, and what was she honoring? Luke chuckled when he realized the religious theme of his first three shots.

As he and Lil approached the marker for the well-worn path that Sophie and Russell had taken ten minutes earlier, Luke's eye caught another sign, one overrun with a tangle of vines from the summer's growth. "Look at this, Nan," he called.

In faded letters the sign read "Les Fortifications de la Valle Du Trient." With his limited high school French, Luke explored the marker with interest. The pictures and words described Switzerland's mountain defenses. It was a story of bunkers, machine guns, and anti-tank obstacles that, along with the rugged terrain, protected the country from invasion by Nazi Germany or fascist Italy.

Luke turned to view the narrow valley and the surrounding mountainsides. Even in the span of six summer days he had walked enough of the Mount Blanc massif to appreciate the incredible challenges of navigating this environment. He imagined trying to move an army with its equipment and machines through the snow-covered passes and narrow rocky paths.

"But I thought Switzerland was neutral during World War II?" he said, turning to his grandmother.

She smiled and recalled the stories she had heard from that summer long ago when the war was a much more recent memory. "Like most things, it's more complicated than that," Lil explained.

"To some, Switzerland was not so neutral. Swiss banks allowed Nazi transactions and housed money stolen from Holocaust victims. Covered boxcars transported war *materiele* between Germany and Italy while not allowing Allied bombers to fly over Swiss airspace," Lil explained to the boy born in a century that had not known one world war, let alone two.

"On the other side, Switzerland accepted thousands of refugees, including many seeking to escape the Holocaust, and housed battalions of Allied soldiers. It was like walking a tightrope in a thunderstorm," Lil said, and then added after a pause, "Did you know that Hitler had plans to invade Switzerland? He called it Operation Tannenbaum. But he never did."

"Why not?" Luke asked.

"Who knows for sure, but part of the reason might be this," she said, pointing to the sign that read "Le Reduit Alpin Suisse." She explained, "The Swiss had this plan in one form or another since the eighteen hundreds, but they built it up in the nineteen thirties. They saw what Hitler was doing to other countries, and they started to prepare. Even used some of the steel and concrete they purchased from Germany. They would give up the low-lying cities, move everyone to the mountains, and fight guerilla style." She paused to look at Luke. "You think the Swiss are all a bunch of happy yodelers? Well, there are more guns per person in Switzerland than Texas, and they had mandatory military training, too," she added.

Luke was enthralled. "Let's go this way," Luke said, his eyes widening, pointing to the path behind the sign. "It says you can still see some of the buildings. And it looks like it goes up to the TMB trail on the top of the ridge."

This was not Lil's original plan for the day. She considered her hesitation. She felt Luke's excitement. As she weighed the choice, she recalled something a colleague had once said to her: "When the grandkids invite me to do something with them, my answer is always yes. For one day they will stop asking." Lil knew her one day was almost here. She headed up the trail behind the sign.

The path was narrow and largely overgrown, but they could still make out the switchbacks up the hillside. As they gained elevation, they earned a commanding view of the Vallée de Forclaz.

At first, they saw no relics or fortifications. They had noted a series of smaller side paths along the route, narrower still than the main trail. Luke's eyes glanced along one of the side paths and then back to his grandmother. She nodded her head and they were off. Their gambit was rewarded. They came to what looked like a concrete mushroom, four feet across and less than three feet high. The cap was chipped and crumbling. While covered with moss and lichen, it was clearly man-made.

Luke knelt down beside it. He began pushing away the brush that had grown up around the perimeter. "It's hollow inside," he announced.

With the enthusiasm of a gold miner, Luke excavated his find. After a few moments, he exposed a lower ring of concrete anchoring the redoubt into the earth and the remnants of four steel bars, like rusted arms, holding the concrete umbrella just off the ground.

"It's like a personal bunker," Luke spoke aloud, partly to Lil and partly to himself. His mind puzzled over the purpose. "But too small for artillery or even a machine gun."

Luke pulled off his backpack. Pressing himself into the space beneath the stem and the cap, he disappeared from view.

Lil's heart skipped a beat.

She resumed breathing when Luke's head popped up in the gap. "There is a perfect view all the way down the valley to Trient and the saddle leading into France. I can even see Lake Emosson and the dam. This is brilliant."

Lil's eye traced the panorama Luke described, sharing in his wonder.

"Nan, can you hand me my phone?" he asked. "It's in the compartment at the top of my bag."

She unzipped the pack, took out the phone, and handed it to him.

He stepped to the back edge of the concrete cylinder. He framed the shot of the lake and valley so the bunker's concrete top and bottom edges were viewable. The decaying steel bar defined the left of the image. He changed the focus from the lake to the point where the rusted steel merged into the crumbling concrete.

"That'll be cool," he said, handing his phone back to Lil.

As Luke reached his arms out of the bunker to pull himself up, Lil instinctively put out her hand. And though it made it more difficult to extract himself, he took his grandmother's hand while pushing with his feet.

"Thanks," he said.

She smiled, brushed the hair out of his eyes, and wiped away the leaves and dirt that clung to his jacket.

"I probably shouldn't have done that, right?" Luke said.

"Yeah, not exactly 'leave no trace,'" Lil replied. "But you'll remember it." Worried about the risk of the young man romanticizing war, she added, "Now think of it surrounded by snow. You are alone. You're maybe a little older, maybe not. Your feet and hands are freezing, your stomach hungry. You hear a noise off to your left, and then . . . Remember that, too."

Luke stood silent, uncertain of what he was supposed to say. He knew his grandmother was pro-choice, a protector of the environment, a supporter of the LGBTQ community, a sustaining member of National Public Radio, and staunchly anti-war. He didn't know if his enthusiasm had offended her.

"Let's find another," she smiled and headed further down the thin trail. After thirty yards they found a second bunker. This was nestled closer to the stone outcropping at the edge of the mountainside. The top had fallen off and broken into several pieces. The hole was completely filled with stone and rubble. If you didn't know what you were looking for you could easily mistake it for just a pile of rock. Without any trees nearby, the view of the Nant Noire valley and the mountainside along the opposite edge was even more striking than the first bunker.

Luke navigated along the back edge. This time he did not disturb anything.

"Be careful," Lil said reflexively.

But Luke did not hear her. He was thinking about Pascal. He composed this picture as he imagined Pascal would, with just the slightest hint of human presence. The angle Luke settled on captured a glacial stream emerging from a shadowed col toward the north edge of the valley. The late spring glacier itself was mottled, tarred with bits of stone and dirt like exposed wounds, memories of an inexorable journey down the mountain unhealed by any fresh snow. There were no houses or roads, just the dark water dancing across a series of rough boulders before settling into a steadier stream. At the bottom corner of the composition, Luke included the remaining hints of the bunker on which he stood. He set the depth of field as wide as it would go. To the casual observer, it might seem like an undisciplined picture from a hurried tourist. But the movement of the water, the slope of the mountain, and the angle of the valley all drew the viewer's eye to the ghost of the bunker. There, if they spent the time to look closely enough, they would find a piece of twisted steel, some smooth fragments of poured concrete, and a single small flower, the only bit of color in an otherwise gray, brown, and black palette. This is for Pascal, Luke thought to himself.

Lil watched admiringly as Luke set about his work—his earnestness, focus, and joy. In that moment, she became uncertain of time and was transported into it. She felt a flicker of her own youth—the excitement, pleasure, and hope. In the same instant, she also remembered her uncertainty, fear, and shame.

"Time to go," Luke declared, calling to her. Lil's moment evaporated, an invisible wisp abandoning her. "Yes, it is," she replied. "Yes, it is."

They traced their way back to the main footpath and headed further up the mountainside. Along the route, they encountered two larger installations, wider and with rusted metal faceplates embedded into the walls. Luke and Lil decided these must have housed small artillery or machine guns.

After continuing for another fifteen minutes along the narrowing path, they saw neither fortifications nor other hikers. Just as they thought their trail of discovery was at an end, they turned a corner and came upon what looked like the remains of a typical Alpine hut built into the face of the mountain. It was the sort of gîte they might find elsewhere along the Tour. Upon closer inspection, though, they noticed some curiosities. The fallen wood facing from the side of the structure revealed not timber framing but gray concrete. And the windows were not windows at all but trompe-l'oeil, the paint long faded and now cracked to reveal still more concrete.

Luke approached the door. He grabbed hold of the handle. It would not budge a fraction. He knocked first with his hand and then, surprisingly to Lil, with a stone. Before she could stop him from damaging the door with the rock, she heard the ring of metal.

"Not everything in these mountains is as it seems to be," Lil said.

"A faux house. Do you think there is something behind it?" Luke added with a tone of excitement.

"I draw the line at darkened caves," Lil added. "Just in case you had any ideas."

Luke feigned disappointment. "Well, the door was locked and nobody was home anyway. Stand by the door so I can get a picture."

Lil obliged, a simple composition this time.

"I'm not certain we can get much better than this anyway. We should get back to the TMB trail. Which way to the blue dot?" he asked his grandmother.

Lil took out her phone. The screen was blank. She pressed the power button. It remained dark.

"Damn," she said.

"I know that feeling," Luke responded quickly. "Apple batteries are still crap. That's why you need the PIXL," Luke added with a flourish, waving his phone in the direction of his grandmother. "Plus, it takes better pictures."

Luke opened Google Maps. He didn't have an international data plan, but after the first day of hiking, he had downloaded some maps of the area.

"That'll work even without a cell signal?" Lil asked.

"Kinda," Luke replied. "I don't have your AllTrails app, but the GPS will still put us on the map."

The image of the map filled the screen, and after a few moments, the pulsing indicator dot appeared as well. "Hello us," Luke said.

Luke zoomed in on the image. "Damn," he said in the same tone his grandmother had used upon finding her battery depleted. "This map does not have all the TMB trails on it. It assumes you are a normal person and driving."

It was Lil's turn to gloat. "That's why you still need this," Lil replied, imitating Luke's smug tone while taking out her well-worn copy of Kev Reynold's trekking bible: *The Tour of Mont Blanc.* She flipped to the section for the day's stage: Col de la Forclaz to Tré le Champ.

While the maps were not to scale, they did provide a detailed description of the main route and some side paths.

"We need to get to Col de Balme and then there are two options for heading to Tré le Champ. Is Col de Balme on your map?" Lil asked her grandson.

"Yeah, and it is not too far. It looks like we are on the slope heading up to it. But it is not like there is a road. I still can't see the trails on this map."

"Weren't you a Boy Scout, and didn't you learn how to use a compass?" Lil teased him.

"Cub Scout. And I quit after losing the Pinewood Derby," Luke replied. A memory invaded his mind. He was building the small wooden car with his dad, making it look like the Batmobile. Luke wanted the Dark Knight while his dad was thinking the TV Series. The good memories were sometimes the hardest.

"Well, we've got two options." Lil determined. "We can either head back down, which will take an hour and a half, and then climb back up following the TMB signs. That'll put us about three hours behind. Or we look for a trail that's heading in the direction of Col de Balme and try our luck . . . So you gotta to ask yourself one question: Do you feel lucky? Well, do you, punk?"

It had been a while since Luke had played the movie quote game with his grandmother. "Clint Eastwood. Dirty Harry," Luke announced. Smiling, he pointed up the hill. They both began looking for a path that headed toward Col de Balme.

The Tour du Mont Blanc is not a single trail. It is more of a spidery network blanketing the massif. While the main path is chock-a-block with signposts, there are multiple variants for folks looking to save a little time, see a particular vista, or challenge themselves. Hundreds of small paths spread like capillaries across the mountainside, usually leading back to one of the major arteries. These paths may have been carved by water sluicing its way to the rivers that inevitably found the valley floor or worn by generations of local feet getting from here to there. Some were simply game trails, etched from the unending search for water, food, shelter, or a mate.

As Luke and Lil circled around the back of the faux cabin, they observed the trace of three distinct paths. One veered right, heading in the direction of a talus field nested beneath a rocky outcropping. The second path led more or less uphill via a series of short zigs and zags. The final option ran east and disappeared around the curve of the mountain.

"Yikes, two goats and a car," Lil quipped, referencing an old line from Monty Hall.

"They probably all head there," suggested Luke optimistically.

"Shortest distance between two points," Lil voiced, and she set off on the uphill path. They walked without noticing the tumble of stones, remnants of the fallen cairn guiding hikers to the path on the right.

For the first thirty minutes their confidence rose. The TMB ran through a series of mountain shoulders. Elevation gain was a requirement to locate the saddles between peaks. This trail, with its tight switchbacks, had the right feel to it.

But doubts resurfaced shortly thereafter when the trail unexpectedly split. They chose left, judging it to be heading west based on the position of the sun. When it split a second time, they chose right, as the other choice headed downhill, which didn't seem right.

All seasoned hikers have experienced the treachery of switchbacks. You walk and walk and walk, certain the top of the mountain is just around the next bend. After a glance upslope suggests you have arrived at the summit, you take what surely must be the final turn only to see the same landscape and yet another switchback ahead.

And so it was that Luke and Lil's hopes were repeatedly punctured. "Check the map again," Lil suggested.

"Damn, Google. No GPS signal," Luke announced, smacking the side of the device.

"That worked with our old Zenith TV," Lil offered.

They briefly considered staying put, hoping someone would find them – the standard counsel for lost hikers. But having made their original choice to move, they decided to walk on. It was a warm day. They had some food. Besides this was the Alps, not an uncharted forest on the edge of nowhere.

As they rounded the turn, they were greeted by the long face of a chamois. Smaller than an ibex, the chamois is distinguished by two features: the brown stripe down its back and the short horns that hook backward at the tip.

Luke and chamois stood unblinking at one another. His blue eyes fixed on the rectangular slits of the creature's dark brown eyes. Luke flinched first. He turned to the side and took a cautious step down the path. The chamois immediately turned and quickly bounded back up.

"We are screwed," Luke said.

"Looks like we chose the goat," Lil added.

They sat down, removed their backpacks, and took out some trail mix.

An Unexpected Escort

Grandmother and grandson spent a few silent moments chewing peanuts and dried fruit. Lil picked out her M&Ms, handing them to Luke, who gratefully accepted.

"Well, we have three choices," Lil began.

"Not three choices again," Luke groaned.

"We go down, we go up, we stay put," Lil continued.

Their contemplation was disturbed by the sound of dirt and rocks tumbling from the path above them.

Jolted by adrenaline, both Lil and Luke jerked their heads up the path, ready to fight a vengeful chamois or quickly flee if the creature had recruited a neighborhood ibex.

It was neither chamois or ibex. Instead they saw a bike. The rider was slowly picking his way down a trail that Lil and Luke had struggled to navigate on foot. As he approached, their surprise turned to astonishment. In a quiet voice, Luke said to Lil, "He's ancient, even older than you."

Noticing his riding was raining scrabble onto the unexpected travelers below, the biker dismounted and walked his cycle toward Luke and Lil.

Lil looked at the man. Luke looked at the bike.

The bike was a Devinci Spartan. We are talking *beaucoup* dollars, many thousands, Luke thought to himself.

"*Ciao signora i signor,*" he greeted them. "*Il mio nome e Giacomo.*"

"I am Lil, and this is my grandson Luke," Lil said.

Luke raised his eyes from the bike and looked at the old man. He was wearing a faded green Giro d'Italia shirt and black biker's shorts. His hair was close-cropped but thick, a dappled grey that reminded Luke of the glacial ice they had passed. His skin was dark brown, the color of someone who had spent much of his life outside with inadequate SPF protection. Beneath the wrinkles, the old man seemed to have no fat. His forearms were a series of sinewy cords. He had a biker's tricep, a tight triangle distinct from the rest of his upper arms. His thighs and calves were similarly well-defined. Luke glanced down at his own arms and legs. This old man is still cut, he thought to himself.

Luke straightened tall and extended his hand. "*Bonjour Monsieur*," he said.

"He is Italian, Luke, not French," Lil said in the tone of a verbal dope smack.

Giacomo smiled and shook Luke's hand. Luke had always thought he had big hands, which gave him an advantage in the pool. Giacomo's hand was immense, the fingers overlapping onto Luke's wrist. And the man's grip was firm, built from many years controlling the handlebars on the narrow, jutted paths of the mountain.

"What brings you two to this little goat path?" Giacomo asked in accented English.

Lil quickly told him of their exploration and unlucky decisions.

Giacomo looked at her intently and smiled as the tale unfolded.

"Might you be able to tell us the way to the main TMB trail or Tré le Champ?" Lil asked.

"It would be an honor," Giacomo replied. "It would be best if I walked with you for a way."

"No, no, no, we do not want to disturb your ride. If you can just point us to the trail," Lil tried to politely object as was the expected custom.

But the gentleman rider responded lightly, "I have ridden enough this morning, and a little walk is always welcomed."

With the dance complete, the biker pointed them up the path he had just descended.

Giacomo was amiable company, and his English was excellent with only an occasional word of Italian or phrase from the Haute Savoie.

Giacomo and Luke fell into an easy conversation. It was clear that Luke was struck by the old man. Surely, the young man's admiration for the elder's athleticism was one factor, but there was also something more. When Luke spoke, Giacomo listened with his whole body. His eyes focused squarely on Luke. The small muscles of the man's face stretched and twitched and curled, reacting to Luke's every word and tone. His way of listening made Luke feel special and important, the way a child feels before they begin to doubt their parents.

Luke told Giacomo about the fake hut and the bunkers he had seen on the hike up. He sprinkled references to the Alpine Retreat and Operation Tannenbaum. Luke talked and talked, not so much to impress the old man, though he did want to impress him, but so the feeling wouldn't end.

When Luke paused, Giacomo spoke. "Those individual bunkers, they are all connected you know," Giacomo said. "The fake chalet marks the entrance to a tunnel that will take you to a cavern, a giant complex inside the mountain. You could get to each of those bunkers from the main cavern."

Luke considered Giacomo's description, his mind imagining a web of darkened tunnels stretching beneath their feet.

"Most of these sites, *grazie Dio*, were never used during the Second World War. But there were some battles along the Little Maginot Line to the south," Giacomo explained. "Much of the real fighting in these mountains happened during the Great War, World War One."

Giacomo paused, gauging Luke's reaction. His attention invited him to continue.

Giacomo pointed to the range across the valley. "Now, there are only a few glaciers left, and most of them sit like wrinkled fruit barely hanging on to the branch. Not so a hundred years ago. Picture every rift, every crack and crevice overflowing with snow and ice. Filled so high you couldn't see the rocky face below. And into this frozen land the Dukes and the Princes, the Emperors and the Kings sent their men, many of whom knew nothing of what it meant to live, or try to live, in the mountains during winter. They dug trenches, dragged artillery, and followed orders from those who had less to lose. More died of frostbite and cold than were taken by bullets and cannon. And even today, when the Alpinniers climb for the higher peaks, or as the ice recedes, they still find a caisson wheel, a rusted gun, or an abandoned helmet. *Che spreco, che spreco . . .*"

The words of past suffering were tinged with real pain. Luke suspected there was something more behind the description, but he did not ask.

As they walked along, the path leveled, joined at intervals by a series of small trails not unlike the one Luke and Lil had taken.

Lil interrupted the silence. "I see you are wearing the Maglia Verde," she observed. It was a statement, not a question.

"*Si,*" he said, and no more.

"Are you a rider?" Luke asked.

"I was *un piccolo uomo*, no more than that. My father taught me how to ride in the mountains. He was *un buon ciclista*," Giacomo said dismissively.

"Signore Bartali," Lil said, using their escort's last name. "You are more than that, and your father was much more than *un buono ciclista . . .*" The lilt in her voice was an invitation.

Giacomo met Lil's eye with a look equal parts knowing and reluctant. After a barely perceptible nod, the corners of his mouth turned down quickly while his gaze fixed on the path before his feet.

"The boy does not want to hear an old man's stories," Giacomo said and started walking on.

Lil spoke, her words briefly trailing behind before catching up with him. "The young need these stories. Today, too often, they are surrounded by misleaders. Some don't believe, and some may never have even heard." Lil paused, hoping her words would take effect. "The boy is interested in history. Telling him would be a great gift so he may keep a truth alive."

Perplexed, Luke watched the exchange between the two.

Giacomo stopped, seeming to wrestle with Lil's words. He turned to face her, "*Conosce la tua storia?*"

She paused and weighed her own moment of hesitation. "*Non ancora,*" she finally replied.

The old man tilted his head. "*E dopo la mia storia,*" he said, touching his chest and then opening his hand in Lil's direction.

"*Lo farò,*" she replied. The deal had been struck.

Lil began. "The Bartalis are one of the most famous families in this area. They are renowned for bicycle racing, yes, but it is what the family did during the war that is truly heroic."

Giacomo started slowly and spoke softly. Luke fell in stride next to him, matching steps so as to better hear the man.

"My father was Gino Bartali. He was born very far from these mountains, in Ponte a Ema, a small village south of Florence," he added with a glance at Luke and a gesture to the south.

"Like most of the boys, he worked on a farm. He was a hard worker. Skinny but strong. Always moving and full of energy. Even as a young boy he could work as long as the older men. He loved being outside." Giacomo paused, as he would do many times throughout the story, the ever-changing emotions apparent on his face as if reliving each moment he described.

"He helped Mamina with her embroidery. But he was also a smart boy. He learned his numbers early – he could do sums in his head – and was the best reader in the village. *I miei nonni* saw how smart he was. So they arranged for him to go to school in Florence."

Giacomo looked directly at Luke. "Those days not everyone went to school, it was not like today. The children were needed at home to work. So this was a big sacrifice, *si*." Luke could see the pride in the old man's face.

"And getting to school, that was a problem. There was no car or bus. And Signore Pasquale, with the cart, did not travel the road every day. So Mamina and Papa and Francesca, his older sister, bought him a bike. His first bike."

Giacomo's face lit up as if he was seeing his father right now on that bicycle. He spoke more quickly. "The road to Florence was long and very hilly. That is where he learned to ride. Every day to school and back again. He was always in a rush with lots to do at school and more to do at home. He would challenge himself to pedal faster and faster. He loved the wind blowing on his face. And he found he never got tired, even going up hills. Legs like steel, *come pistoni sulle ruote di un treno*, always going around and around. Even as a boy, he was a Giant on the Mountains," Giacomo laughed, using the nickname his father would earn later in his cycling career. "He got a job working with Signore Casamonti in a bicycle shop in Florence. Signore Casamonte is the one who convinced *mieie nonni* to let Papa race.

"How old are you, Luke?" Giacomo asked.

"Seventeen," Luke answered.

"That's how old my father was when he won his first race in nineteen thirty-one," Giacomo said, slapping the boy gently on the shoulder with the back of his hand.

"He became a *professionale* in nineteen thirty-five. He married my mama five years later. He lived in Florence to keep close to the *famiglia*. But he always trained in the mountains, *les Apennininca*, *les Pirenei*, *Dolomiti* and *les Alpi*. He used his money from racing to take care of our whole family. He learned what it meant to take care of others from Mamina and Papa.

"He won his first Giro D'Italia in nineteen thirty-six. Do you know of the Giro?" Giacomo asked.

"No sir," Luke replied.

"Think of the Tour de France, only more difficult," Giacomo replied.

Luke laughed. Giacomo's look told him he was not joking.

"After he won the Giro, the Federacion Bicyclette Italian demanded, for the glory of Italy, that he race in the Tour de France. Now Papa loved to ride and compete, and he was always fierce. But he was not boastful. He said his legs and lungs were a gift from God and that he was just *un piccolo uomo*." Giacomo paused.

"You see, Luke, this was before the war, but the Fascists were in power. Mussolini was *vanaglorioso* – a big talker. And he was cruel. He ruled Italy with a fist. You stood in his way, the *squadristi* – the blackshirts – would crush you. He controlled everything: the military, the factories, the trains, the newspapers and, yes, the Federacion Sportif, too. Many Italians, it is true, liked the big man, especially at first. He talked a lot about the glory of Italy and the greatness of Rome. Mussolini called himself Il Duce – the leader. But Papa called him Il Due – number two, a shit." Giacomo laughed as he remembered the family joke.

"In nineteen thirty-eight, Papa won the Tour de France. It was *magnifico*. That is when he earned his name, The Giant of the Mountains. Mussolini saw the victory as a trophy for the Fascists. On the night before the final leg, when it was clear he would win the Tour, a member of the Federacion visited Papa and told him what to say when he accepted the yellow jersey: 'Signore Bartali, when you are at the podium tomorrow, and they hand you the *maillot jaune*, you are to dedicate the victory to Il Duce and the greatness of Italy.'"

Giacomo paused to look at Luke. He stood up tall and squared his shoulders. "Instead, when he accepted the jersey and gave his speech, my father said he was grateful to his family, to the people of Italy, and to God." Giacomo nodded his head as if he had just spoken the words himself.

"Mussolini was furious and wanted to punish Papa. But Papa had won the love of the people. Mussolini could not harm him, so he decided he would ignore him. There were no parades, no celebrations, no national awards. Mussolini thought that would hurt Papa. But the funny thing, Papa preferred it that way. He did not want attention or celebration. He just wanted to ride.

"Papa continued to ride, but things got worse in Italy. Mussolini sent *le truppes* to Africa, Greece. He joined Hitler and started to enforce anti-Jewish laws. When Hitler went to war with Inghilterra and France, Italy joined the war on Germany's side.

"Like most Italian men, Papa was called to serve in the army. But, and this always makes the family laugh, he was not fit enough to fight – *battito cardiaco irregolare*. The greatest bike racer in the world *inidoneo*." Giacomo shook his head and laughed. "So he was assigned *comme corriere*. He would ride his bike delivering messages for the Italian army. For his three years in the army he kept doing what he loved to do – to ride, to train and to race.

"People know of Auschwitz, Belec, and Treblinka, but there was also a concentration camp in Italy, San Sabba in Trieste. Just like in Francia there was also an Italian Resistance, *capisci*. Cardinal Dalla Costa met with my father and asked for his help – the Cardinal knew our family, he had married my grandparents. My father was a very pious man. You see, Luke, the Cardinal, and the church had been helping the Jews. The Friars in Assisi would make false IDs and paperwork. But it was difficult to move these from place to place. So the Cardinal asked my father to hide the documents in the frame of his bicycle and carry them from city to city to help the Jews escape. This was very dangerous. If he was caught, he could be killed. But he did not hesitate.

"At first, it was a good plan. Papa knew the roads. And everyone knew Gino Bartali. When he got to a checkpoint, he would tell the guards he was *allenamento per una gara*, and they would let him through.

"As the war went on and races were canceled, people grew suspicious. 'What is he training for?' they would ask. They also knew Papa was a very devout man and loyal to the Church. There was one time he was arrested and taken to Villa Trieste, the House of Sorrow, where local Fascists tortured their prisoners. Papa was accused of being a traitor and helping the Resistance.

"But good virtue shined on my father – Papa said it was the hand of God. One of the *ufficiali* was Papa's former *comandante*. He convinced the other *interrogati* that papa was innocent and he was released. Papa then hid in Umbria under another name. A few months later, Italy was liberated."

"Did your father race after the war?"

Giacomo's face lightened, the sly smile returning to his face. "A little bit. He won the Giro D'Italia in nineteen forty-six, a second Tour de France in forty-eight, the Milan San Remo in fifty."

"Your father was a hero," said Luke.

Giacomo hesitated. "Yes, I think so," he said. "But then every boy imagines their father is a hero, *non*?" The old man paused before adding cautiously, "And then you find out the truth. That he is just a man."

Giacomo stopped again, the silence longer this time. He lifted his eyes and looked squarely at Luke. He decided to continue. "My father could also be a *difficile*. Impatient. Selfish. He would curse and honk the horn when he was driving. He spent days away from the family at the big races, even when he was no longer competing. As a boy, if he missed a birthday or special event, I would think maybe if I were a better *figlio* or a better *ciclista* he would want to be around more. And then, when I got older and saw how he could neglect his family, I would silently curse him for not being a *meglio padre* or *nonno*.

"Heroes are for the stories we need to tell ourselves," Giacomo said, looking at both Luke and Lil. "Right after he died, I found I was angry all the time. I started speaking with a *lingua amara*, and to drink. I stopped riding and disrespected my own family. One day my wife said to me 'when will you let this pass?' I reminded her of his *offese e mancanza*, of all he had done wrong. She listened, looking at me with her big brown eyes, and said, 'Giacomo, you might as well get angry with the crickets for chirping or the petals for falling from the rose. We are each *imperfecto*. We do the best we can, and that is only on a good day.' She was right. On that good day, I started to forgive. First, and gradually, my father. Later, and more slowly, myself. To forgive – that is how we keep the love alive."

The trio had stopped walking. They had arrived at a crossroad marked with the familiar TMB signpost. The old man rested his bike against the post and said, "So for me, Luke, Gino Bartali is no longer a hero. He is now a man, and will always be my father." Giacomo glanced up beneath the shroud of his overgrown eyebrows. "And as long as I have breath, he will still ride with me through these mountains."

Lil's face softened as she struggled to hold a strong emotion. She reached out both her hands toward Giacomo. He held them lightly and kissed her once upon each cheek. Luke heard the old man whisper something but could not make out the words. Lil reluctantly nodded, her mouth drawn tight while looking to the sky.

The old man then turned toward Luke and extended his hand. Luke took the hand and hurriedly embraced the man. He hugged him like a lost relative, members of a universal family bound together by the loss of a father. The old man who had found his way to forgive and the young man still lost in the pain. Giacomo cradled Luke's head in one hand while gently patting his back with his other.

When they separated, Lil could see Luke's eyes were moist. She saw a hurt little boy in the young man's face. She approached her grandson and stood by his side. The three shared a final smile before the old man got on his bike and returned to the path they had just walked together.

A Confession

Luke and Lil headed down the path toward Tré le Champ. Lil placed both walking sticks together and reached out to her grandson. They walked silently, hand-in-hand, along several gentle switchbacks.

In the quietness of his steps, Luke's mind drifted. He had begun the Tour a reluctant traveler. As the days passed, the miles accumulated and the final destination approached, Luke realized he was not as hurried to have it end. He replayed his encounters with the people and stories he had discovered. His thoughts then returned to his father.

Lil, too, was thinking of the journey's end. For her, time truly was running out, with much yet to do. When Luke glanced at her, she turned her head to meet him. "I love you," she said. "I love your mom . . . and I loved your dad." It was a simple message and a true one. It was the message she had hoped to send by taking this final walk.

Unexpectedly, tears flooded Luke's face. She had not seen her grandson cry since he was a little boy falling off the slide at the playground – not even at the funeral. She pulled him close.

"I miss him . . ." Luke managed between the sobs.

Lil nodded and held him tighter. Together, they stepped to the side of the trail and leaned against a boulder.

Luke did not hear if his grandmother said anything. He was no longer on the trail. He was back again in that familiar scene: Visiting his dad at the lake house. Opening the box. Seeing the pipe. Closing the box. Returning it to the closet. Finding the pills.

Luke risked the words. The words that had taken root in his head: "And

191

it's my fault... I could have done something . . . I knew he was still using . . ." He did not hear if his grandmother replied. He continued. "I could've told someone, but I didn't. Then he could have gotten help, but I was too *stupid*." These were the words he had desperately felt, the ones that gnawed at him but he never said aloud. Not to his mom. Not to Sean. Not to anyone.

"I could have saved him. If I had done something, he would still be alive. But I didn't, I didn't do anything . . ." Luke relived for the thousandth time the details of the conversation with his dad that night. "Have you ever lied, you know, to help a client?" He saw again his dad shifting in his chair. He remembered the answer: "Luke, sometimes I have had to keep things to myself. To protect the person, to help them."

Luke was uncertain if his father knew that he knew. Either way, he had his answer. He said nothing more that night or in the two weeks before the overdose. He said nothing about it at the funeral, nor in the past 18 months. He said nothing to anyone except himself. And those words were unforgiving: *I killed him.* The cancer of guilt ensnared his every day. Luke might find temporary refuge, but then the same thought would eventually return.

Lil and Luke rocked together against the stone, Luke's pain flowing out along with his tears. Luke eventually heard the words his grandmother had been softly repeating while she stroked his hair. At first, it was a distant whisper, and then clearer and clearer still. "It's not your fault . . . it's not your fault . . . it's not your fault . . ."

Luke had tried saying these words to himself but never believed. He knew he was a coward for remaining silent, that he was a fool for thinking the problem would disappear, and that he was to blame.

Yet the words sounded different coming from his grandmother.

Lil held Luke's face lightly in her hands. "We all knew about your dad's addiction," she confessed. "We did what we thought we could, or we should. But none of us had the magic key. What he needed, we didn't have to give, and what we had to give wasn't what he needed. And when Mom thought his using would harm you, that's when she sent him away."

Luke listened without speaking.

"Baby, you can love him, and be angry with him, and have a hundred other feelings all at the same time. But please, please, please do not blame yourself," Lil continued. "We do not have to shoulder the weight of other people's choices, even those we love."

Luke slowly found his breath. He didn't feel better. Not exactly. He wasn't cured. He was exhausted. And he still hurt. But he did feel some relief. He had told that darkest secret, the thing he had been carrying by himself, alone, for almost two years, the truth he had been ashamed to admit to others. And when he spoke it, the world did not crack open. His grandmother was still there. She still loved him. It wasn't that she forgave him. Not really. Because she said there was nothing to forgive, that he was not responsible for his father's overdose. Could that really be true? Luke considered the possibility, rolling it over in his mind. Finally, he said, "I'm very hungry."

"Well, we'd better be walking, then," Lil replied. They left the boulder, and a little bit of the pain, at the side of the trail and headed toward Tré le Champ.

The sign indicated it was another 30 minutes to their destination. As they walked they talked, but it was lighter talk. In what seemed like a blink, they first saw one house and then another. They were nearing the tiny hamlet.

Lil approached a young woman playing in a backyard with her children. "*Excusez-moi, s'il vous plait. Est-ce-que tu connais ou est l'Auberge de Boerne?*" Lil asked.

"*Mais oui*," the young woman replied before continuing in English. "You can either walk along the road for two kilometers. When you pass across the railroad track, turn to the right, and you will see the Auberge, or you can stay on the cart path," she said, gesturing to the right. "It is a little longer and curves along the canal but will take you right there." She paused before adding, "I recommend the path. Madame Brienz is home today. Maybe you will be lucky?"

"*Merci*," Luke added quickly and turned toward Lil, a which-way-do-you-want-to-go look on his face.

The reference to Madame Brienz had no meaning to either Luke or Lil.

"A cardinal rule of traveling, my boy: Always follow the recommendation of the locals," Lil added, heading toward the cart path.

Madame Brienz

The cart path was a well-worn track that never ventured far from the hamlet, a comforting sight given their adventuresome wandering earlier in the day. Light ruts on either side of a grassy median hinted at its origin as a route for wheeled vehicles of some sort. But now it seemed tamped more by feet than carts. It hugged a narrow waterway tracing the edge of the hillside. The water was not the milky color of the glacial streams. That and the uniform width suggested it was a man-made canal rather than a natural feature. Later, they would learn that the canal followed the route of a Roman aqueduct first built more than 1500 years ago.

They heard Madame Brienz before they saw her. A faint echo, like a woodpecker in the distance, grew into a more substantial 'thwunk, thwunk' as they drew closer. To Luke, it was the sound of a fungo bat hitting a baseball. For Lil, it was more like beating a woolen rug with a broom handle. They found their steps marching to the cadence of the continuing percussion.

The path curved gently to the left. Through a copse of trees they could see hints of a structure, the first they had encountered directly on the cart path. As they approached, the hints became a stone house capped with a thick timber roof. It looked small, no more than two rooms, and clearly had been there for a very long time. It had a certain weight or, rather, a presence. Luke's mind imagined a home for a canal master. Lil immediately thought of a church. Neither was prepared for the sight they beheld when they rounded the final bend.

"We walked all the way to Easter Island," Luke muttered aloud. A stone bridge connected the house to a large clearing on the other side of the canal.

The clearing was divided into a series of five cascading terraces, with an irregular line of totems on each. The smallest of the carved wooden poles was six feet, and the largest was easily twelve feet. All told, 30 or more sculptures graced the space. Lil and Luke stood frozen in place. The display simultaneously captured their breath and compelled them to smile.

As they marveled at the sight, they only noticed the silence when a woman stepped out from behind a totem on the third terrace.

"*Bonjour*," the woman said, wiping her forehead with a gloved hand. She placed down a large wooden mallet and an ancient chisel. She took two steps toward the two travelers. "*Je m'appelle Madame Brienz. Bienvenue à le jardin*," she said.

Lil and Luke introduced themselves. Madame Brienz invited them to sit on a wooden bench located at the base of the first terrace.

Madame Brienz turned to Luke and asked, "So, young man, what do you see?"

Luke's face turned red, feeling as if he were back at school confronted with a pop quiz. He resisted the temptation to panic and blurt out something, anything to fill the silence. Instead, he remembered his conversation with Pascal. Luke drew his breath and let his eye wander. Eventually he spoke, looking neither at Madame Brienz or Lil, but beholding the scene before him, listening for what the totems might tell him.

"Well, there is the obvious thing: five terraces with a series of carved poles or totems. At first, they look similar to one another, but they are very much not. Each one is unique for sure. They all look like they grow up from the earth, but some have wider roots. And they are not all the same wood. Most are looking toward the mountains, but some are looking away. This one over here looks very sad, its eyes are down. That one looks angry, but then if you turn your head, it looks more determined or proud. I am not certain what else I see yet. But this is beautiful."

"I see a family," Lil added. "I see a history."

Now it was Madame Brienz who smiled. She looked pleased. Slapping both hands on her knees, she said, "Come, let's have some café." She stood up, wrapped a hand around each guest, and escorted Luke and Lil across the bridge and into her home.

The interior was a study in contrast. The stone and framing, striking from the outside, was as impressive inside. The wooden countertop, a single live edge slab a good three inches thick, appeared to be the same type and age as the eight beams that supported the ceiling. What little furniture there was – a kitchen table with four chairs, a couch with two side arms positioned in front of the fireplace – were all wood, but for the cushions on the couch. Not delicate, but with less mass and more curves than the framing of the house. The appliances, on the other hand, featured a who's who of high-end European manufacturers: a Liebherr refrigerator, a Bertozzoni range, and a Nuova Simonelli espresso machine.

Madame Brienz removed her work coat and hung it on a wooden peg on the wall. She invited Lil and Luke to place their bags by the door and gestured them toward the table. A small plate of pastries was already out as if she were expecting guests.

She moved to the counter and set to making three espressos, talking as she packed the grinds into the portafilter. "Though I work alone, I prefer company when I take my breaks. You two seem interesting. It is nice to see the generations walking together. So, thank you for joining me."

The potent smell of the coffee quickly filled the small house. Lil closed her eyes, inhaled deeply, and savored the moment. Reflectively she swallowed in anticipation of the treat. Luke smiled as he looked at his grandmother. Though he was embarrassed by the thought, Luke recalled how he swallowed like that whenever he thought about sex. So that's why adults like coffee so much, he laughed to himself.

The woodcarver returned to the table with three espressos and took her seat. She passed around the pastries. Lil chose the *pain au chocolat*. Luke selected the almond croissant topped with an abundance of powdered sugar while Madame Brienz tore half of the plain croissant.

"So, what calls you to the mountains?" their host asked.

Lil smiled and began. "The voices of the past," she said. "We are traveling as a family. Me, my grandson Luke, my daughter, and my husband. I wanted them to see it before I died. We have been walking for seven days, and the Tour is almost over." This was as honest an answer as Lil had ever given when asked about the trip.

Madame Brienz studied Lil closely. Much as she would when she would carve, Brienz narrowed her eyes, shutting out the background of the world so she could concentrate on the essence before her. Madame Brienz asked no follow-up. She accepted what was given and mulled it over in her mind.

"And what of you, Monsieur grandson," the host asked.

Luke had only been partially listening. He was more focused on the pastry. "Do you have any milk and sugar?" he asked. "I still can't drink this stuff black."

Lil looked disapprovingly at Luke, but Madame Brienz only chuckled. "*Venez-ici*," she directed, motioning Luke toward the refrigerator. "Well, if you're not yet enough of a man for an espresso, you might as well learn how to make a good cappuccino."

She handed him a stainless steel cup and filled it halfway with milk. "Whole milk," she instructed, "and always cold." She guided him to the espresso machine and pointed to the steam wand. She briefly turned it on. It sputtered to life, expelling some drops of water before settling into a steady hiss. She then turned off the steam. "Two parts. First, you get the milk warm. Keep the wand low. The steam heats the milk. Then you get the tip of the wand just below the surface and you tilt the container. Now, you are starting to build your froth. You should see the milk spin and you hear the sucking sound. And no big bubbles. If you see the big bubbles, change the angles. Okay, do it."

Lil had left the table and stepped behind her grandson. Luke gave a yeah-right look, shook his shoulder, placed the wand in the milk, and turned on the steam.

"Lower," Brienz instructed. Luke lifted the cup. "Now make the froth."

Luke changed the angle and lowered the cup to bring the steamer closer to the surface of the milk. What began as a slight hiss and the start of the whirlpool quickly transformed into a cacophony of large bubbles. Brienz smiled. She placed her hand on top of Luke's and gently guided the cup into the proper position. The mixture returned to a gentle hiss as the milky foam steadily crept toward the top of the frothing cup.

"That's enough," Brienz concluded as she turned off the machine. "Not bad for an amateur," she joked to the boy.

She emptied his espresso into a larger white china cup, then poured the foam down the side of the cup, and the crema folded over itself. She added a final twist of foam to the center and quickly stopped the stream with a twist of her wrist.

Luke looked down and saw a perfect heart floating in the middle of his cup. He shook his head.

"Life is filled with art," Brienz remarked. "Now, don't forget to wipe the tip of your wand," Brienz instructed, handing Luke a wet cloth and pointing to the coating of milk on the steamer.

Luke swallowed and couldn't help but smirk.

The three returned to the table. Luke sipped his drink. Still needs sugar, he thought to himself but decided it wise to say nothing.

Instead, he asked Madame Brienz the question she had presented to Luke and Lil when they first sat down. "So what calls you?"

The artist was grateful Luke did not ask the questions she had been asked ad nauseam for the past thirty years: So what are they? What do they mean? Those sorts of questions disappointed her. Lately, they had begun to annoy her. Invariably, she would answer cryptically and not untruthfully, "It is what you make of it." Brienz lived firmly in the camp that the artist alone does not create art. Rather it exists, however fleetingly, at the intersection between the viewer and the object, born anew each moment, much like life itself. Yes, when she was asked those banal questions she would quickly end the conversation and send the pilgrims on their way.

Brienz liked these two visitors. "Let's go back outside," she said.

The party crossed the stone bridge. They started walking amongst the terraces. "I am also called by the voices of the past," she began, looking at Lil and referring to Lil's earlier response. She turned to Luke and added, "And by the voices of the future."

Brienz continued. "A careless eye sees each as much the same. We satisfy ourselves by finding an easy pattern. We deceive ourselves and conclude this is the meaning.

"Lil, you said you saw a family and a history. My family has lived in the mountains for many generations. Our roots were in Switzerland. And always we were wood smiths and carvers," Brienz began. "At first, it was just the men. Famous for making tables or chairs or decorations. Whatever the people wanted, the Brienz could make. It was a good living and the family prospered."

The tone in her voice changed as she continued. "My grandfather grew tired of merely making furniture for money. He saw war and industry and cities as destruction. In his lifetime he witnessed the forest retreat out of the valleys and up the mountainside. So he, his wife, their two children, and his sister moved from our home to here at Tré le Champ. For a while he worked the canal as a lock-keeper and kept a small garden," she pointed to the terraces.

"But wood still called to him. He started milling and building again. Not many pieces, just a few. And he was very selective. To him, each tree, each board, possessed its own individual beauty, to be studied, understood, and respected. Through the craftsman's hand the wood is reborn. And then, there is the third life when the piece is embraced by the client and delivered to its new home. In our family, we never say sold, for how can a spirit ever be owned?" she said before adding with an ironic twinkle, "Though we did charge them a lot of money."

"So your grandfather carved these totems?" Luke added with youthful impatience.

"No, my young friend," she corrected. "That was his sister, my grand-aunt, Giulia. She was two years younger than grandfather and never married. She was always close to grandfather and grandmother. So when they left the village and came here, she moved with them."

Brienz paused. This time Luke did not interrupt with a question.

"Though the rest of the family remained in the village, great-grandmother was heartbroken to see two of her children leave. That summer, after Giulia left, there was a great storm, and Giulia woke with a start. Lightning had struck a giant larch tree," Brienz gestured in the direction of one of the smaller totems on the edge of the first terrace. "Giulia had lived in the mountains all her life. Storms and lightning were not unusual, especially during the summer. But that night, Giulia was filled with dread, and she could not go back to sleep. Two days later, she learned her mother had died. She went back home – her first visit since leaving. When she returned from the funeral she set to carving. She created the first of the mémoriaux. Giulia said she was creating a home for the soul of the beloved."

Together they walked to the edge of the terrace. Luke looked at the sculpted wood. He tried to imagine the personality revealed in each. Words seemed inadequate for the task. He abandoned that effort. Instead, he settled on feelings.

"And in the years that followed, when Giulia found herself moved by the passing of another loved one, she created a second and third. Each time she would search for a tree that had recently fallen. And in the wood, with the patient kiss of the mallet, she would reveal the soul of the lost, and place it here in the garden."

Pointing to the various totems, Brienz introduced the travelers to "my grandfather and grandmother," two totems perched at an odd angle so the tops of their foreheads touched. "My mother," and in the second level, "my father. . a niece . . . a nephew . . . a dear family friend."

"Giulia, she taught my mother, and my mother she taught me. In our family, it is the women who tend to the garden of memories."

The three sat on the stone wall at the edge of the third terrace. "Every time I sit, I hear them. They tell me a story. Sometimes it is the same one, over and over again," gesturing toward her father. "Other times it is something I almost forgot." Brienz grew silent.

As they sat together, Lil risked the question. Looking toward the totem Brienz was tending when they first arrived, Lil ventured, "May I ask, who is this?"

"This is Giada, my sister."

Lil reached out her hand, and Brienz accepted it warmly.

"It took me a while to find the right tree. This is a spruce. But it was up high on the mountainside, where you usually only find the larch. It was no easy feat getting it down here. My sister, she was a free spirit, always on her own path . . . Thank you for asking so kindly," Brienz added. Brienz held Lil's hand for several heartbeats

Luke, who had been listening closely, broke the silence. "What, or who, are those over there?" he asked, pointing to a series of three totems at the base of the clearing. They were set apart from the rest, adjacent to the small stream that flowed along the northern edge of terraces.

Brienz's face lit up. "Come," she said. "Those are for the people of the village, and for the travelers."

Brienz walked quickly. Luke fell in step with her while Lil, her legs feeling unexpectedly tired, followed behind.

This series of totems was clearly different. Unlike the others they had no faces. Instead, they were a mass of carvings of all different shapes and sizes. There were many initials or numbers, an abundance of hearts, and an occasional scene. Some of the symbols looked Celtic, Cyrillic, or Asian. It reminded Lil of a circular kiosk from her college days with flyers stapled haphazardly, one next to or over another, announcing an upcoming concert, a sofa for sale, a roommate or lab subject wanted. Individual messages created by multiple authors at different times.

"These are for the people," Brienz explained. "Sometimes friends or strangers would ask us, 'Brienz please make a totem for my loved one, like you make for your family. We will pay you good money.' But we always refused. The memory must flow through the hand of the one who loved. A few times a year, we host a workshop where we invite people to create their own, and that was nice, but it takes a lot of time. So my mother, she started this, *le jardin des mémoriaux*. Here, everyone is welcome to stop by and remember that which was loved and thought lost." Brienz smiled and looked at both of her guests. "We always have a small chisel and mallet in the arolla box," she said pointing to a wooden toolkit by the base of a totem.

Luke and Lil spent several minutes examining each of the poles. Instinctively, they touched some of the carvings and closed their eyes, imagining the hundreds of stories captured in the wood.

"This is beautiful," Luke said. "May I take some pictures?"

"*Bien sur*," Brienz replied. "This is for the people. And perhaps before you pass you two will add your own."

As Luke framed some images, Brienz and Lil chatted. "We get a lot of randonneurs, you know. And each has a different story. Some are walking away and some are walking toward. In the end it is part of the same circle, *non*?" Brienz remarked.

"*Oui*," Lil replied.

"But not so many grandmothers with their grandsons. This has been a very pleasant visit, Elizabetta," Brienz said.

"And for me as well. Thank you for honoring us with your story."

As Luke returned from the first terrace, he saw the two women embrace. Nan's becoming quite the hugger on this trip, he thought to himself.

They had separated by the time he arrived. He approached and said, "Thank you so much, Madame Brienz." She reached out and embraced the young man, kissing him lightly on the cheeks as Giacomo had with Lil.

Anticipating his question, Lil replied without him asking: "Tonight after dinner. First, we have to get to the Auberge. Your mother and Russell have to be wondering what happened to us." With that, they continued down the cart path and on to their destination for the night.

L'Auberge de Boerne

The Auberge was less than a five-minute walk from la place de Madame Brienz. Like the very first refuge, it was located on the edge of a village. With its stone foundation, massive side timbers, and low-pitched roof, l'Auberge de Boerne sat rooted strongly to the earth. Every window was framed with flowers – vibrant reds, blues, and yellows. A half dozen bright umbrellas spread across a double flagstone terrace. The colorful sight, along with the smell of roasting meat, made for an enticing welcome.

Lil and Luke approached unseen toward Sophie and Russell. They were seated under the umbrella at the largest of the picnic tables, sipping a latte and chatting with another family. A half-eaten fruit tart sat on the plate in front of Sophie.

"Nice to see you were worried about us," Luke remarked with mock annoyance. "We were lost in the wilderness, and here you are with your feet up, filling your faces."

"About time you two arrived," Russell said as he stood up and gave Lil a light kiss. "We were a little worried in the morning, but then we ran into an ancient man on a bike. Said he had given you a lift, and set you in the right direction. He assured us you should be by shortly. Still, it took you a bit longer than we thought it would."

Russell took care of introductions. "Lil and Luke, these are the Nilssons, Karl and Anna, and their children Per and Cora. They are from Sweden. This summer, they are doing the Haute Route all the way to Zermatt."

Karl and Anna stood up and shook hands, first with Lil and then with Luke.

Per and Cora energetically grabbed hold of Luke's arms and pulled him to the opposite side of the terrace. "Did you see these?" the younger boy squealed as he pointed to the wall. Framing the entire length of the terrace was a stacked wall of wood, easily thirty feet long and six feet high. What sparked the children's enthusiasm was not the wood but the weapons. Displayed behind two locked steel bands was an arsenal worthy of a crazed medieval lumberjack. A dozen axes, some short-handled and others longer than a short man, hinted at the history of this homestead. Though rusted, the blades appeared still capable of considerable damage. The collection also included rakes with wooden tines, a two-person trunk saw with one-inch teeth, and a scythe that would make the Grim Reaper proud.

"*Toppen!*" Per exclaimed before running after some chickens in the grass next to the terrace. Cora took Luke's hand and walked back to her parents.

Luke picked up the remaining piece of tart from his mother's plate and plopped it into his mouth. He swallowed the treat whole and licked his fingers. "Is dinner ready yet?" he asked.

"Let me show you your space. And then you can get showered before I let you sit at the table with us," Sophie teased her son. "You stink," she said not untruthfully.

The solid framing visible from the outside was equally evident on the interior. The supporting columns of the walls were more than a foot thick with the ceiling beams almost the same size. The joints were set with a foot of overlap and a trio of three-inch wood pegs to finish the connection. This made for low ceilings and narrow hallways. The dining area, the largest open space on the first floor, was situated near the front, taking advantage of the light from the three windows on the south-facing wall. Even this open expanse was interrupted by what looked like two tree trunks supporting a center beam that spanned the width of the structure.

"Our nests are upstairs," Sophie added, first turning left, then right, and then left again up three half flights of stairs. Once at the top they were confronted with a labyrinth of options. A longer hallway continued to what Luke took as the back of the building. Two shorter spurs led in opposite directions. "Keep going straight," Sophie directed.

They walked past two rooms, each crammed with a set of four platforms, two upper and two lower, bunk-bed style. A few folks were lying down, one reading and a second mid-nap. Backpacks and sleeping bags announced that other spots were already taken. In the second room Luke saw Russell's yellow hat and headed in. "Nope," his mother corrected. "There was only one lower bunk left, and that was for Lil. Russell and I are on the top. Your room is down a little further," she added with a smile.

Luke exited. Turning to the right, he passed two bunks tucked under an eave and fully open to the hallway — you would see and hear everyone walking down the hallway to the bathroom. A gear bag claimed the lower full-sized bunk. The second bunk was three-quarter length, shortened by the slope of the eave. It was unclaimed. With downcast eyes Luke pointed apprehensively to this upper bunk. His mother shook her head. "Tempting, yes, but I wouldn't do that to my baby," she said. "Just a little farther."

Luke arrived at the end of the hallway. There were no more rooms.

"So, do I sleep on the floor or against the wall?" Luke asked.

His mother pointed to a large circular door about three feet off the ground. Luke took it to be a storage nook or torpedo tube. He opened the door and stuck his head inside, revealing a full-sized room with six single bunks built into the side walls.

"A hobbit hole, way cool!" Luke exclaimed.

"There is actually a door on the other side that leads to another hallway, but I thought you would like this entrance better," Sophie added. "If you go out the regular door, the bathroom is on the left. The showers are downstairs on the main level. Dinner is in half an hour."

Luke placed his backpack in the corner of the room and tossed his sleeping bag on an open bunk. He gathered his shower gear and headed back downstairs.

The showers were located at the far end of the first floor. A series of framed black and white photos lined the hall leading there. The sequence of pictures provided a history of the home. A single squat rectangular building was centered in the first image. Though there was no terrace nor flowers, it was obviously the main portion of the Auberge in which they now stood. Five men, two holding a trunk saw and the others with axes, posed in front of the home with three women and some children off to one side and a stack of logs on the other. Subsequent photos captured the additions to the west side of the home. Two pictures caught Luke's eye. In one, a tent with a cross imprinted on the top covered the yard at the entrance to the home. It was an unstaged photo with nurses in their smocks and men in uniform scattered throughout. In the second image snow was piled past the roof line. A man standing on the snow was passing a goat to another man standing at a window in the top gable. "That's a shitload of snow," Luke whispered aloud. It helped him appreciate why the timbers and framing were so stout.

Luke showered quickly and rejoined his family in the dining room.

"That boy has got a talent for arriving just when the food is served," Russell joked as Luke arrived.

"Everybody has their gifts," Luke replied. "Mine are eating and looking good," he added as he slid onto the bench and gently nudged his grandfather with his hip.

This was their last night on the trail. While traditionally, the TMB begins and ends in Les Houches, Chamonix, a quintessential Alpine village that has evolved into a four-season destination, was a much more inviting location. Tomorrow they would trek across what is perhaps the most scenic and challenging portion of the trail. It promised a steady ascent along a series of ladders and hand holds up to Lake Lac. Once at the lake, if the weather gods permit, you stand high in the heavens with a blessed view across the valley framed by the Mount Blanc massif and all the peaks you had passed throughout the hike. A few hours later, mostly downhill, and they would enter Chamonix where they had reservations in a hotel.

When the meal was over, Lil savored this moment. When she began, she was uncertain what this walk would hold for her. Now, she felt it was more than she could have hoped. In seven days she had come to know her family in ways lost in the past. And in that timeless fraction it takes for a thought to erupt, an internal voice chastised her: Foolish woman, you have not yet done all you need to do.

As Lil sat silent, Luke quietly watched his grandmother. He saw a flicker across her face. He didn't know what it was, just that it was different from the serenity of the moment before.

"Come on, Nan," Luke said, reaching across the table and extending his hand. "We have a job to do, remember."

She took his hand, and the smile returned to her face. "Yes, let's go," she said to Luke. Turning to Sophie and Russell she added, "We'll be back."

Le Jardin des Mémoriaux

Nighttime descends more quickly in the woods. As the sun slides behind the frame of the mountain, shadows gather well before the orb's final bow below the horizon. Each tree casts its own twin upon the earth, a temporary gift of the fading light. It is a time that is neither day nor night. It was into the not-this-nor-that that Lil and Luke returned to Le Jardin des Mémoriaux.

When they arrived at the lower grove, they noticed two chisels had been placed on the wood bench where earlier there was only one. Though they did not see Brienz, they silently thanked her. Without speaking they each took a chisel and mallet and moved to opposite sides of the same totem.

With the moon now cresting over the eastern ridge, they found they could turn off the headlamps they had used when walking from the Auberge to this grove. The evening's silver light was more than enough to guide their hand.

In this wordless time, the only outside sound was the soft wind in the trees and the gentle tapping of the mallets.

With each tap, Luke's father returned to him. And as a small chip of wood flaked off and fell to the ground, the absent space was replaced by a memory. Tap . . . his dad's smile. Tap . . . his dad's voice. Tap . . . his dad's embrace.

On the opposite side, Lil worked more quickly. Her deft hand carved a series of arcing letters, the ends of each touching the other and together forming a circle. As she cut, the memories raced. At 3:00 an R: The day they first met at the park, a summer morning planting flowers, their midday lunches at Le Fournil, sitting together at Cathedral Rock. At 6 an S: The day she was born, her first day of school, packing for college, their embrace on the bus.

At 9:00 an L: Resting in Sophie's arms, running in the backyard, jumping into the pool, his stoic face at the funeral, their conversation by the boulder. Finally, at 12, an F: A first love, the ache of joy at what was briefly so, the hollow emptiness of what might have been. Her final image: A body at the base of the mountainside, and, as she approached, the face she saw was not Frederico's but her own.

Lil finished first. She waited silently until Luke stopped. She stepped to the side of the totem and asked, "May I?"

With his jaw still quivering, Luke nodded. It was a simple carving. A heart encircling the word DAD. The old woman embraced the young man. A fresh wave of tears rushed down Luke's face. "I miss him so much," he managed between sobs.

She took his face in her hands, looked into his eyes and said softly, "And I pray you always will. That's how you keep him with you, how you remain together over time."

"Can I see yours?" he asked. Lil nodded, and they walked to the other side.

Luke studied the carving, noting its shape, the letters, and their position. He nodded and paused, allowing Lil some time.

"I never felt truly close to my parents. A little too judgmental and preachy," she said with a flick of her hand. "Your grandfather, he was like the morning light for me – optimistic, accepting, shining down on everything. I could be what I was, and know that he would be there day after day, steady and dependable . . . And then with your mom. When she was born, I still remember the flood of emotions: joy and fear, hope and concern. God, how I didn't want to be like my parents. In some ways I was, and sometimes worse. I desperately wanted her to be strong and independent. Sometimes I forgot to remind her she was loved. As she grew I let her slip away . . . And you, my boy. There is nothing like a grandchild. To see that new life. To hold you. The smiles, the coos. The reaching out into the world. That is a joy beyond words."

Lil arrived at the F and took a deep breath. "Frederico was my first love."

Luke's eyes widened. He had only half-listened to the storyteller. His mind now scrambled to recall the details. "Elizabetta?" he mouthed the name softly.

Lil looked at her grandson, her lips drawn tight. After several seconds, she gave a slow nod and continued. The words rushed out as if anxious to be finally released. "For me, that summer, when I felt apart from my own family, that was freedom. I was reborn. At last my own person. And then, that quickly, he wanted me to join with him. I was afraid. Part of me craved 'yes,' and another part relished being on my own. That is why I could not answer on that night. I wanted both – together and apart, united and independent. But I was young and didn't know how to respond. I didn't know then – not until Russell – that with trust and time, both are truly possible. And when Frederico died, at first I blamed myself. Whenever I thought of it, I felt like I was killing him again, and again, and again. Over the years, I have come to accept some things. I still mourn, but I no longer carry the responsibility."

"Holy crap," Luke muttered. The connections then came quickly. "That's why you speak . . . and everything is familiar . . . and people know you." In his next heartbeat, the initial jolt of astonishment was replaced by the implications. "And you never told anyone?"

"No," Lil shrugged. "I did what I felt was the best thing possible. I cut myself off from that past, or tried to. I kept the memory buried, or tried to. I did not speak of it. Not to Russell, not to my friends, and certainly not to my family . . . Not a soul, until now."

"Why not?" Luke added, fully aware he had been asking himself the same question for more than a year.

"When we have a secret, Luke, we think we are hiding it from others, but actually, we are trying to keep it from ourselves. Maybe we are not ready, or we don't know how, not yet. I am not sure." Lil lifted her head and looked at her grandson. "But I know this now. We may try to hide from the pain, but we cannot escape it. It is woven into our skin. The more we hide it, the more it scars."

"But you chose this trip. You came back here . . ." Luke said aloud, wrestling with a jumble of thoughts in his head.

Lil shook her head. "But not to tell you about Frederico. Seeing Maria and confronting the past – that was unexpected." And then, nodding, Lil said,

"Yes, I intended this as a healing trip, a way to reconcile with your mom for the past and to prepare for the future. But I never expected to tell the full story, Luke. With this Tour I just wanted to tell you, your mom, and Russell . . . to tell you that I love you."

After releasing these memories in Le Jardin des Mémoriaux, gifting them to the totems for all to see, Luke and Elizabetta placed the tools back on the bench and returned to their refuge for the night.

Day 8 - Breakfast

Lil spent another restless night in her lower bunk. Her body and mind conspired against her. Low waves of nausea unsettled her stomach. The ache in her back defied any easy description – not a cramp, nor throb, nor stabbing pain, but with the worst features of all three. While she was relieved at finally speaking aloud what had been swirling in her private mind, new concerns scrambled to replace them. All focused on a central reality: The end of this walk is almost here.

Unable to truly sleep, Lil rose early before the others. She dressed, adding an extra layer to resist the chilly air that had settled overnight. Undetected, she went downstairs, headed outside, and set out alone through the hamlet.

About an hour later, Sophie and Russell awoke to the steady bustle of roommates shuffling to the bathroom and pulling on clothes. Russell lay awake in his top bunk and looked at his daughter. He held his smile as Sophie stretched her arms and rubbed her face. It reminded him of weekend mornings when she was a child, and he would quietly watch her from the bedroom doorway. Sophie was not a morning person. As a youth, she was a reluctant outcast from the world of sleep. Gently tossing and turning, she would pull the covers up tight as she struggled to remain in the comfort of her bed. When she finally did awake, it looked much like this moment: a final grand stretch and a rub of the face. At least that is how he remembered it.

Russell mouthed a silent "Good morning."

Sophie replied in kind and whispered in her ironic voice, "And thank you for not yanking the covers down the way mom would."

Russell had forgotten that aspect of their contrasting parenting styles. But he was often out of the house early before Sophie had to get up for school. His knowledge of the morning battles was second-hand and colored by the teller's perspective. Part of the negotiated truce from the long-ago was that Russell would assume primary parenting duty on weekend mornings. Beyond making breakfast – waffles on Saturday and omelets on Sunday – it included getting Sophie out of bed. Usually, he would let her get up whenever she wanted as long as it was before 9:00.

To exit his bunk, Russell first grabbed hold of the strap suspended from the rafters, like the loop on an old-time subway car. His foot then found the first rung on the ladder. He sustained no injury as he cautiously climbed down to the floor – a victorious start to the new day, he thought – and started pulling on his clothes. Scanning the lower rows of bunks, his eyes came to rest on the spot where he expected to find Lil. "Did you see your mother?" he asked.

"Not this morning. She is probably downstairs already. You know how much she loves granola," Sophie joked. "Let's go join her."

The breakfast area was already crowded. Sophie and Russell did not see Lil. However, they were surprised to see Luke. He was in good spirits, speaking with the Swedish family they had met on the terrace yesterday.

Luke waved to them enthusiastically and greeted them with a 'god morgon' he had just learned from his tablemates. Sophie grabbed his hand and placed a kiss atop his head. Beyond a slight flinch in his eyes, Luke did not react to the public display of maternal affection. Karl and Anna exchanged a smile. Russell's eyes were still darting back and forth even as he took a seat.

"Have you seen your grandmother?" Sophie asked Luke.

"No," he said. "I thought she was with you."

Russell was in the middle of standing up when he saw Lil enter through the front door. Her face was vacant. She took a step toward the dining area and stopped. She appeared lost, as if uncertain about what to do next.

He made his way swiftly toward her, bumping into a guest at an adjacent table, causing him to spill some of his coffee onto his lap.

When she saw Russell, Lil refocused. She strained to smile lightly.

214

"Are you alright?" Russell asked.

"Yes," she replied slowly, as if trying to convince herself to say the words. Then, after a pause, she added, "I'm just not feeling up to the nines today," looking into her husband's face.

Noticing a slight shake to her lower jaw, he guided her toward Luke and Sophie. "Here, let's sit down and get you something to eat."

They sat with their backs against the wall. Luke was excitedly talking with Per and Cora about recent superhero films. Per was trying to convince Luke that Thor was actually Swedish. Cora said Per was *tokig*.

"Sophie, would you get some juice and cereal for your mother?" Russell asked.

"And I'll take some more coffee," Luke added.

"No more caffeine for you, boy," Sophie responded. "Since when did you start drinking coffee, anyway?"

"Sean and I stop at Starbucks all the time when we drive to school," he replied with a grin before he thought the better of it.

With a shake of her head, Sophie walked away toward the serving table. When she returned she placed the bowl and drink in front of Lil. She thought Lil's color was better. As she looked away from her mother and toward her son, her thoughts wandered back toward his comment about the coffee. Her mind jostled by a dozen different topics: *He has changed so much these past few years. Look at that peach fuzz - he is no longer my little boy. Funny how, as a teenager, they grow into a stranger you struggle to recognize . . . Who am I kidding – even as a child, you don't know what they are thinking. How do you know what anyone is truly feeling? Hell, I do not know what I am feeling half the time . . . Does he miss Rick – of course he does. Does he love me . . .* Sophie caught the cascade before it carried her too far downstream. She looked back at her man-boy, and she knew, at least in this moment, he was happy. That would have to be enough. She went and got him another coffee.

Lil sat at the table quietly. She attempted a few sips and bites, but neither sat well with her. She struggled to focus on the conversation around her, but her attention was elsewhere. She caught herself taking shallow breaths and noticed Russell gently massaging the palm of her hand. She looked in his

215

eyes and heard him say, in a voice that sounded like Debbie, 'breathe, Lil, breathe."

After sipping the coffee sugar at the bottom of his cup, Luke excitedly described the hike ahead. "Today, when we get near the top, Karl said you hit a wall of rock. The only way up is to climb some ladders while holding on to metal rings pounded into the stone." As Luke spoke, Per gestured with an imaginary hammer, securing imaginary rungs into the wall of the Auberge.

"Just like Thor," Per added.

"That is the '*passage delicat*'" Anna explained. "It is challenging for sure, and if the weather is bad, it is unsafe. But it gives you an incredible view of Valle d'Argentière and leads directly to Lac Blanc. Of course, there are alternate routes," she added, glancing toward Lil. "You could walk through Tré le Champ to the Col de Montets, or even take the train to Chamonix and the gondola to La Flégère, and skip the ladders and Lac Blanc . . ."

"We are going to Lac Blanc," Lil interrupted with a little more force than she had intended.

Anna shifted uncomfortably in her seat.

With an apologetic glance toward Anna, Lil added in a determined voice. "We came all this way and have walked this far. I'll be damned if we miss that view from heaven."

Luke, who couldn't remember the last time he heard his grandmother swear, even if it was only a "damn," punctuated her sentence with an excited "Cool!"

"But before we leave, we have to take them to the garden," Luke suggested, looking at Lil.

"You take them, Luke. I need more time to force down some of this granola." Her resolve on the day's route seemed to fortify Lil, at least for the moment.

"Come on," Luke gestured to his mother and grandfather as he stood up. "I will take you to Madame Brienz's place. It is incredible. Will you come too?" Luke added, looking at Anna and her family.

Per and Cora were already up and heading to the door. Anna said to Karl, "You go with the kids but not too long, we need to leave by eight-thirty. I will get their packs ready."

Russell added, speaking to Sophie, "I will stay here with Lil."

Lil responded quickly. "You go on with your daughter and grandson. It's okay to leave me. I am feeling better now. Go. . ." She pushed him gently forward.

With a doubtful eye, Russell stepped away from the table and toward his remaining family.

Once they left, Lil drew a heavy breath and pushed the bowl of granola away from her.

Anna slid from her chair to sit next to Lil on the bench. "I apologize. I did not mean any offense by suggesting the alternate route," Anna began.

"Oh, sweet child, I am the one who needs to apologize. You were just trying to help, and my tone was way too bitchy . . . How do you say that in Swedish?" Lil asked.

"Bitchy!" Anna added with a laugh.

"I don't have much further to go," Lil said. "I think I can do this."

"When I was young, my mormor would tell us, especially the girls, 'You are not as strong as you think, you are even stronger. And when the time comes, you will be as strong as you need to be.' As a child, I didn't know what she was talking about, and then I got married, had a baby and worked while raising a family. I have come to understand a little bit more. I see this quality in you, Mormor Lil." Anna squeezed the hand of the old woman and left the table.

Lil sat alone. She observed the fellow travelers getting along with the busyness of living. She tried another nibble of cereal and nearly gagged. What I could really use, she thought, is a joint.

A Truth Revealed

Luke led them along the canal path toward Madame Brienz. He resisted the temptation to tell them more than he already had at the Auberge.

As they turned around the final bend and were confronted by the terraces, their faces shared the same look of startled amazement that Luke and Lil had experienced the previous afternoon.

After they crossed the canal bridge Per and Cora started dancing around the totems.

"They are like the runestones," Cora said, "But with faces."

Karl explained, "You can find runestones scattered across Sweden, most of them in Uppland. Some have pictures and symbols. Some are just all runes. The stone might commemorate an event, but most are carved in the memory of a person. 'Holmfast had this path cleared in memory of Inge his good mother' or 'In memory of my father Finnvid,' that sort of thing."

Per added, "My favorite one is from Ragnarok with Ferris eating Odin. We saw that in Ostergoland. It was huge, as big as two dads."

"That's exactly what these are," Luke explained. "Brienz carves them when someone she loves has died. She picks the wood out special, and it becomes a place for a piece of their soul – like a Horcrux, but in a good way."

After a few minutes, Karl gathered Per and Cora and said his goodbyes. "We will have to be going if we will make it to the next hut on time. *Sakra resor*, my friends." Per and Cora hugged Luke before heading back across the bridge and toward the Auberge.

"We best be getting back, too," Russell added.

"Just one more thing," Luke said cautiously. Sophie and Russell heard the hesitation in his voice.

Luke held each of his family members by the hand and walked to the lower grove. As they approached, he explained how these totems were different and that this was where he and Lil went last night.

Sophie's eye immediately knew which carving was Luke's. The missing flakes of wood were fresh, and their meaning was clear. Her face drew tight as she reached out to touch the heart her son had carved into the wood. Luke placed his hand on hers, and the son's tears joined those of his mother as they slowly traced the D and the A and the final D.

In between the sobs, Luke managed to say, "I miss him so much, Mom."

"I know, baby, I do too." Those simple words. That feeling shared by all who have lost one they loved.

"I used to be so angry at him for what he did," Luke began, and after an extended pause, quietly added, "And at you for not helping him. And at myself." Another pause. "I knew, and I should've stopped him." As Luke spoke, he found that releasing these words of utter sadness made room for a small foothold of relief.

"I am still angry at him. And I know you tried to help him, and you wanted to keep me safe. I get that now. And I don't blame myself, at least not as much." Luke weighed his next words. As he spoke, he felt the anger rush out. "He did what he did, and it was so stupid, and a fucking waste." And the sense of relief grew. "But that doesn't mean I have to stop loving him, and it doesn't mean I can't miss him, and it doesn't mean everything is all better and will stop hurting. Right?" He asked without meaning it to be a question. "That's what I carved in the tree."

Russell had moved toward mother and son while Luke was speaking. As Sophie was holding tight to her boy, her hand reached out to clasp her father's hand.

While listening to Luke, a corner of Russell's mind was drawn to the other side of the pole. Sophie and Luke continued their whispered conversation. He gently separated himself and moved slowly around the totem.

He imagined what it might contain, but he was uncertain. Though together for over 40 years, parts of Lil remained a mystery. Russell saw the four engravings oriented like compass points. Each consisted of a single letter. His initial, R, was on the east side. To the south an S. To the west and L. Those all made sense. But at the top? He stared at that fourth letter. Not her parents, he thought to himself. Their names both began with M. And she had no siblings.

Sophie and Luke stepped over to join him. Sophie stared at the carvings. She smiled and shook her head, "Well, it's good to see we all made the cut – but F?"

"Frederico Bonatti," Luke blurted out. "The story is true, you know. She told me last night."

Russell's face blanched. He pictured Lil standing here, carving these tokens, a dying woman's testament to the ones she loved. The weight of her choices carried by the mallet as it chewed into the wood. He imagined her abandonment. Of her body failing her. The terror of an infinite future of nothing, knowing that you will and will not miss it all. Luke's revelation, though, sparked a different response, part of an emotional palette from which he usually did not draw.

The story is true. That's what Luke had said. Why did she never tell me? Forty years – not a word! This whole trip – that's why she chose this place! She knew the storyteller. They were friends – why didn't she just say something? Anger drowned his sadness.

The initial shock on Sophie's face gave way to a wry smile. "That woman is quite the keeper of secrets," Sophie said. Turning to her father, she asked, "Did you know?"

Russell looked down and shook his head, "No," he said softly.

Detecting the hurt, she embraced him.

As his daughter held him tight, Russell struggled to slow his own breath. A familiar series of questions returned. Why is this happening? Why does she have to die first? What am I going to do when she is gone?

With each exhale, as he tamped down the sharp edges of his own feelings, his focus shifted back to Lil. How had she felt here, etching her memorial to life? What was it like this whole week, with the shadow of the tragic past behind every step on this walk? What courage it must have taken to finally reveal what she had kept hidden for so long. This pause allowed the anger to ebb just enough to reveal his essential truths: He loved Lil. They had enjoyed a good life together. Soon he would be alone.

Sophie released her father. She shook her head and, with a lighthearted edge to her voice, added, "Well, she's got some explaining to do, doesn't she?"

Owning Up

After Anna left, Lil struggled with one more spoonful of cereal. She gagged and pushed the bowl away. Her comment to Russell about feeling a little better wasn't true, just another in the string of little lies. Not nearly as grand as the omissions she had kept from others and tried to hide from herself.

Lil had fully expected to take the story of that summer to her grave. To finally bury it with her body. She never imagined her past would confront her, not now after so many years. Maria's appearance had taken her by surprise. After the first night, Lil had wondered if she'd recognized her – God, we had some fun that summer, she'd mused to herself. Since leaving almost fifty years ago, Lil had not received nor initiated contact with anyone in Frederico's village – no family, no friends. While the tug of the events and the frequency with which she revisited them had declined over the years, the shadow never fully disappeared. Periodically, the past would cloud over her – triggered by a random sight, smell or phrase – and then eventually pass. Maria's story brought it all back. The excitement, the courtship, the consummation, the tragedy, the grief. She heard his voice more clearly than she had in years, and felt his touch. She shook her head, still haunted by her answer at the final picnic. She imagined his body at the base of the path, inert and as broken as her heart. She remembered the pain at leaving, the loneliness of the flight home, the desolation at the clinic, and the depression. But Maria's story also shined light on the joy, a joy that Lil buried even deeper beneath the tragedy—a time of youth when everything was new and fresh. The promise of endless tomorrows where nothing was yet written, and anything was possible. Having savored first love on her initial visit, Lil was not expecting to rediscover this during her final tour. She simply wanted one last adventure before walking away and wished to spend it with the people she now loved. Returning to the Alps, she thought, would be like closing the circle, and the mountains would make a great place to die. Having Frederico and her past find her in the present was unexpected. But so was her cancer. That's the thing about dying: everyone knows it will happen, but the absoluteness makes it unknowable.

This morning, those she still loved would go to the garden. They would see the initials. And she would have to tell them. Tell them what they might already know. She could have avoided it. She didn't have to carve anything; just go there with Luke. She could have simply carved three initials and wiped her hands. Done! But that just didn't seem right. Perhaps she was now ready to share this one secret? Maybe she had wanted to tell all along? But what words to say, and how much? "Hell, they already heard the story. Just tell them it is true," she whispered aloud to herself. Yes, that approach seemed reassuring, and simple. And what of all the other truths? Lil did not have a simple answer to that question.

She wrestled with these thoughts and made another decision: I really need that joint. She left the table and went upstairs. Grabbing her pack she sat down on her bunk. Uncertain how long her family would be gone, she fumbled hastily through the contents, depositing some clothes, a dry sack with her toiletries, and a bag of trail mix onto her bunk. A flash of fear sparked through her – Where is it? A moment later, she found the purple kit ensnared beneath some dirty laundry. Relieved, she hurriedly headed outside.

Usually, Lil did not smoke during the day. She briefly considered parking herself right on the terrace. Europe was surely more tolerant than America, and after all, she was an old woman who would soon be exiting this stage. However, she was dissuaded by the thought of having to explain something else to Sophie and Luke. One secret for today is enough she thought as she looked for a spot with a little more privacy.

She walked down the path leading to a stone basin. A simple pipe routed water from a glacial stream. The basin was a mere way-stop. The overflowing water gently sloshed above the rim and back into the earth, rejoining the unseen currents that make life possible.

Lil cupped her hands beneath the pipe and sipped the cold water. She heard some voices from behind a screen of trees. A deep inhale delivered the familiar odor. Lil smiled. She turned the corner and saw three young souls enjoying the fellowship of the weed. With their backpacks at their side, two were clearly hikers. The second young man looked a little younger and had an apron tied to his waist. They nodded a welcome which Lil returned before settling against a large rock and taking out her stash. The young man in the apron walked over and, with an admiring look, offered her a light, which Lil accepted gratefully. That's right, I'm a real badass, she joked to herself.

Lil smoked in silence. She found herself lingering in the haze a bit longer than expected. But the treatment did the trick. She felt more relaxed and even a little hungry. She glanced at her watch, hurriedly packed away her paraphernalia, nodded goodbye to her cannabis comrades, and walked around to the front of the Auberge. As she crossed the terrace she glanced down the path. In the distance, she saw Sophie, Luke, and Russell approaching.

"Oh, shit!" she exclaimed. In a rush, she threw open the door, pushed past some hikers, and started up the staircase, taking two steps at a time before rapidly losing her breath and having to slow down. She laughed at herself, feeling like a child worried about being caught smoking in her bedroom.

Lil grabbed the clothes, the trail mix, and the dry bag and stuffed them in the backpack. She fumbled with the purple case, quickly placing it on top. She was in the process of zipping the pack closed when Luke plopped down in the bunk next to her and stretched out with his hands behind his head.

"Well, is there something you need to tell us, Ms. Elizabetta?" she heard Sophie say.

Lil was not certain what she would see when she looked up. In this moment she wasn't even certain how she felt. She took a breath and looked up anyway. She looked up into her daughter's face, her only surviving child. She looked up into the face of Russell, the second man she had loved. Though Sophie had her arms crossed, there was an openness in her eyes.

"Yes," Lil said, nodding her head. "It's true."

Sophie had rehearsed a series of snarky comments, practicing them in her head as she walked back from the garden to the hut. She said none of them. She looked down at her mother—the one who was always strong, independent, and free-spirited. Sophie saw a vulnerability she had not recognized in the past. She could feel the pain and regret. In the walk back from the Jardin to the Auberge, Sophie had focused on discovering a secret and forgotten the tragedy behind Lil's story – the death of a beloved. She was embarrassed by the light tone she had just used when speaking with Lil. Kneeling down, she hugged her mother like a friend or a sister. There were no questions, not even the obvious ones, just the moment of communion.

Lil lifted her head and, through tear-glazed eyes, found Russell. Lil extended her hand. Russell reached out and took hold of the hand he had held thousands of times before. He sat on the bed beside her and bowed his head onto her shoulder. They rested cheek-to-cheek. Lil wasn't sure how he felt, as if it was one thing or was even knowable.

Luke sat up and observed the scene awkwardly. He wasn't sure what to do but figured as they were all hugging, he might as well join them. He was almost able to encircle his family in his youthful arms. He did not cry. Instead, he thought, my grandmother is a legend!

It was Lil who spoke to end the moment when their world changed. "I'm sorry. I didn't know what to say."

Her family did not interrupt her. "I tried to forget it, to put it behind me, like it never happened . . . and make a new life."

This morning, when confronted with the choice of how to respond, Sophie chose compassion: "Well, you are a remarkable and mysterious woman, Elizabeth. And I am proud to be your daughter."

Lil looked at Russell. Lil imagined how to interpret his silence. She sensed a sadness in the curve of his brow.

"We should be moving on," Russell said finally. "We have a lot of miles before us, and," looking at Lil with a narrow eye, "not much time."

To the Wall

The sun had already crested the low range east of the Auberge. The forecast called for building clouds at midday with possible clearing in the afternoon. The travelers hoped the sun would remain, as the Tour promised some of its finest views for the final day.

They followed the path that circled around the back of the Auberge and past the screen of trees that Lil had visited a short time before. The hikers had left, but the young man in the apron was still there. "*Au revoire, ma soeur,*" he called out. Lil waved a trekking pole in response and continued on.

The first hour was glorious hiking. Though a steady ascent with cool temperatures, the sun and exertion kept the hikers warm without overheating. Luke was the only one in shorts.

At Sophie's request, they stopped once after thirty minutes. Sophie, Russell, and Luke removed their outer jacket and placed them in their backpacks. Lil kept hers on. She felt clammy; her stomach was uncomfortable, whether due to illness or hunger, she couldn't tell. She took a chocolate square from the small pocket on her hip belt where she kept her nibbles. That only made it worse. She drank some more water instead. After this short break they quickly returned to the path.

While this segment was wooded, the frequent turns on the switchbacks allowed uninterrupted views of the Argentière valley set against the backdrop of Aiguille Rouge, a mere hint of the scenic vistas found in the higher elevations in Le Grand Balcon Sud.

After two hours, the group approached the halfway point of their ascent to Lac Blanc. They had been moving west/southwest across the southern face of the Aiguillette Argentière. At this elevation the trees gradually thinned and the path forward was bare and rocky. They again removed their packs and rested. They took some water and opened up a snack. Luke noticed his grandmother was not eating.

"Still not feeling well?" he asked. "Try one of these," he said, breaking off a gel block. "You just suck it. It's like an energy boost. I will sometimes use it before a race or after a long swim."

Lil twisted her head slightly and cast a skeptical eye.

"It's nothing illegal," he reassured her. "Mom buys it at Whole Foods."

Lil took the block and popped it in her mouth. It tasted a little cherry with a hint of cranberry, and her stomach did not immediately object. "Not bad," she said, grabbing the remaining package from her grandson's hand.

He smiled. "The most I've eaten was four in a day. But if you like those, I also have some Clif Shots you can try."

Russell looked ahead and up along the path before him. He could see the stony ridge line of three Aiguilles – de Mesure, la Tête Plate, and de la Floria. These peaks frame the bowl in which Lac Blanc rests, the run-off from their glaciers feeding Lac Blanc and the lesser Lacs de Chéserys. Earlier, he had noticed the wisps of clouds struggling to rise above the western silhouette, their initial efforts to overrun the peaks denied by the warm air on the eastern side of the valley. As the morning progressed, what were once occasional strands knitted into solid bands. And now Russell observed the blankets of white overtake the peaks and begin a steady descent down the mountainside toward them.

Pointing at the approaching clouds, Russell said, "Looks like we are going to lose our sunny day."

"Will we need our waterproofs?" Luke asked in the direction of his grandmother. "It would really suck if we got rained on."

"Don't think so," Lil replied as she stood up. "They look more white than gray. But they may ruin our view for a bit."

It was quiet walking for the next hour. Truth was, there was little conversation even earlier in the morning. Perhaps it was the revelations from the garden or maybe the impending end of the Tour. Regardless, each traveler seemed preoccupied with their own thoughts.

Lil noted how Russell chose to walk next to Sophie for much of the morning. She gave him that space. She wondered if he was surprised or angry. And if he was angry, was he angry that she had another love or that she didn't tell him about it? He had always confessed that she was his first love, and only his second lover. He was twenty-five when they met. At first, she didn't believe him, but then, as she came to know him, his gentle nature, his sweet soul, and his awkwardness with his own body, she accepted it as true. Lil never raised the topic of her past loves, and Russell never pressed. Surely, he had to know there were others. But what did it matter, she convinced herself. There was only the now. And she had remained, as she was sure he had, faithful. How would she feel? She couldn't imagine. And if he was a little angry with me, she thought, that may help him to move on. If he were to connect with Sophie, that would help him, too.

Initially, Sophie's mind was centered on her mother. She didn't feel angry or betrayed, not in any deep way. If anything, she felt amused. Her mother had this whole other life and didn't tell a soul. And she gives me shit for not being a communicator, Sophie thought. Sophie then felt a slow bubble of anger rising in her. This was followed almost immediately by, "Well, this apple didn't fall far from the tree, Ms. Eliza-not-much-betta." This self-realization helped calm her spleen. No, she was not angry at her mom. She found her own reaction strangely liberating. Like when you get 75 on a test and then find out that class average was a D, or when you see a photo of a movie star without two hours of make-up and they look just as frumpy as you do. "Perfection isn't reality," her therapist had said at a recent session. "If you can't embrace the flaws, at least accept them." Sophie found a greater empathy for her dad. What must he be feeling? He was always the patient, kind, and trusting one, balancing the emotional swings of her mother. What had mom told him? Was he pissed? Sophie wasn't certain. But she knew she wanted to be there for him, whatever he felt, much like he had been there for her growing up. So she remained close to him, periodically holding his hand as they walked on their way.

For much of the morning, they encountered few other hikers. They passed an elderly couple they recognized from the Auberge and were passed by a group of five young friends speaking German. An hour after their last break, they approached the twin pitons mentioned in the guidebook and saw a back jam of people standing together along a rope barrier where the trail appeared to end.

"That must be the wall," Luke said excitedly, picking up his pace and moving toward the crowd.

An Accident

Luke arrived just as Lyndon was giving directions to the members of his tour group.

"Lyndon, hi!" he called. Lyndon winked and nodded in return before focusing his attention back on his group.

"The ladders and platforms are safe, well anchored into the stone. Matteo tested them this morning just to be sure. This is a non-technical climb, so there is no need for ropes. But there are a few basic safety rules. First, only one person at a time on each section of ladder or each platform. Wait until the person ahead of you exits the ladder or platform before you begin. Second, control your body. Focus on your breath, breathing in through the nose and out through the mouth. Keep at least three points of contact at all times - two hands and a foot or two feet and a hand. Eyes ahead or up. Don't look down. Look at where you're going, not where you've been. Third, these routes are pretty clean but if you hear rocks falling, or someone calls out a warning – *rock, rock, rock!* – press your body against the stone with one hand on the ladder and one hand over your head. Do NOT look up!"

Lyndon had each group member repeat one of the safety reminders before sending the first one up the initial ladder.

"Roger, you're up first," Lyndon said, adding, "No photos in the middle."

Luke recognized the first climber as the man Lyndon had to save from the local crowd at le Refuge des Ciels.

Lil, Sophie, and Russell had arrived by the time the final member of Lyndon's team had started up the first ladder. Lyndon walked toward them and shook Luke's hand.

"Hi Luke. I couldn't really talk back there. I had to keep on my serious face." And then, turning to the others, he added, "Well, if it isn't my favorite hiking family. I was hoping I might see you again." He shook Russell's hand, kissed Lil on the cheek, and hugged Sophie.

"Luke, give them the safety talk, and let's get you on your way," Lyndon said.

"No, no," Sophie added. "You go ahead with your group."

"Are you kidding?" he replied. "Some of those guys have been a pain in my butt all trip. I'd rather hike with you."

Luke faithfully repeated the instructions he had heard Lyndon deliver to his group.

"That's my boy," Lyndon said, patting Luke on the back. "When you are ready for a summer job, you give me a call."

"Okay, our order is Russell, Lil, Sophie then Luke. Time to climb! Off you go, Russell," Lyndon directed.

"I really don't like heights," Russell said as he slowly placed his foot on the first rung.

"Take your time, remember your breathing, and try singing yourself a little song. Take it one step, then one step, then another, just like climbing up to your bunk in the hut," Lyndon coached.

Luke could see Russell's leg quiver as he lifted his feet to each of the first half dozen rungs. After the initial ladder, either the quivering stopped, or Russell was too far away for Luke to see the shaking. Luke found he was laughing to himself. When Russell reached the first platform, Luke yelled out, "Way to go, mountain goat." If he hadn't known better, Luke could have sworn Russell gave him the finger.

Lyndon thought Lil was looking a little paler. While he admired her determination, given her condition the last time he saw her, he was surprised to still see her on the trail. Gotta give her credit, she's quite the Dench, he thought to himself.

"You ready?" he asked Lil. She was on the first step before the second word was out of his mouth. "That'll be a yes," he said.

Lil was making steady progress through the first six rungs. Though her legs were not quivering like Russell's, Luke found himself anxious in a way he wasn't when his grandfather was climbing.

"I'm going to go up next and stay a bit close quarters," Lyndon said, turning to Luke. "You go up after mom the same way."

"What about the first rule, 'one person at a time'?" Luke asked.

"That's for beginners. You and I are professionals," Lyndon replied, quickly heading up the same ladder as Lil. He paused and matched her speed when he was within three rungs.

Without looking down, Lil felt his presence and found it reassuring.

From bottom to top, it was a fifteen-minute climb. The first of Lyndon's clients and one of his assistants had already completed the ascent.

Sophie was on the middle of the first ladder when the warning rang out. "ROCK, ROCK, ROCK, ROCK."

There were eight people on the ladders and another four on the platforms. Ten remembered the training and pressed themselves against the rockface. Two looked up. It was a single stone, about the size of a softball, dislodged by Roger as he stood close to the edge to take a photo of a friend who was climbing the final ladder.

Luke joined the chorus, "ROCK" that accompanied the projectile on its descent. It passed by the first four climbers, its initial path taking it harmlessly through the open air. The stone bounced off a ledge, slowed a bit, and changed course to the left. Russell pressed himself into a hollow beneath a curve in the rockface. Sophie quickly jumped down the bottom four rungs, grabbed Luke, and pushed him toward the path. Lil was exposed as the stone approached, her body tight to the flat wall, a hand over her head, her back slightly curved. Lyndon quickly scrambled up the rungs that separated him from Lil, one arm holding the ladder while his second hand pressed her hip toward the wall.

The stone struck her. The way she had curved her back, it contacted her backpack and not her body. She let out an audible grunt, heard a crack, and felt the wetness running down her back – the plastic of her water bottle breaking. The top zipper of her pack burst open and the contents followed the stone to the ground.

Lil's eye looked to the left. She watched her purple kit descend through the air, as if in slow motion, and disappear behind the rope at the edge of the wall.

She wailed as a mourner would for a loved one. Luke heard her scream the words, "My kit!" as clearly as he had heard the initial warning.

Lyndon looked up and saw a wild look in Lil's eyes.

Russell looked down. He had seen the rock make contact. He instinctively cringed and closed his eyes. When he dared reopen them, he saw her still clinging to the ladder. Relief coursed through his body.

Sophie stood safely on the ground, her eyes fixed on her mother and Lyndon's arms cradled around Lil.

Luke threw down his backpack and sprinted away from Sophie, following the trajectory of his grandmother's possessions. He hopped over the warning rope at the base of the wall and disappeared from view.

Lil did not see Russell's relief, Sophie's terror, or Luke disappear. She looked down at Lyndon. She saw the care in his face and felt the strong arm around her. For a flash, she thought of Frederico. Her wild look washed away. She smiled warmly and touched his face. And in that moment, too, it was undeniable: She was glad her kit was gone.

Panic returned to her when she heard Sophie's cry, "Luke!"

The footpaths along the TMB are largely open, with safe routes designated through frequent signage and ensured by a hiker's good judgment. The area around the base of the ladders was an exception. Ropes cordoned off the zone to the left of the stone face. Not that you could mistake that direction, with its sharply descending slope, as an alternate path. There was no worn trace on the rocky surface, not even a goat path. The reclining mountain pines clung precariously to the outcroppings. The tops of the trees were at eye level when you stood on the ladder base. The lower trunks were only visible if you were bold enough to lean over the cautionary rope.

It was into this terrain that the purple kit floated. It was onto this slope that Luke jumped, hoping to retrieve the object.

There are no words to capture the feeling that swallows a parent when they see their child in danger and know they are powerless to save them. Sophie saw her son running. She screamed his name – the name she and Rick had given him 17 years ago, the name she had uttered thousands of times in the days since, uttered to get his attention, to give him direction, to make a correction, and not nearly enough to tell him she loved him – and she saw him jump over the rope only to disappear.

Sophie ran to the rope. "God no. God no. God no," a desperate plea from a faithless soul. "Please, please, please," a hopeful prayer ringing in her head. "Luke, Luke, Luke," a fervent wish streaming from her lips. She cast the words toward her son as if they could pull him back to her.

Though neither Lyndon nor Lil had witnessed the boy disappear, Sophie's voice and that one word, "Luke," told them all they needed to know. Lyndon guided Lil to a platform and slid down the final two ladders. He then rushed to join Sophie.

Sophie had not crossed the barrier, not out of fear but of uncertainty as to where to go. She would have, she was sure of it – at least that is what she told herself – but there was no sign of her son.

Lyndon's gaze was drawn down the slope. His practiced eye saw a patch of broken branches in the underbrush about five feet to the left. That must have been where he landed, but the angle was too steep to see solid ground further down.

Lyndon looked at Sophie. He placed one hand on her shoulder and pushed the rope with his free hand. He was about to step over onto the slope when he heard the voice.

"Where are you going? I already got it." Luke was five yards uphill, scrambling on all fours, using some of the underbrush as handholds, the purple kit tucked into the back of his pants.

Lyndon ducked under the rope and, while still holding on to it, side-stepped toward Luke. He reached out. When the boy was in range, he grabbed him firmly on the forearm and pulled him to level ground.

Sophie's first instinct had been to scream at him. Instead she held him tight, as tight as she ever had..

Luke resisted his instinct to push her away. Instead, he wrapped his arms around his mother's shoulders and reassured her, "It's ok, it's ok, it's ok."

When his mother finally released him, Lyndon smacked the boy on the side of his head. He pointed his finger in Luke's face and said, "That's for being stupid."

Luke put up his hands and replied, "I know, I know, I know . . ."

Lyndon's face softened, and he grabbed the boy firmly by the shoulder. "Rule one: Be safe. It would've been a hell of a vacation if you died out here."

Luke smiled. He reached behind his back and pulled out the purple kit. "Would you give this to Lil. She seems mighty fond of it," Luke said to Lyndon.

"You give it to her. You're next up," Lyndon said. "Clearly, you can't be trusted down here alone."

"Are you all right?" his mother asked, unsettled at the prospect of him now climbing the ladders.

The only evidence of his misadventure was a slight scratch on the cheek where he must have caught a branch. "Except for the broken ribs when you hugged me, I'm fine," Luke replied.

Luke proceeded up the ladder without incident and was followed in order by his mother and Lyndon.

Lil was waiting for him on the third platform.

"I think this belongs to you," he said, handing her the purple kit. "Sorry I couldn't get all the other things," he said.

With her right hand she touched the boy's cheekbone just below the scratch. She slowly raised an ambivalent left hand and reclaimed her comfort kit. She looked down and contemplated the purple case. She looked at it as an archeologist might examine a mysterious artifact. A voice in her head said, "Throw it away."

Lil lifted her left hand. She returned the kit to her backpack and zippered the pack closed.

"Time to move on," Lil said to Luke and she started back up the rungs. The certainty of her steps contrasted with the uncertainty in her head.

Russell was waiting at the top of the wall. He reached down and helped each one in turn as they climbed the final steps before reaching level ground.

Matteo, Lyndon's assistant, was pacing back and forth. Roger was seated at a bench about ten yards away with a cloth placed against the side of his face and some bruising already visible around his eye.

As Lyndon made the landing, Matteo approached, agitated. "I'm sorry, boss. He was just being a shit again with the pictures, leaning over and not paying attention. I told him to move back but he wasn't watching. That's when he kicked over the stone," Matteo explained. "When it hit her I thought she was dead."

"Yes, Roger was irresponsible," Lyndon replied. "But you didn't have to punch him. You're a professional."

"It wasn't me, boss," Matteo replied. "It was the old guy," he said, pointing to Russell. "He was hot. I had to pull him off and keep him away."

Lyndon looked at Russell and then down at Russell's scraped and swollen hand. "I want to apologize for what happened. We should have been more careful, supervising them."

Lil interrupted. "Accidents happen in the mountains. It's not your fault. Everyone is fine except for that one over there," she said, pointing at Roger.

Russell looked pleadingly at Lyndon. "I'm so sorry for hitting your client. I hope it will not create a problem for you."

Lyndon shook his head, "Way I see it, he's bloody lucky you didn't push him over the edge. I'll get my team going. Give us about ten minutes before you move on, and we can keep some space between the groups." Lyndon then left to speak with Matteo and Roger.

Luke wondered what Lyndon was saying. What may have begun as a sympathetic check on the man's injury now looked more like a stern talking to.

Lil and her family waited at the top of the wall. They decided to give Lyndon a 15-minute head start. A thick bank of clouds had settled atop them, obscuring any view of the valley below and the jagged peaks above.

Russell sat next to Lil with his arm firmly around her shoulder. "I thought I had lost you," he said.

"Not just yet," she replied. "Not just yet." Wanting to change the tone, Lil added, "So when did you start with the boxing lessons, my noble champion? I don't think I have ever seen you get into a fight before."

Russell didn't smile at her jab. He spoke without lifting his head. "I was so angry." And he was. Angry at the stupid man for not being careful. Angry at the cancer for its cruelty. Angry at Lil for her secrets, for not telling Luke and Sophie, and for leaving him. Russell found these strong emotions disorienting.

Lil sensed the wider meaning of his words. She stroked the side of his face with the back of her hand. "I love you, my dear Galahad," she said.

Ten yards away sat Luke and Sophie close to each other. The burst of adrenaline having run its course, Luke was suddenly tired, like he would feel after swimming a 3200. But his mind was a whirl. That was stupid, he acknowledged silently with hindsight. I could have slipped and fallen all the way to the bottom. And Nan didn't seem all that happy when I gave her stuff back.

Sophie's mind also flitted from one person to the next. The rock hitting Mom. Luke jumping over the rope. The image of her father punching that stupid man. And in the shadow of all these thoughts about her family, she also found herself thinking about Lyndon. It seemed as if every time her family needed some help, he would appear. That thought warmed her.

Luke strained to listen to the discussion between his grandparents. The fog of the clouds carried their conversation but muffled the words. He could only make out snippets. "Lost . . . angry . . . tell Luke. . ."

It was Sophie who announced they'd waited long enough. "Let's get going."

Rapprochement

The guidebook indicated another thirty minutes before they reached le Refuge du Lac Blanc. Here, above the tree line, the stone path picked its way across the rock face, the shroud of clouds hiding the view. The hikers passed the time looking at their feet and listening to the click of their poles.

Luke stepped around a piton and spied a small pool of water about 20 yards wide. "Is that it?" he asked disappointingly.

"No," Lil answered. "Those are just some of the Lacs de Chesery. But we are almost there," she added.

They passed another half dozen of these small pools, remnants of glacial carving from a past era. Luke saw the sky in the water. The reflection of the clouds painted across the wind-drawn ripples seemed indecisive, shaking right to left and up then down as if uncertain about their future.

Luke couldn't resist reaching down and scooping the water with his bare hand. The chill ran up his arm, and his eyes widened as his body shivered.

Sophie noticed Luke lagging behind. She gestured to her parents to stop. In that moment of waiting, the clouds thinned. The scene emerged like a Polaroid. First, the outline of the hut anchored to a rocky finger that jutted into the now visible mountain lake. Then, the silhouette of the mountain surrounding the lake on three sides, holding the water in the palm of its ancient hand. As the blue sky triumphed above, the colors of Lac Blanc transformed from a steely gray to turquoise blue. The winds faded and the surface calmed. From where he stood, Luke beheld the mirror image of the distant Mont Blanc massif reflected in the stillness before him. Earth and sky were one. The water curved both down over the edge of the world and on up into the endless heavens. Of all the remarkable views the family had seen throughout the Tour, this was the most profoundly inspiring.

Luke said excitedly, "We have to take a picture. Now!" He directed his family to a stone ridge separating the lake's two portions. He framed the image so the refuge was visible in the top right corner. Mont Blanc and its reflected image encircled them.

Luke took two shots and was preparing for a third when a stranger said, "Here, you get in. I'll take the picture." After the briefest hesitation, Luke handed them his phone and joined his family. Lil and Sophie in the middle, Luke and Russell on either side, their arms draped, each touching the other three. Their faces shared the same broad smile. This was to be the picture next to Lil's urn at the Life Celebration later that summer. The picture Russell will talk to each evening before going to bed. The picture Sophie will display on her office desk. The picture Luke will keep as the backdrop on his phone until he replaces it on the day his first daughter, Elizabeth, is born.

Luke accepted the phone back from the kind stranger. With a swipe of his fingers, he enlarged the image and nodded his approval. That's dope, he said to himself.

Strutting back to his family, Luke held up the phone and declared smugly, "We look good." And they did. Any disappointment, resentment, or frustration from the day, or the days before, put aside, at least in that moment. They were a family, together.

Lil raised her arm and let out a triumphant cheer. Luke hugged his grandmother and lifted her slightly in the air. Sophie and Russell laughed, enjoying the joy between Luke and Lil. After catching her breath, Lil announced, "Time to eat!" and they headed toward the open-air patio.

Like most of the other huts, le Refuge du Lac Blanc was a simple structure. It was divided into two separate buildings. The dining area and deck on the upper building sat atop the stone finger. A small walkway led to a second building housing the sleeping dorms, bathrooms, and showers. However simple, it was graced with the same advantage that benefitted the Rifugio de Bonatti: an unequaled view. Russell had wondered, as do many Tour du Mont Blanc hikers, why the standard route proceeds counterclockwise south and east from Les Houches. What seemed arbitrary was apparent as they rested on the deck warmed by the sun and soaked in the world around them. The vibrant blue of the sky, the vistas of mountain peaks with the dark stones cutting up and through the still visible snow fields – to see this first would render the later views disappointing by comparison. Far better, Russell thought, to have this as your reward on the final day of walking.

Lil nibbled on a croissant and found that food still did not agree with her stomach. She stayed with the tea.

Luke had finished his pasta before Sophie was halfway through her salad. "Be back in a sec," Luke stated, returning shortly with a fruit tart and a slice of chocolate cake.

"You are not going to eat both of those," Sophie admonished.

"Silly woman," Luke replied. "They are to share." He sliced them into four almost equal pieces.

Russell selected a portion of the fruit tart and the largest piece of the cake. He placed them on the side of his dish, muttering, "Better claim it now. I've seen that boy eat."

Lil took stock of her body. She was suddenly exhausted and felt chilled even under the warming sun. Her stomach was uneasy. "Excuse me for a moment; I'll be right back," she said as she pushed away from the picnic table and headed toward the bathrooms of the lower building.

She just made it to the stall when she retched. The initial clenching in her stomach brought up a foul mouthful. The subsequent heaves, each more insistent than the one before, yielded little else. The wave passed, and she sat on the toilet to catch her breath. Her abdominal muscles were sore from the exertion.

"*Est-ce que ça va?*" a gentle voice inquired from outside the stall door.

"Oui," Lil said after a brief hesitation.

Lil took a piece of toilet paper and wiped her mouth. She noticed the red flecks. She stood up slowly and looked into the bowl. She studied the range of colors and shapes as one might contemplate a puzzle. Dispersed among the mix of browns and greens were several black clumps with crimson tendrils spreading across the surface of the water.

"Shit," she said to herself. The sight and the thought triggered a second wave of nausea that she suppressed by closing her eyes and breathing.

It hadn't disappeared. Lil knew that. Despite the magical thinking, that faint hope bolstered by an occasional good day: Maybe the doctors were wrong. Maybe there will be a miracle. Maybe if I am strong enough. Maybe if I am good enough, kind enough, penitent enough, God will forgive me . . . But Lil had known there would be no maybes. The only uncertainty was when. When would fate draw the final curtain and escort her off the stage? Her relief when the falling stone freed her from her medical kit. Her ambivalence when Luke handed it back. Those feelings were what disappeared. She flushed them away with the bile her body had just expelled. She – not fate nor accident – would author her final scene. The time. The location. And the terms.

Russell had been keeping a cautious eye on the walkway to the second building. When Lil reappeared, he thought she was walking slowly, though he was uncertain if she was struggling or just contemplating.

As she neared the table, he saw that she looked pale. "Are you okay?" he mouthed.

Lil nodded her head. Her firm eye stood in contrast to a slight trembling in her hand. She took her seat and Russell took hold of her arm, patting it gently.

"It's another thirty minutes to Le Flégère and another hour and a half to Chamonix," Sophie said, falling into her newfound role as group leader. "We should be going."

With Russell's assistance, Lil rose to her feet. She looked at her pack next to her and sighed slightly.

Like many couples who have spent a lifetime together, words were not always the primary means of communication. But Russell had learned long ago that his efforts to translate Lil's nonverbals did not always result in accurate understanding. He wondered if she was in pain, tired, or just resolved. Should I lift the bag? Or let her do it? Russell often struggled to deal with Lil's unpredictable emotions. In the past, the wrong guess might lead to an abrupt correction. What the hell, he said to himself. He picked the bag up and placed it on the table.

Lil smiled. Russell was encouraged. He took items from the outer pockets and placed them into his backpack.

Lil smacked his hand lightly, though this was gentler than many "that's enough" messages he had received in the past.

"Luke," Lil said. "Come here."

Luke approached.

She reached into her pack and removed the dry sack, her waterproof jacket, a pair of sneakers, and some dirty clothes. "Be a dear, and carry these for me."

"Sure," he said, cinching the sneakers to the outer loops and stuffing the rest into the top half of his backpack.

Lil cast a mischievous smile in Russell's direction. She pulled the drawstring tight and clipped the mostly empty bag shut. Backing up to the table, she placed her arms through the straps. She cautiously buckled the waist belt and found the pressure helped lessen the discomfort in her abdomen.

"I'm ready," she said. Holding both poles in her right hand, she took Russell's arm with her left, and they set off for the final walk to the valley.

The route to Flégère was largely a slow descent with only short uphill stretches along the contour of the mountainside. The views were stunning throughout. Each turn and curve provided a slightly different panorama.

Even with the pack's reduced weight, Lil struggled. Though she had been drinking water steadily, she had eaten no more than a mouthful between breakfast and lunch. She found herself short of breath and with cramps in her stomach. What should have taken 30 minutes to Flégère required ninety, and Lil was exhausted. At this rate, Chamonix was still hours away.

A Shortcut

By comparison to most other refuges along the TMB, Le Flégère is a crowded bustle. Its location just to the north and east of Chamonix, along with its magnificent vistas, accounts for its appeal. It is also served by a large-capacity gondola making it accessible to day hikers who prefer to gain the 800 meters without breaking a sweat. Once disembarked, these casual randonneurs could enjoy the dozens of shorter paths that track across the mountainside. Some simply choose to head straight to one of the restaurants for a sandwich or gelato. Visitors not prone to vertigo could walk to an observation platform perched at the mountain's edge. From this eyrie they are graced with a view of the entire Chamonix Valley.

The clear skies that found the family at Lac Blanc remained with them all the way to Le Flégère. An expansive patio was set with a score of picnic tables, each one adorned by a royal blue umbrella that complemented the now cloudless sky. Several dozen wooden lounge chairs were strategically placed on three separate decks, each below the other so as not to interrupt the view afforded to the temporary residents.

Lil took a seat in one of the loungers. The subtle throbbing in her legs was now accompanied by twitching in her calves. She began flexing her feet, bringing her toes toward her shins, and then extending her feet away from her body. That helped lessen the throbbing but the twitching remained. She thought her ankles looked swollen. Lil noticed her breath was quick, with shallow huffs of air flowing in and out through her open mouth. She closed her eyes, concentrating on slowing her breathing, mentally coaching herself: In through the nose . . . one, two . . . out through the mouth. She lowered her head against the back of the chair, tightened the muscles in her upper back and then released them. She felt exhausted. Exhausted in a way she had not felt earlier in the trip. It felt good to simply lie down and rest. "I could stay here forever," she caught herself saying.

A sudden sharp pain jolted her. She gasped audibly and reached down. The contraction knifed through her lower leg, and she felt her foot curl as if being rolled up. Her eyes watered. Lil rubbed at the center of the cramp and tried straightening her foot.

Pain is a commanding master. It consumes our attention and alters time. Lil closed her eyes and prayed for it to end. The twenty seconds required for her muscle to relax felt like an eternal instant. When Lil opened her eyes, she found the crown of her head was pressed against her daughter. Sophie's hands were massaging the muscle of Lil's right calf.

Lil kissed the top of Sophie's head, taking in the smell of her daughter's hair. The memory of bathing Sophie in the kitchen sink flashed through her mind. The young baby splashing her hands against the surface of the water. The suds spraying across the counter top, and Lil not minding. "Oh, that is much better. Thank you, sweet pea," Lil said.

"Leg cramps are a bitch," Sophie said, a satisfied smile settling on her face.

Lil didn't know what image Sophie had in her mind at that moment. But she found herself wishing it was the one of the bath, the suds, and the shared happiness.

After the cramp released her, Lil's attention shifted to the emptiness of her stomach. It was a new gnawing, not the swirling rejection of nausea but more the call of her body demanding sustenance.

"It's my own damn fault," Lil remarked. "I haven't eaten much today and I must be dehydrated. Russell, would you be a dear and get me some tea and toast?"

Russell was glad to now be of service. When Lil cramped and gasped, he was next to her, and froze. Uncertain what to do, he did nothing. He watched. It was Sophie who acted. Helpless. Though he didn't use the word, that is how he felt. The same feeling he had regularly experienced over the past four months. So to be needed, even if only to get tea and toast, lightened his spirit.

Russell returned a few moments later with a cup of tea in one hand and a plate with croissant and jam in the other.

Lil smiled and accepted them gladly.

"That looks good," Luke commented, looking at the food.

"Come on," his mother said, correctly interpreting the code. "Let's get you something before you fade away."

When they were alone, Russell asked, "How are you doing . . . really?"

Lil paused a moment before answering. "Better," she said, pointing to the tea and croissant. "But not great." Another pause. "I do not feel much like walking anymore . . . today."

Russell nodded. He was heartened, not so much by the content of the message, but by the honest answer.

"I think I will be taking the lift down to the valley," she added.

"Sounds good. We'll take the lift," he replied.

"You can keep walking," Lil said. "With Sophie and Luke."

"No," Russell replied, using a word he rarely said to Lil. "I'm coming with you."

Lil smiled and was grateful for his response. The truth was that she was not quite feeling "better" in the slightest. Once in the valley, she feared she might need a little assistance making it to the hotel. Besides, she only needed to be alone later that evening and not right now. She grabbed Russell's hand and nodded.

Sophie and Luke returned from the cafe. Sophie had the same tea and croissant as her mother. Luke balanced a slightly larger plate containing a pain au chocolat and a bowl of soup in his right hand and his second cappuccino of the day in his left.

Russell explained their plan to take the gondola down to Chamonix and then head to the hotel. "Your choice if you want to ride or finish on foot."

Sophie glanced at her mother. She thought she saw the faintest shake of her head. But before she could respond, Luke interrupted. "Ah, we're walking, thank you. I didn't haul my ass over 104 miles of mountains to wuss out the last three miles." What Sophie thought she may have seen, Luke had clearly observed. "You two enjoy your comfy ride. Me and my girlfriend," he said, linking his arm through his mother's, "have a little more trail to burn."

Lil grinned at her grandson.

"We best be going," Lil said, announcing her departure. Russell helped her rise from her lounge. For the second time she did not shake him off. "We will see you tonight at dinner." With that, she and Russell proceeded to the gondola station.

III

Part Three

The Final Walk

Le Faucigny

L e Faucigny is tucked into a quiet impasse connecting Allée Recteur Payot and Rue Joseph Vallot, two main streets in Chamonix. The nondescript entrance on the north side, just past the local Super-U marche, belied the charming hotel Lil and Russell discovered upon entering the door. The light stain on the wide-planked floor gently contrasted with the muted gray of the walls and ceiling. Four wooden chairs, two singles and two doubles, beckoned travelers to nest among their oversized cushions. The long side of the room featured a mantelled half-wall, with cultured stone beneath and scalloped waves of fabric above. The opposite wall of open shelves, made of the same wood as the desk, housed a series of black and white photographs in wooden frames. The room was brightened with pops of red – red gladiola, red-spined books, red wire for the pendant lights.

Collette stood behind a birch table which served as a reception desk. The young host was dressed sharply in a blouse and skirt, both of which effortlessly matched the colors in the room. She greeted Lil and Russell warmly: "Welcome to Le Faucigny, my dear friends."

After check-in, Collette invited Lil and Russell to the community room. "We have tea each afternoon as well as breakfast in the morning. Of course, coffee is available anytime. I, myself, especially like to sit outside in the courtyard," she said, pointing to the door opposite the one they had entered. "You will find the pool, sauna, and spa downstairs and to the right. If you require anything at all, just ask and we will be happy to assist."

Russell accepted the key. It was attached to a wooden fob, slightly smaller than a door knob. The room number was engraved on a metal disk embedded into the wood. Collette saw Russell staring at the key. "Those were original to the building. It was a former boarding house for sheep shearers."

The community room was as charming as the lobby. While the walls and curtains used the same color palette, one wall was partitioned floor to ceiling with a series of cubbies built from reclaimed wood, each space home to a select number of magazines, books, pictures, games, or red-glazed ceramics. Two double chairs – the ones with the nesting cushions – were stationed immediately in front of a large fireplace. The servery, watched over by an illuminated glass moosehead, anchored the left side. A series of ten tables provided plenty of seating on the north wall, but the room was empty at this hour except for Lil and Russell.

"I think I will try some chamomile," Lil said, moving to the assortment of teas by Mariage Frères. Russell followed her lead and filled a plate with two small cakes and some chocolate.

"I can't believe the room only cost eighty-four euros," the accountant in Russell said absently. He then glanced at Lil sheepishly, remembering his pledge not to reduce everything to numbers.

Lil smiled and said, "Let's sit outside."

As impressed as they were with the hotel's interior, they were even more enchanted with the courtyard. The cobblestone space was framed on two sides by the hotel. A tall, slender screen of evergreens backed against an adjacent building to complete the U-shape. A flagstone path led to a series of metal arches providing access to la Place de l'Eglise, which, though a mere 20 yards away, seemed a world apart.

Lil and Russell sat down at one of the three red bistro tables.

"Are you feeling better?" Russell asked between bites of his cake.

"A little," she replied, her eyes looking at the outline of Mont Blanc visible in the distance above the courtyard. "It is certainly good to be off my feet," she added, glancing back at her husband.

"Got that right," he replied with a light nod.

Lil reached out her hand and cupped it over Russell's. "Thank you for doing this," she said.

He heard the words – thank you. These were not words Lil spoke often. Usually, he was the one who expressed appreciation: A thank you to Lil for some small kindness. A word of gratitude to the mailman, the waitstaff, or the stranger who held open the door, a routine of appreciation that he said accounted for the good fortune in his life. Yes, it was usually he who gave thanks. Not that Lil wasn't grateful, or at least he didn't think she wasn't. It was that she usually didn't say it, at least not in words.

As Russell sat there his smile slowly faded. In that shadowed moment, he struggled to keep hold of what to be grateful for. His wife was dying. She would soon be gone and he would be alone. Alone in a way he had not been these past 45 years. Russell knew that too soon, his normal life would be no more. It would be buried with Lil. The edges of his emotions turned to fear and then to anger. He felt himself standing back at the totem, staring at the names, stung again by a secret revealed.

"I love you," she said.

He heard the words – love you. These, too, were words Lil did not often speak. For as long as they had been together, and they had been married longer than most couples they knew, he did not recall her utter those words more than a dozen times. When they were younger, he wondered why. He would profess his love, both because it was true, and he thought perhaps his words might serve to model, coach, or prompt. On some occasions, he struggled to now recall when, she replied in kind. Though more often, he recollected, she would reply, "Me, too," avoiding the four-letter word. Over time, he had to admit, he stopped saying the words himself.

So, in this moment, when they were together, and he knew these opportunities would soon disappear, in this moment, when she had said the words he had wished she had said more frequently, Russell found himself bitter.

Me too, he thought. Russell had meant to say it using the words she had taught him. Instead, he pulled his hands back, folded his arms across his chest, and said, "When are you going to tell them? Time is almost up." The words came out more sharply than he had intended.

Lil paused. Debbie had prepared her: "Your loved ones, they'll get angry too, just like you. It's natural and all part of the process. It's not easy. But truth is, some of the grieving happens before you're even gone."

More words tumbled out, biting again as they left his mouth. "When are you going to tell them you've got cancer and you're dying?"

Lil drew up her jaw and turned her eye to the mountains.

"To tell them you're going to kill yourself?" he continued, with the corners of his lips pulled taut. He grasped the edge of the table with both hands and leaned in toward Lil. "They deserve to know."

Her husband's pain had spoken its truth. And when he had finished, Lil's eye returned to his dependable face. "I've told them what I've come to tell them," Lil began. "I've told them I love them," she paused. "That was the purpose of this trip," she concluded.

Russell shook his head. His grip tightened, knuckles a bloodless white against the table's red. "That's not fair," he said, his voice insistent.

"NOTHING about this mess is deserved. And there is no fair," Lil said, reaching out and placing her hands atop his. "You know that," she added. "I do not want them treating me with pity. If I had told them those things, this whole trip would have been about dying. And I wanted it to be about living."

Russell did not reply. He felt drained, left with a nagging emptiness.

"Let's go upstairs," she said. He acquiesced and released the table. She led him to their room. They lay down in the bed together. Russell's arm draped over her shoulder. Lil held it tight as they both fell asleep.

Lil woke an hour later. She lifted herself quietly from the bed. Still, Russell sensed the movement, stirred, and patted her on the shoulder as she rose. The anger, at least for the moment, had left him. For the briefest instant, he felt as he often did when he woke in the morning: Content and grateful, happily surprised at his good fortune to lie next to the one he loved. And then, just as quickly, the present intruded. He thought not of his anger and fear but of his current dread of a clock ticking down. He shook his head, a hopeless attempt to cast off the unwelcome thought.

"What time is it?" he asked.

"Almost five o'clock," Lil replied. "They should be here by now."

"Aha," Russell agreed. "Almost time for dinner. I guess we should get ready."

Lil had practiced for this moment. She had scripted what to say and how to respond to each objection. She would do it calmly, sympathetically, with perhaps a gentle touch to the arm if necessary. Impatience would be her last resort.

"I am still not feeling well. It would be best if you went along without me. I'll just rest here in the room and maybe sleep a little more. I'll be here when you get back," she said, presenting the ruse.

"But this is the final day with everyone. Luke and Sophie have to catch the train tomorrow for Geneva and their flight back. This was going to be our last meal together. We made reservations at the restaurant you selected," Russell replied.

"I know, and I am disappointed. I just don't feel up to it," she gently persisted.

Russell paused. "Okay. I'll let Sophie know. I will get something light and stay here with you. She and Luke can go out together," he replied genuinely.

"No," she said. "You are right. This is the last night together as a family. You should join them," she added. "I'll be here when you get back." That last line didn't sound quite right – a little too melodramatic, and she had used it already. Of course she would be here when he returned. Why wouldn't she?

Russell looked at her slightly askance. Lil sensed the doubt in his mind. Was he hesitant to leave her because she was not feeling well? Or did he suspect?

"Look, I'll rest a little longer," she said, touching him gently on the arm. "And if I feel better, I will join you later, maybe for dessert. That will save my accountant a little money on the dinner bill." She smiled sweetly and, with just the slightest of pressure, pushed him away.

Russell showered and dressed quietly. Nothing too formal. Though this was one of the finer restaurants in the valley, Chamonix was a relaxed mountain village.

"They are in room eighteen," Lil offered while Russell buttoned his shirt. "I checked with the front desk and they arrived about an hour ago."

"I'm still not sure this is a good idea. I can stay, you know. It's alright,"

Russell said.

"Go," she commanded in a soft voice. "I'll rest and be fine."

Resolved to his fate, Russell kissed her on the cheek and said, "I'll be back no later than eight. If you need anything, text."

Lil nodded, closed the door behind him, and exhaled.

The Preparation

Lil went to her pack and removed the purple pouch. She emptied the contents onto the wooden writing table tucked into the corner of the room. She lined them up and began to take inventory.

Lil's planning was interrupted by a knock at the door. For a moment she thought about not responding. If it were a staff member from Le Faucigny, perhaps they would simply go away. She chided herself, thinking I should have placed the Do Not Disturb sign on the handle. But maybe it was Russell. She had latched the chain lock on the door so he couldn't simply barge in. There was a second knock, this time a bit softer, and accompanied by a voice: "Nan, it's me, Luke."

Lil's heart beat faster. She thought again about not responding. Instead, she said, "Just a minute." She quickly swiped the contents off the table with her arm. Most returned safely into the purple pouch and three bottles fell to the floor. Lil took a deep breath, wiped her face, and smoothed her hair with her hands. She went to the door and let Luke in.

"Sorry to interrupt," Luke began. "Russell said you still weren't feeling well and wouldn't be coming to dinner."

"Yes, I'm sorry about that . . ." Lil replied.

"No trouble, makes perfect sense," Luke said. "I just wanted to come by and give you something," Luke said, reaching into his pants pocket.

He was dressed smartly, with a light blue button shirt and a pair of skinny jeans. His hair was combed, and it looked like he had applied some gel or something to keep the front curve in place. He is a handsome boy, Lil thought silently – even if a little too thin. And in the flash of that moment, she imagined him as the man he would come to be, the one she would never see.

She reached out her hand and lightly touched his face. "You did not need to do that," she said, her eyes starting to glisten. She felt the complex swirl of emotions the old often have when they look at the young ones they love – that mix of joy, pride, and nostalgia, with just a tinge of envy.

"I know," he said with a shrug of his head, his wave of hair moving only slightly. "But I thought...."

Luke sat on the corner of the bed. "I never wanted to go on this trip, you know," he began over. "I wanted to stay home with my friends. Hanging out, swimming, video games. I even told Mom I would get a job," he added with a laugh. "Walk a hundred miles? Share a room with a bunch of strangers and no internet? I thought it would suck. And at first, I'm not gonna lie, it did." He paused. "My legs were so sore the first two days, after walking up and up and up. I still remember getting splashed with cow shit and all the people farting in the dorm room." They both laughed. "And then something changed. I got to thinking about the people we'd met, and all the messed up things that happened to them. But then I would think about all the beautiful things, too. And I started to think about Mom and Dad, and you and Russell, and me. It began, you know, to feel different. What started out as one of the worst things in my life became one of the best . . . It's like you said. You take some things with you, and you leave some things behind, right?"

Luke paused. "So I wanted to thank you, Nan, and give you this." Luke handed Lil a small box.

"I wanted to get everyone something but didn't know what. I thought a T-shirt or a cowbell would be stupid."

Lil opened the cover and removed the gauze. Inside was a pendant, or more correctly a portion of pendant, attached to a gold link chain.

"So when we walked into town, I saw this jewelry store. Jewelry is not really my thing. Anyway, there was this necklace, and it had a medallion with Mont Blanc in the middle. After we checked in, I told Mom I had to run an errand, and I went back. I asked the guy if he could cut the pendant in quarters and drill a hole in each one. He looked at me funny, and then I told him why, and he said sure." Luke was smiling. "Mom's is attached to a bracelet. Russell's has a pin so he can stick it to his backpack. You have the necklace, and mine is on a choker," he said, showing her the braided black cord already affixed to his neck. "I hope you like it."

"I was going to give these to everyone tonight at dinner. But since you're not coming, I wanted to stop by and drop it off now. And to say thank you, and I love you!"

"It is the perfect remembrance," she said, embracing the boy. "Here, help me put it on."

She turned around so her back was toward Luke and went to hand him the necklace. She released the necklace too soon, and it dropped to the floor. As Luke went to retrieve the necklace, he noticed the medicine bottles on the floor next to the bed. He picked up the necklace and affixed it to her neck.

"Thank you, Luke. I have had the most marvelous adventure. It is something I will cherish forever," Lil said. "You best be going; the other two are waiting."

"Three," Luke said. "Mom ran into Lyndon and invited him to join us for dinner. Between you and me, I think she likes him."

"I suspect the feeling is mutual," Lil added, smiling.

After a final hug, Luke left. Lil returned to her inventory. It was 6:00.

Lil took the largest bottle. The label included an oversized skull and crossbones. The words "THIS SUBSTANCE WILL CAUSE DEATH" were written above the image. She sliced through the first of two safety tapes that secured the cap to the bottle. She shook the bottle for no particular reason and heard the rhythmic rattle of one hundred pills. She felt her body moving as if commanded to dance by some macabre marimba, but then realized her hand was shaking.

The first step was to open each of the capsules and empty the contents into a ziplock bag. The first capsule burst open when she tried to separate the two pieces. The contents spilled to the floor. "Damn," she said aloud, panicking. She kneeled down and tried retrieving the powder by pinching it between her thumb and forefinger. It proved a poor strategy, more effective at spreading the mess around than moving it to the bag. Her mind instinctively considered what other floor crap she was collecting in her efforts to pinch the powder. She laughed at the absurdity of the concern. I don't think there is a five-second rule for death pills, Elizabeth, she told herself.

In the end, she was able to retrieve a little less than half the content from the first pill. The rest was spread in a light coating across the wood floor. She studied her fingers which had the same coating of pill dust. Hesitating for a moment as she looked at the lethal powder, her future, her choice – she refused to call it medicine. Lil brought her hand to her mouth and touched her tongue to the tip of her finger. Her face immediately twisted tight. It was bitter, like uncoated aspirin flavored with castor oil. She wiped her tongue immediately on her shirt sleeve. She stepped away from the bed and to the mini-fridge. It was empty. She settled on a cup of water. It didn't help much; it just spread the nasty taste throughout her mouth.

She took another sip. It was a cautious swallow. She waited. Nothing. She wasn't certain what to expect. She thought there would be something, especially with all the ominous labeling. The rational part of her brain engaged: You have to open one hundred of these to do the trick and you just took a little lick. What were you expecting, silly woman?

She smiled at her foolishness and returned to the task at hand. She wet a paper towel and wiped the floor to remove the thin layer that still remained on the wood. She debated whether to flush the towel down the toilet or place it in the trash bag. Either way, I'm poisoning the environment, she told herself. She opted for the trash, deciding she liked fish more than garbage rats.

Fearing that her same approach would yield similar results, Lil took a plastic bag the hotel provided for laundry service, spread it on the floor, and began opening the pills onto the larger plastic sheet.

It was painstakingly slow. The capsules resisted her efforts to pry them apart. She had brought a second bag to store the empty plastic hulls but chided herself for not thinking of bringing some nitrile gloves.

After she emptied the first twenty pills, she lifted the sheet, creasing it carefully along the midpoint, and poured the powder into the plastic bag. The thinnest cloud of dust entered her mouth and nostrils. She pursed her lips tight. "Well, now I know why they give you the Valium and anti-puke med. This stuff is nasty."

6:20. It had taken her twenty minutes for the first twenty pills. Eighty left. She did the math, factored in some expected time-savings for her improving skills in capsule-bursting, and set back to work.

* * *

La Fin du Parcours was a small establishment on the ground level of an historic building. The restaurant avoided the traditional cuisine of Haute Savoie, with its overreliance on ham and cheese and dark wood decor, opting instead for a lighter farm-to-table fare and a view into the open kitchen.

Lyndon had already arrived and was at the bar when Russell, Sophie and Luke entered. Not surprisingly, he was chatting with a middle-aged couple, his ready smile and easy manner once again creating some newfound friends, despite his frequent glances to the front door.

Sophie caught his eye during one of these glances. She smiled and waved. Lyndon made his excuses, patted his bar mates on the shoulder, and walked toward the group.

Luke watched Lyndon approach, a jumble of thoughts bouncing in his head. He liked Lyndon, for sure. Though the man was a good twenty years older, Luke felt that Lyndon treated him like a friend. But Lyndon seemed to be that way with almost everyone. And then Luke thought of his father, who also had that same gift of immediate likeability, of being everyone's friend, at least until the last year when the drugs took over. When Lyndon was halfway to the group, Luke found himself doubting the man. He's just a smooth salesman selling packaged tours to wannabe adventurers, he thought. And then he saw Lyndon bite his lower lip and glance at the floor as he approached Sophie. Luke recognized that look. It was that moment of doubt, that hesitancy Luke felt when he was about to ask a girl out and was uncertain how she felt, uncertain if he deserved to spend time with her. Luke glanced toward his mom. He thought he recognized that same look on her face, too.

Lyndon shook hands with Russell. He then extended his arm to Luke and patted Luke on the shoulder with his other hand. And slightly awkwardly, Luke did the same. They both smiled. Lyndon then turned to Sophie. He kissed her on the side of her cheek in a way that seemed to Luke to be more than a European greeting and said, "Thank you for inviting me," followed quickly by, "Where's Ms. Lil?"

"Not feeling well," Russell said. "But she insisted we go out for our final dinner." He paused, "And if there is one thing I have learned over the past forty-four years, she is not a woman to be disobeyed."

"I thought you've been married for forty-five years?" Luke quickly corrected his grandfather.

"It took me one year to learn that lesson," Russell replied with a wink.

The troupe followed the hostess to their table.

* * *

6:40. The contents of thirty more pills had been released and added to the baggie without further incident. Halfway there. Lil's calculation was correct. She was getting better at this.

* * *

When they arrived at the table, Luke immediately pulled out a chair and moved to sit down. Lyndon shot him a look accompanied by a subtle movement of his hand. Message delivered. Luke stopped mid-bend and slowly straightened. Russell stood behind the seat closest to the exit door. Lyndon pulled out the chair next to Russell for Sophie and pushed it in slightly as she sat down. She was followed in quick order by Russell, Lyndon, and finally, Luke. Even while part of his brain was telling him that this etiquette stuff was bullshit, Luke was taking mental notes.

By comparison to their first day on the trail, the conversation on this final day was easy. It began with the typical small talk around the menu and then shifted to some moments from the past week.

It was Sophie who ventured into new territory. "So, how did you get into this adventure guide business?" There were many other questions, much more personal than this, that she wanted to ask Lyndon, but Sophie thought business was the best first bet.

"By disappointing my dad, I suppose," Lyndon said with a look toward Russell. "I was at university, studying economics. My dad wanted me to get into business. Finance, banking, that sort of thing. That's what he did." A slight pause. "Not exactly my strong suit, though. I was more into football, palling with mates, or chatting up the ladies. University was alright, though, 'cause you could do those other things too," he laughed. "My mum, she always said I was more of a card than a scholar. She's the one who encouraged me and my sibs to try new things, follow our dreams, and all that."

Sophie found herself thinking about the different messages she received from her parents. She always viewed Russell as the encouraging one. In the past, she'd imagined Lil was indifferent. But this trip had caused her to question that narrative. Perhaps her mom's laissez-faire was just Lil's way of giving Sophie her freedom. Perhaps it was Sophie who built her own cage.

"So what happened?" Luke asked impatiently.

"In my third year I had a chance to knockabout some, backpacking through Europe. And I was hooked. I thought it was the greatest thing, and I had found what I wanted to do for the rest of my life. I was going to tramp across the world: New Zealand, Asia, South America, wherever the wind took me. When I got back, I told my folks I was going to drop out and scamp across the globe. Now that was a row. I still hear my dad: 'No boy of mine is going to be some second-rate roustabout.' That was the biggest fight we ever got into, and we got into some big fights. I told him that I was my own man, and I would do what I pleased with my own life. That's when he reached his hand toward his trousers – I thought he was going to take off his belt and try to strap me. But he pulled out his wallet and tossed it toward the bin. His message was clear. I stormed out, telling myself I didn't need him, and I didn't need his money."

"Ow," Luke exclaimed. "That is cold."

Lyndon nodded and smiled. "About an hour later, my mum walks into the pub. I had already had a few. She ordered herself a pint. That's the only time we ever went drinking together in a pub – God's honest truth. And she said to me, 'Lyndon, I am going to tell you the same thing I told your father: You are the most pigheaded man I know, and the both of you are cut from the same cloth. You two need to get together and fix this or, sure as I am sitting here, you will regret it for the rest of your life . . . and I will never forgive you.' She took her last sip, put down her glass, and left the pub."

"So what did you do?" Sophie asked.

"The next day, my dad came to see me. Said my mother sent him, a little smile tucked in the corner of his mouth. I was hungover, and he didn't look like he got much sleep on his end – probably spent the night on the couch. We apologized to each other, and we agreed that I would finish university and then pursue my path as I saw fit. So I graduated with an economics degree and then got a job with Butterfield and Robinson. Worked for them for two years. Had some fun but didn't make much money, but B & R was making bank. After a bit I said to myself, 'I can do that.' I set up my own firm, and here I am. My old economics degree came in handy after all. And don't you know, my dad reminds me of that fact about twice a year, at least."

Without missing a beat, Luke turned to Sophie and said, "Mom, I'm thinking about quitting school, and . . ."

"Don't you even say it, young man," she quickly interrupted.

"Listen to your mother, lad," Lyndon replied with a wink toward Sophie. "But if you ever want a summer job, give me a ring. You just have to promise you won't be jumping over any cliffs or losing the clients off the trail."

Luke's eyes lit up. He glanced at his mom and nodded his head before turning to Lyndon and said, "Those things were all Nan's doing."

"Here, here, a toast to Ms. Lil," Lyndon announced. "To she who brought you all here. A gem of a woman if ever there was one." They all raised their glasses.

"I have something else to say," Luke followed the toast. "I stopped by to see her before dinner. I had something to tell her, and to give her. And I, uh, wanted to tell you as well," he said, looking at Russell and Sophie.

"You probably know I wasn't too keen on this trip. And at the start, I was probably a pain in the arse – if you will excuse my Queen's English. But I just wanted to tell you, I had a really good time. This was the best trip ever. It is something I will remember for the rest of my life. And, hopefully, when I have kids of my own, I will take them on a trip like this, and Mom, you will come along. And I would tell them stories about their great-grandpa Russell and great-Nan Lil."

Russell gestured toward Luke with his glass. Lyndon clapped him on the back. Sophie looked at her son and wiped the moisture from her eyes.

"So when I stopped by, she was busy playing with her meds. I told her how I felt about the Tour, how I was grateful we had this adventure, and I wanted to give her something. I have something to give you two as well," he said with a nod at Russell and his mom.

With that, he presented them each with a box identical to the one he had given Lil earlier in the evening.

Russell's heart had started to race when Luke mentioned medications. He struggled to maintain his composure. He knew she wasn't feeling well, and that medication was now a routine part of life. Still, he felt uneasy.

Russell and Sophie opened their gifts simultaneously. Russell admired the pin with the words Mont Blanc visible on the lower curve. Sophie held out the bracelet. As she brought it closer for Russell to see, he pressed his pin next to it forming half of the original medallion. Luke lifted his choker out from behind his undershirt to reveal the third portion. "Nan has the final piece."

"Best gift ever," Russell said quietly. "Well done."

Luke smiled a satisfied grin. He turned to Lyndon and, with upturned hands, said, "Sorry. Got nothing for you, friend."

Lyndon laughed and responded smoothly, "Meeting your family was gift enough for me." He raised his glass for a final toast. "Here's to climbing with friends and family."

Around 7:45, as they finished their entrees, the waitstaff returned and asked if they would like some dessert. Russell quickly announced, "Not for me." Turning to his dinner companions he added, "You all, please stay. I want to go check on Lil." He then handed the waiter his credit card. The waiter declined, "*Non Monsieur, s'il vous plait. The dinner for le parte de la*

263

Belle Elizabetta was already paid for in advance."

Russell cast a look at Lyndon.

"That would have been a smooth idea," Lyndon said, nodding. "And seeing as I recruited my latest tour guide, I could have written it off as a business expense, but, eh, not me."

Russell glanced about the room but observed no obvious indication of the benefactor.

Luke stood up. "I'll go with you," he said to Russell. "I can't be eating too much dessert. I have to start getting back into swimming shape. You two stay and enjoy," he said to Sophie and Lyndon. And with a glance at his mother, added, "Curfew is at eleven."

Russell and Luke left the table and headed toward the door. "That was very gallant of you," Russell said as they stepped onto the street.

"Not too obvious?" Luke asked.

"No, it was obvious. But still good. She didn't protest or get up to leave," Russell added.

"Yea. I think she likes him." Luke concluded as he hustled to keep pace with his grandfather.

At 7:55 they arrived at Le Faucigny and took the stairs to the second floor. As Luke entered his room, Russell reached into his pocket for his own key. It was not there. He felt in his other pockets and came up empty. "Damn, I lost my key," he said silently before remembering they had requested only one room key and he had left it with Lil.

He knocked lightly at the door. No answer. He knocked a second time. More forcefully. Again, there was no response.

The anxiety he had struggled to suppress for the past five months crept to the surface. He cursed himself for leaving her and going to dinner, for agreeing to go on this trip, for not insisting she get treatment. He cursed himself for doing what she had wanted. Russell started pounding on the door. "Lil, wake up. Let me in. I'm here."

The noise drew the attention of other guests on the floor. Several came into the hallway including Luke who was already in his boxers and t-shirt.

"*Ist alles in ordnung?*" a middle-aged woman asked.

"*Monsieur, est-ce que ça va?*" said another.

"Russell?" Luke said as he approached his grandfather.

Russell heard none of them. The only voice he heard was the one behind him. "What is all the ruckus?"

Russell, his face red with exertion and fear, stopped pounding at the door. Swinging round, he saw her. She'd entered the hall from the stairs, having just returned from dumping the capsule husks in a recycling bin several streets away from the hotel.

"I thought I had lost you," he managed to say as he approached and embraced her.

"My sweet, lovely, silly man," Lil said as she hugged him back. "Let's go inside," she whispered in his ear.

"*Un peu trop boire,*" commented the second woman.

Lil nodded sympathetically. She turned the key in the lock, entered the room with Russell, and closed the door gently.

Confused at the scene he had just witnessed, Luke returned to his room after everyone else had left the hallway.

"I thought I had lost you," Russell repeated. "That you were gone. And I wasn't ready. I am not ready," Russell said honestly as he sat on the bed beside his wife.

Lil paused for a moment, and then shared what she had concluded privately some time ago. "There is no such thing as ready," she said. "Not for this."

"It is nothing you can truly know or prepare for," she said aloud to her husband. These were the exact words she had repeatedly told herself. Lil had come to catalog death along with some other existential life experiences like being born or having a baby, yet made even greater by the finality, the infinite span of time you will be unable to know. "But at least we had the gift of knowing it was right around the next curve, and we walked to it with eyes open, together. We lived as we wanted, all the way to the end." Lil didn't have God. But she found comfort in these practiced words, even as she doubted them.

Russell spoke. "I imagined you were on the bed, not breathing. I saw myself shaking you, trying to wake you. Taking you to the shower and running cold water on you like that would do something. And then calling nine-one-one or whatever number they have in France and asking that they pump your stomach. And I was afraid, and angry. And ashamed because I know what you want. But it is not what I want." He looked at his beloved and asked, "Is that so wrong?"

Lil turned on her side, cradled her husband's head in her arm, and stroked his hair as you might a newborn. "No, it is not wrong, nor weak, nor shameful. It's love."

When a beloved dies, so too does the life for those who remain. Living prepares us for this lesson at every turn. But too often, we do not heed the message delivered in small doses across the years. We deny the change in our bodies, our circumstances, or the world around us. We cling instead to the nostalgia for the imagined past, or fail to recognize the reality of a narrowing future.

Lil had quietly worried that the final moment would be too much for Russell to bear. That he would intervene in some way and try to stop her, tricked by a misguided belief that he could stop the inevitable. That is why she had decided that her final moment would be lived alone, surrounded and comforted by the memory, but not the company, of all those she loved. Tonight, though, was not that moment.

Russell and Lil fell asleep in one another's arms.

Inside the room next door Luke tossed in his bed, his racing mind moving from one topic to another. He had called Sean, and said the words, "You were right," and asked the question, "Can you forgive me?" He had tried calling Nikki and Katie, but they didn't pick up, so he texted them instead, "I'm sorry." Eleven o'clock came and went. Later, when he heard the key fitted into the lock, he glanced at his watch: 12:10. Now that's a naughty girl, he thought to himself, smiling in the darkness and pretending to be asleep.

The Last Breakfast

By 7:00 all four members of the family were awake. Only one had enjoyed a satisfying sleep. Sophie and Luke were scheduled on the 12:05 train from Chamonix to St. Gervaise les Bains with a transfer to Geneva and the flight home. Russell and Lil would remain in Chamonix a little longer. This was to be their last morning together.

Lil, who had been awake for the better part of an hour, rose from bed around 6:10. She opened the room-darkening curtain slightly and moved the chair to catch the light. She sat in the warming rays, leafing through the inaugural issue of *Super Alpine*, a glorious two-hundred-and-fourteen-page compendium of photographs and stories from Chamonix.

The images were a mix of the historic and the contemporary. Some black and white stills featured wood and stone homes in the original village with the same low roofs and massive beams evident today. Several pages were dedicated to the very first Winter Olympics in 1924, when two hundred and fifty-eight athletes from sixteen countries assembled in the Chamonix Valley to compete in sixteen events. Lil chuckled as she read about the second-place finish by the US Hockey team, who won their first three matches by scores of 19-0, 22-0, and 11-0 before losing in the finals to, of course, the Canadians.

Lil's eye was drawn to the second chapter of the magazine, "The Death Sports Capital of the World," a name coined by Mark Twight, an American climber, author, and photographer who now worked as a personal trainer to movie stars. The article highlighted an increasing number of outdoor enthusiasts who had failed to fully respect the dangers inherent in their quest for adventure. As she drifted from image to image, she recognized some, including a handful she had met personally during her summer long ago. The mountains were an unforgiving teacher.

Walter Bonatti was prominently featured in chapter two and cited as a counterpoint. He had stepped away from extreme climbing at age 35 and lived past his 81st birthday. She was curious whether there were any references to Frederico. There were not.

As she was about to close the magazine, she saw a header buried on one of the final pages: Mountain Stories and Legends. She skimmed through a half dozen profiles when her heart skipped. The capsule under his name mentioned "a promising climber," "a tragic accident," and "family heartbreak," along with a reference to his American girlfriend, "La Belle Elizabetta, who returned to the United States shortly after the accident, never to return to the valley."

Shows how much they know, Lil laughed to herself, reacting without anger or tears.

At least, she thought, there was no talk of suicide. While there was no note, through the years Lil had long wrestled with that doubt. It was not a technically challenging climb for someone of Frederico's skill. The possibility had initially been another burden of blame Lil had placed on herself.

She closed the pages when she heard the rustle of the bedsheets. Returning the magazine to the table beneath a stack of other guides and tour books, she walked over to her husband, smoothed his hair, and kissed him on the forehead.

Awake though not well-rested, he managed a smile at his wife's unusual morning greeting.

"I am going to take a tub before breakfast," Lil said. She had been waiting for Russell to stir, fearing that the sound of running water would awaken him. He nodded sleepily.

She went into the bathroom and closed the door partway. She turned the water spigot to extra hot. Lavender Morning. She had found the packet yesterday when looking through the basket of toiletries provided by the hotel. What an inviting name, she had thought at the time. She waited until the tub was a third full before pouring the crystals. Scented dust from the package mingled with the thin steam from the water. Lil placed her face into the cloud and inhaled deeply. It smells as good as the name, she thought. With the tub filled close to the top, she turned off the water, removed her robe, and slid into the warmth. Lil always liked a hot bath, but this morning was especially sweet. She closed her eyes and lowered her body under the water up to her chin, thinking this is heavenly – I will miss my tubs.

A short time later, she heard the creak of the door gently opening. Still, she kept her eyes closed. Russell drew up a small stool behind the edge of the freestanding tub. He placed his hands in the water to warm them and then began massaging Lil's shoulders, his thumbs finding the small knots of tension in her back and shoulders.

Lil lifted her right arm from under the water and patted his hand. She tilted her head back and opened her eyes. Russell saw the contented smile on her face.

"You are a dear," Lil said. "I so love you," she added, blowing a kiss to him.

Russell leaned over the edge of the tub. As he went to return the kiss, he missed her mouth and kissed her nose instead.

Lil laughed and flicked a splash of water at him. She then lowered her body fully beneath the surface. She spun around so that when she emerged, she was facing her husband. She brushed her hand across her head, pushing back her hair, the excess water dripping down her back. She then placed her hands on either side of his face and kissed him fully on the lips.

The clock read 8:20 before they left the room and headed downstairs for breakfast. Luke was seated at a corner table immediately adjacent to the serving stations. A small pile of plates was already scattered along the edge of the table to his left.

"'Bout time you got here," he said casually to his grandparents. "I am on my third breakfast. I'm not certain how much longer I can go. Oh, and next time we do this hike, we should skip the huts and just stay here. In case you didn't know, you can take the ski lift or train to any of the trails and come back, sleep in a real bed, and have an actual breakfast," he said, popping a

269

forkful of egg and prosciutto into his still moving mouth.

Lil smiled and lifted a piece of fruit from Luke's plate. Russell went to the serving tables and surveyed the array of pastries, eggs, and quiche, all artfully presented.

"Where's Mom?" Lil asked as she sat next to Luke and wrapped her arm around his, the one not holding his fork.

"Not up yet," and after a brief pause, he added with a smirk, "She got in a little late last night."

Lil nodded with a smirk of her own and squeezed his upper arm before joining Russell at the food tables. When they returned, Lil had a few berries and a plain croissant on a small dish.

"Weak," Luke pronounced, pointing at Lil's selection. "Gimme a high five, champ," he proclaimed to Russell, looking at his grandfather's overflowing plate. A fluffy omelet firmly anchored the center of the dish. It was surrounded by a petit muffin, a thick slice of quiche, a small ramekin of yogurt topped with granola, and a single lonely section of grapefruit.

"Some of that is for your grandmother," Russell lied with a nod.

Sophie entered the room a few minutes later. Her hair was not pulled back into her signature ponytail the way she usually did when going out in public. Instead, it hung loosely on her shoulders, like she preferred on weekend mornings at home.

Luke caught her eye and beckoned her to the table. As she was halfway across the floor, he pointed to his watch.

"I made it in time. They are still serving for another hour," she said.

"Not talking about that, young lady. I'm talking about curfew," Luke teased his mother. "You know how I can't sleep when you are out at night," he added in an exaggerated imitation of a lecture he had received multiple times at home.

Sophie raised her eyebrows and changed the topic. "So, what is on the agenda before we have to catch the train?" she asked.

"Russell and I were going to walk through town. We will meet you at the train station to see you off," Lil replied.

"I am going shopping," Luke added. "They've got Helly Hansen, Saloman,

Patagonia, Arc'teryx, Volcom, Mammut, one right after the other. Mom, you'll have to give me your credit card; I'm tapped out."

Sophie shot him a no-way-nice-try look.

"What about you?" Russell asked.

She cleared her throat. "I told Lyndon I would meet him for coffee around ten," she managed to say with a look that was slightly sheepish but not fully embarrassed.

"Good for you," Lil quickly added before anyone else could say a word. "I like that boy."

"My work here is done," Luke said, adding his fourth plate to his pile. "I'll meet you in the lobby at eleven. That should give you enough time," he said to his mother with the same snarky tone he had used earlier.

Lil and Russell also excused themselves and walked out with Luke. "You go on ahead, dear," Lil said to Russell. "I have a small bit of business with Luke."

When Russell rounded the corner and headed up the stairs, Lil turned to Luke. "I wanted to thank you properly. It meant a lot to me. The whole thing. You being here, to have you along on this trip." She was rambling. "More than you may ever know, at least until you get to be an old man."

"Like I said last night, it's been the best. I'll have to be in charge of planning the next one. Though it might not have quite so much walking. I'm thinking more like the beach. Costa Rica or Hawaii," Luke said.

Lil looked down. "I'll be right there with you," she replied. "And take this," she said, pressing two 100-euro bills into his hand. "Go get yourself something at one of those nice stores."

"I can't do that, Nan, that's too much. I was just joking with mom. I thought she would want to see him 'cause that's what I would want to do if I met a girl I liked. The shopping stuff, I just made that up. You know, to give her some space."

"Make an old woman happy, and take it. At my age, I don't need the money. Get something to wear on your future adventures." Lil wrapped his fingers around the bills and kissed the back of his hand.

To the Train Station

That morning for the first time in nine days they went their separate ways. Luke wandered the stores along La Rue de Docteur Paccard. He stopped first at the Arc'teryx store and drooled over a waterproof shell which he bought twenty minutes later in Snell Sports for thirty euros less. Sophie met Lyndon at l'Hotel Le Chamonix. They sat together sipping cappuccinos at a sidewalk table. Lil and Russell, hand-in-hand, wandered slowly about town, splitting their time people-watching and window-shopping.

As they walked north toward la Place de l'Eglise, Lil suddenly tugged on Russell's arm, pulling him behind a tall shrub in a curbside planter. "There they are," she whispered, urgently pointing to the bistro table where she spied Sophie and Lyndon about a block away.

Russell squinted in the direction Lil had indicated.

"They look happy," Lil said.

"Yup," Russell replied, mimicking Lil's whispered tone. "And why are we hiding? Let's go say hello." He started walking toward them.

"No, no, no. Let them be," Lil replied, pulling him back into concealment. "If they wanted company, they would have invited us."

Russell shook his head and laughed silently. Lil and her mysteries, he thought to himself.

"We'll go this way," Lil added, ushering Russell to the left. She glanced one more time over her shoulder before turning down Allée du Majestic which fronted a wide plaza adjacent to the Hotel Mont Blanc. This morning the green space was home to a series of white tents, a pop-up market featuring farmers and provisioners from Chamonix Valley and nearby villages. Russell and Lil sampled some raspberries bursting with flavor, sipped a little wine from a nearby vineyard, and nibbled on a slice of brioche dappled with honey.

A peal of the bell tower from St Michel signaled 11:00. "We best be headed to the train station," Lil announced. "We do not want to miss them."

As they turned back to Allée de Majestic, they encountered a series of displays. It was a timeline of sorts, featuring alpinists from Chamonix's history. All the luminaries were there, along with a host of lesser-known climbers.

They slowed to read the descriptions. At the second board, Russell shook his head. "Maria would not be pleased," he commented, reading the narrative below the picture of Balmat and Paccard, which portrayed Paccard as the hero and relegated Balmat to local sidekick. Among the many images they lingered over was Walter Bonatti. Russell stood beside Lil and placed his arm around her waist. Lil touched the words as she read them silently. The description did not mention Frederico. When she finished reading she exhaled slowly. She placed her arm around Russell's and they left the allée together.

It was less than a quarter-mile to the train station. Along the way, they again passed Balmat and Paccard, this time as bronze statues with eyes permanently affixed on the summit of Mont Blanc. They arrived early at La Gare de Chamonix Mont Blanc.

The station, completed in 1904, was a gorgeous building with much of the original ironwork and stone framing still intact. Nineteen gables stretched along the front facade, nine on either side of the central clock tower, inlaid with stone reading CHAMONIX-MONT-BLANC. Positioned along the southern edge of town, the mountain peaks rose majestically behind the depot. The view north was equally striking. The green slopes gave way to a serrated ridge of rock that defined the valley's northern edge, with yet another row of snow-capped peaks visible in the distance.

Russell and Lil took a seat on a bench. "That's where we were yesterday," Lil said, pointing to the lift across the valley and to their right.

They sat in silence for a few minutes, each with their own thoughts. Lil placed her hands inside her oversized jacket pockets. She fiddled with the two letters she had written. She looked impatiently at her watch. Eleven-forty. They should be here by now, she said to herself.

Russell leaned back into the bench and tilted his head to catch the full sun on his face. He closed his eyes and let the wash of orange flood across his lids before opening them, allowing the valley to slowly return to focus. He repeated the sequence several times, all the while leaning gently against Lil. He wasn't thinking of anything in particular. Just being there with her.

"Look," he said, pointing to the left.

Lil thought he had spied Luke and Sophie so she looked down the street.

"No, higher," Russell said, raising his hand toward the sky.

Lil cast her eyes up and saw one, then two, then a dozen or more. She followed the brightly colored chutes of the paragliders as they carved swooping arcs through the sky. The conditions in Chamonix were ideal. The sheer faces of the mountains offered multiple launching points, many readily accessible via chairlifts. The variation in temperatures between the bowl of the valley and the walls of the mountain created the thermal lifts, allowing the gliders to float down toward the base and up above the peaks along the entire length of Chamonix. And then there was the view. An airborne adventurer could look down and see not just Mont Blanc but range upon range of the Alps beyond France and into Italy and Switzerland.

They sat tracing the invisible lines as the gliders rose and fell, and then slid gently to the right only to bank sharply in the opposite direction. All told they counted 18 but the constant movement made it difficult to determine the exact number. The effect was hypnotic.

"Oh, how I would like to do that," Lil suddenly said aloud. "After the kids get on the train, we will get our tickets and have lunch. I think I will need a glass of wine or two. And then we will go floating in the heavens together. Me and you."

His wife's voice shook him from his trance. Russell paused and contemplated the idea. As he sat there on the bench he suddenly felt very tired. He was uncertain about the source of the fatigue that had seeped into his bones. The end of their adventure? The departure of Sophie and Luke? The toll of

Lil's cancer? Likely all three, and more. He was suddenly afraid. He felt his own heart beating and noticed he was sweating. He shook his head in a quick series of twists from side to side.

Lil saw the sadness and the fear. She dismissed the instinct to push a little further. Instead, she wiped his forehead and kissed his cheek. He reached out and held her hand. "I'm sorry," he said.

"Go easy with the lovey-dovey PDAs," Luke said as he and Sophie approached without his grandparents noticing. With their shorts and backpacks, Luke and Sophie could easily have been mistaken for two adventurers about to start their journey rather than travelers coming to an end.

"We were just discussing our plans for this afternoon," Lil replied.

Luke's face turned red. He was not ready for the image of his grandparents that involuntarily flashed through his mind.

"You two best be getting to your train," Lil said. As she stood, she felt a slice of pain in her abdomen, and her knees buckled slightly. Hoping no one had noticed, she slid one arm into her daughter's arm and the other into Luke's.

Unlike flying, with its security checks and restricted zones, travel by rail allows you to escort your loved ones to the platform and see them off properly.

The train pulled in at 12:05 sharp. SCNF had a well-deserved reputation for punctuality. This reputation was built on its predictability with everything happening at the appointed time.

As they turned to say their goodbyes, Lil reached into her pocket and retrieved the two envelopes she had prepared. She pressed one into the hand of her daughter and the second into the hand of her grandson.

"Here. These are for you. But you have to promise me. You can't open them until you get home," Lil said, still grasping one end of the letter.

"So dramatic," Sophie said.

"Promise!" Lil repeated firmly.

Sophie looked at her mother. The conductor rang a bell and announced, "*Tous a bord.*"

"We promise," Luke said with a light tug at the envelope. He kissed his grandparents, picked up the two backpacks, and headed toward the train.

Lil released Sophie's letter. Sophie kissed her father and turned to her mom. She saw herself reflected in her mother's eye, and hugged her. "Thank you," they both said together. Walking away from her parents, Sophie heard her mother's words following her: "I love you." As she was about to leave the platform, she turned in the doorway and said, "I love you, too, Mom," and meant it. The door closed and the train departed at 12:10 just as scheduled.

Russell knew Lil had been preparing some letters. She had told him of her intent when they walked into La Plume du Montagne. He had not pressed her for more than that. Though he didn't know the exact words, he knew the general message. That she had cancer, that she was dying, that she refused treatment, and that she loved them. That last part was the most important; it was her purpose for taking this trip in the first place. It wasn't the way he would have chosen, but he was coming to accept it as her way.

They left the train station and walked a block to a small bistro, Moo et Co. In addition to the bread and cheese, they ordered a squash soup and a plate of roasted vegetables. Russell picked lightly at the food. His anxiety still gnawed at him even after his second glass of wine. Lil moved the food around the plate with her fork, taking only a few nibbles. As lunch wore on she felt increasingly nauseous. She struggled to resist the urge to cough. While Russell paid the tab, Lil headed to the restroom.

She coughed into the wad of toilet paper and saw the same dots of blood she had observed yesterday at Lac Blanc. Today, she also saw flecks of red mixed in with her loose stool. She did not panic. Instead she took comfort in this new symptom, a validation of her decision. Further evidence that the cancer was real and would consume her if she let it. Lil flushed the toilet and felt strangely better.

As she approached him, Russell noticed that Lil was smiling. He could not help but smile in return.

"I have a new idea," Lil said. "And it doesn't involve parachutes."

They left the cafe and walked a few doors down into an adjacent building. The amiable tanned young man behind the counter said, "You're in luck. Most folks make reservations in advance. But we had a cancellation and have an opening at two o'clock."

A Final Toast

I t was after 6:00 when they returned to the hotel. As Russell opened the door they found a bottle of champagne chilling in a silver bucket. Beneath two white roses read a card: *Compliments of l'Hotel de Faucigny.*

"I fibbed and told them we were celebrating a special anniversary," Lil explained. "I also took the liberty of arranging for dinner to be delivered. It should arrive at seven-thirty. That will still give us time to get cleaned up."

"That was very sweet of you," Russell said.

He gestured to the bottle. Lil nodded. "Just a small one, for now. I want to save some for the lamb," she said, partially true.

Russell popped the cork which flew into the curtain across the room. Startled, he laughed. "I wasn't expecting that much force."

Lil smiled widely at his surprise. The fizz of the bubbles sang in her ear as Russell poured a small quantity into the flutes and handed Lil her glass.

"To my most beautiful woman," Russell toasted.

"To us," Lil replied, tapping her glass to Russell's.

After finishing half her champagne, Lil said, "I'll shower first. I won't be long."

Fifteen minutes later she returned. Like the other details for the evening, she had given much thought to what she would wear. She considered a dress but thought the formality might arouse suspicion. She opted instead for her favorite pair of hiking pants and a long-sleeved button shirt with the cuffs rolled and secured to the loop on her upper sleeve. It was the same outfit she planned to wear very early the following day.

Russell gathered his bath kit and headed into the bathroom.

Lil waited until she heard the shower running before she poured the second glass of champagne. She reached into her purple bag and removed the vial she had prepared the night before. She added the small quantity of morphine to Russell's drink. She had researched this detail carefully. It would not cause him any harm but it would ensure he experienced a deep sleep, perhaps with some more vivid dreams than usual. This would allow her to make her exit without waking him.

She had long debated if Russell would be able to resist the temptation to intervene. Though he had grown supportive of her decision, she knew her husband well enough to also know, as it was with much of their life together, that her way was not truly his. His panicked reaction the previous night only reinforced her concern. She imagined, or more accurately feared, he might try to talk her out of it or, worse yet, try to stop her or resuscitate her. She didn't want to put him through that trial, or so she rationalized. She also recognized the truth – that she did not want to put herself through it either.

She stirred the elixir slowly. Some bubbles rose to the top, their gentle burst releasing the champagne's bouquet. Doesn't smell any different, she thought to herself. The water was still running in the shower. When she had practiced at home she didn't notice a change in the taste, but that was a different brand of champagne. With a mix of anxiety and curiosity, she tilted the glass and dipped her tongue in. Pretty much the same, she concluded.

There was a knock at the door. She opened it and was met by a young man wearing a buttoned serving jacket and carrying a wicker hamper.

"*Bonjour. J'ai une livraison pour monsieur and madame,*" he said.

"*Oui, dans ici. Merci,*" Lil replied.

As he entered, Lil gestured to a round table just beneath the window. He unfolded a crisp white linen and laid it across the surface. The young man positioned a small candle in the center and set the napkins and cutlery on opposite sides. After placing the individually plated meals next to each napkin, he lit the candle and asked Lil, "*Y aura-t-il autre chose, madame?*"

"*Non, merci,*" she replied.

He instructed Lil to return the dishes to the hamper when they were done and place it outside the door "*Je le ramasserai le matin.*" With that, the server

278

nodded lightly and left the room.

"Welcome to your table," Lil said as she gestured a returning Russell to his seat. She pulled out his chair the way he had for her on so many occasions over the course of their life together. "Tonight, we celebrate the end of our adventure."

The meal was truly delicious. The fresh asparagus and beets added a pop of color to the risotto. The sharp bite of the shaved cheese complemented the sweetness of the beets. The flavor combination, along with the roasted lamb, easily masked any tartness the morphine may have added to the champagne.

The conversation between husband and wife was easy and relaxed. Over the years they had accumulated their share of struggles. On this evening none found their way into their conversation. They were like a couple newly in love. But instead of imagining all the things they would do with their life together, they celebrated all they had done. It was a wonderful dinner.

Russell had another glass of champagne, his third of the evening. This, like the first before taking his shower, was unenhanced. Lil's research told her one dose would be sufficient. Russell was already starting to yawn before Lil took out the two small chocolate truffles she had purchased for dessert.

After the meal, despite feeling exceptionally tired, Russell helped Lil clear the table and place the dishes back in the hamper. They changed for bed. Lil suggested they watch a little of the news. She propped some pillows against the headboard and sat back. Russell turned on his side to face her. He was soundly asleep before the anchor had completed the headlines. Lil shut off the TV and lay awake, listening to the sound of his breathing. She tried matching her breath to his but found her heart was beating too fast for that. She pushed slightly away from him and closer to the edge of the bed. This location would make it easier to get out without disturbing him. She again focused on her breath, this time at her own pace, and slipped into sleep.

The Walk Away

Though for the past few months she had routinely been getting up before 5:00 AM, she had set her watch alarm to vibrate at 5, just in case. She roused from her sleep and looked at her watch. Four forty-five, she said to herself. Perfect.

Much like the night before, Lil had also carefully planned for this morning. The first cable to Aiguille du Midi left at 6:00. She had already purchased her ticket. Having removed the top section of her backpack last night, it would serve as a small daypack. She didn't need to carry much with her, anyway. It easily accommodated her purple comfort kit, a bottle of water, a piccolo of wine, and the book she had selected for the occasion.

Lil reached into the body of the backpack slumped against the leg of the bed. She pulled out the carefully wrapped gift box and placed it on the pillow that had cradled her head through its final night of sleep. She put the envelope addressed to Russell atop the box.

Lil clasped on the necklace Luke had given to her two nights earlier. It seemed an age ago. She grabbed her fleece along with a hardshell. The sun was not yet up, and it would be cold both in the valley and at the top of the mountain, at least until the warming rays of the sun crept over the opposing ridgeline. Fortunately, the forecast called for nothing more than thin clouds throughout the day with but a chance of thunderstorms in the early evening. It should be a glorious sunrise, Lil thought. And everything will be finished well before any storms might arrive.

As Lil walked toward the door she turned to look at her husband. She felt the urge to approach and kiss him, just lightly – a last goodbye. No, she told herself firmly. He might awaken. He would be confused and perhaps angry. Stay with the plan, she commanded her feet. With the dosage she administered, he should sleep for 12 hours.

She couldn't find the words to describe how she felt as she left the room, put on her jackets and walked out the rear door of Le Faucigny. Afraid? Yes, a bit. She also felt vividly alive, and with a trace of excitement. Her excitement was flavored with a faint but undeniable rush of power. She was in control. The author of her destiny. One thing missing was doubt. This morning, Lil had no final reservations. That moment of hesitation, the second thought she had experienced when her purple case flew away from her at the ladders, that doubt had evaporated and not returned. She was at peace with her decision. And this was a great comfort.

Though it was still dark and the streets were empty, she put on her sunglasses. She was on a mission and did not feel much like talking to other people. It reminded her of the feeling when Sophie was born. People all around you. Many telling you what to do, trying to comfort and support you – not helpful. She remembered swiping Russell's hands away from her shoulders and telling a nurse to shut up. That moment it was you and your body. Together. Alone. Nothing else.

One difference this morning, though: She did not feel alone. On her mile walk to the cable station, her mind welcomed a stream of visitors from across her life. With some, she revisited a specific event. With others, it was simply the warmth of their presence.

She walked west along l'Allée Rector Payot, passing all the unopened shops that would soon be catering to the bustling Chamonix crowd. Glancing in the window of the sporting goods store where Luke had purchased his jacket, she imagined him wearing the coat, hiking the Laugavegur Trail in Iceland, walking along the Champs Élysées in Paris, and tramping the Milford Track in New Zealand. She turned left onto l'Avenue de l'Aiguille du Midi, which would take her directly to the cable station.

She had seen only a few individuals in the tourist center of Chamonix: One elderly gentleman chatted with his dog, walking together in perfect cadence with the pet taking four quick steps for each of the man's slow strides. From the end of the leash, the furrier partner twisted his head in rapt attention and breathed excitedly, agreeing enthusiastically with everything the old man was saying. A younger man with a wrinkled shirt and disheveled hair, the corners of his mouth turned down in the same direction as his shoulders, seemed lost as he leaned against a stone wall. A young woman, arms wrestled around two bags of laundry, struggled to open the door to the 24-Hour Wash and Fold. None of these morning wanderers were interested in speaking with the old woman wearing sunglasses before sunrise. In fact, they did not seem to even notice her. This suited Lil just fine.

As she crossed the bridge over the Arve River, the number of people out and about increased, and so did their friendliness. The majority, like Lil, were heading to the station, eager to get an early start on their plans for the day. It was an eclectic mix. They ranged in age from twentysomethings, their toned and tanned legs advertising their youthful vigor, to an elderly gent whose corded muscles suggested he had been enjoying an active lifestyle for many, many years. Some sported carbon sticks and brand name labels on their well-coordinated clothing. Others carried gear so well-used that its color was best described as dirt. More than a few had ice picks and crampons attached to the loops of their packs – they had challenge on their mind. Regardless of the differences, these early arrivers were members of the same tribe. They tended to greet one another with at least a nod if not a conversation.

Lil did not object to the nods. She responded in kind. When someone did attempt to engage in conversation she replied with a single word or pretended she did not hear them.

Le Fournil Chamonaird sat a block away from the station. The embroidery on the edge of the awning read *Pain de Tradition*. These simple words were an inadequate description of the baked treasures inside. When she arrived in Chamonix a week ago, she was surprised to find it had remained largely unchanged from decades ago. Baguettes whose crust cracked with an assured snap. Croissants with their golden brown skin guarding the buttery layers beneath. The bakers had been at work since 3:00 AM shaping the loaves by hand. By 5:45, the scents from the first trays had trickled onto the adjacent streets, ready to ensnare the early-morning adventurers. Lil had planned

282

this stop. It was, after all, where she had first met Rene. She removed her sunglasses and joined the small queue that had already formed inside the store.

When it was her turn at the front of the line, she spoke to the young woman behind the counter. "*Je voudrais une petit baguette,*" Lil said. Looking down at the display counter to her right, she added, "And an almond croissant, *aussi.*"

The young woman smiled. She handed Lil a small bag with the croissant and passed her the unwrapped loaf. Lil felt the warmth of the bread pass through the crust and into her hand. She pressed it against her face, taking in the smell. Lil then placed the loaf in the outside pouch of her daypack. She bid the counter girl *au revoir* and left the store.

In astronomical terms, the sun rose at 5:47 along some unseen horizon hidden from the citizens of Chamonix. In reality, it would not peek above the outline of the mountains until several hours later than that. However, even now the rays bounced down from the upper atmosphere and filled the bowl of the valley. With the warm bread at her back and the growing light all around, Lil entered the first car.

The Aiguille du Midi is a mountain and part of the Mont Blanc massif. At 12,600 feet, it is not the tallest peak in the area. That title goes to Mont Blanc, the White Mountain itself, at 15,700 feet. And there are 11 other summits that exceed 13,000 feet. What makes the Needle at Midi so appealing is that old adage: Location, Location, Location. Location 1: It sits directly above Chamonix along the southern ridge that defines the valley. Location 2: Draw a straight line from Chamonix in France to Courmayeur in Italy and you pass right through the Aiguille du Midi. Location 3: The peak may be accessed by a cable car that whisks visitors from the bottom of the valley to the top of the mountain in twenty minutes.

Built in 1955, the Telepherique remains one of the most popular attractions in the valley. Adventurers may disembark at the first station, le Plan de l'Aiguille, at 7,600 feet a preferred start for many hikes or a launching point for tandem paragliding. Remain in the car, and ten minutes later you will arrive at the summit. There, tourists enjoy a panoramic vista deep into Switzerland, France, and Italy. Those with no fear of heights might venture onto a glass skywalk with a 3,000-foot view straight down. True Alpine adventurers, with the requisite skills and equipment, may exit the platform via a tunnel leading to an exposed ice ridge and then descend to the glacier and trails below.

A dozen of the riders exited at the first stop. They were the day hikers eager to get a jump on the crowds while avoiding the fatigue of ascending the first several thousand feet. Among those that remained, Lil stood out. She had no ice pick, no rope, nor helmet. There were no carabiners snapped to her small day pack. It was also too early for the strictly tourist crowd looking to summit without breaking a sweat, snap a few trophy pictures, and return to the valley in time for lunch. Lil was journeying to a destination all her own.

When she arrived at the summit, she walked the short distance to the Vallée Blanche Cable Car. She alone boarded the recently renovated Funivie Monte Bianco that would take her down the Italian side. Lil's plan called for her to depart midway at Le Pavillon de Mont Fréty.

The cable station at Le Pavillon bore little resemblance to the one she remembered from her youth. Gone were the dark, cramped station house and heavy stone blocks that had anchored the cable into the mountainside since the 1940s. The new station of steel and glass sparkled, reflecting the colors of the mountains around it. Its open architecture invited travelers to look up and out and beyond. Despite the sparkle, Lil did not linger long. She exited the station. Her eye was momentarily drawn to the flowered paths of the Saussurea Alpine Botanical Garden. The cluster of colors hugging close to the rocks beneath the cloudless blue sky was an unexpected gift even as she searched for the desired path.

She saw the sign just outside the eastern edge of the garden. The wooden pillar announced multiple options. Only two concerned her: Entrèves and Dent du Geant. That morning years ago, he would have walked up from Entrèves with his rope and pack. She had saved herself time and miles by using the cable cars. She followed the arrow toward Dent du Geant. She didn't have any rope. She had no intent of climbing to the top.

It was a path much like the dozens of miles she had walked over the past ten days. She listened to her body. She weighed each breath and counted the beats of her heart in her chest. She felt the sole of her foot contact the firmament of the earth. She detected the first drops of perspiration beading on her forehead. Resisting the urge to wipe them away, she traced the sensation as they rolled down her face. After a reflexive shiver, she watched the drops fall to the ground. This morning she chose to feel alive.

Lil did not know how long she had been walking. But she knew when she arrived.

There is a Madonna at the top of the Giant's tooth. Lil had never seen it herself. It is located on the easternmost spire, requiring a technical climb with ropes and crampons. No, she had never seen it. But Frederico had described it to her. "The Madonna, she stands on high. Her arms spread gently, eyes looking down across the valley, watching over everyone." He confessed that he would sometimes climb up just to pray. He would sit at her feet. Some days the sun would shine warmly on his face. On other days the buffeting wind threatened to cast him down the mountainside. But there the Madonna stood, anchored to the earth, offering steady comfort to all. That is what he was doing that morning 50 years ago. She was sure of it. But this is where they found his body. She was sure of that as well. There was no Madonna here, but there was a small shrine. The stones were roughly mortared to create a box about 16 inches wide and 12 inches tall with a simple gabled roof. It was tucked under an overhang at the base of the wall, offering some protection from the elements.

Elizabetta had come here once before. But she had not found the body – that part of Maria's story was not true. It was a blessing. Stone is unforgiving. She was spared that image. Instead, the picture she preserved in her mind was of the young man, his handsome face, ready smile, and wavy hair, unmarked neither by granite nor the passing of time.

She had visited this spot the day before her return to America. She had come alone that day, just as she was alone today. The shrine was not here then. But she was sure it was for him.

She knelt down to better see inside. She reached in. The dark space contained a carved stone statue of St. Bernard of Menthon. The patron saint of mountain climbers. She remembered the stories. How in the 11th century the monk had established a monastery serving travelers and pilgrims crossing through the Aosta valley. Some five hundred years later, members of his order raised and bred the famous mountain dogs that still bear the Saint's name. Over the centuries the monks and the Saint Bernards saved scores of lost travelers. They were not there to save Frederico that day. Instead, the little statue of Saint Bernard now stood watch over the spot where his body came to rest.

The corners of the shrine were filled with debris. Lil cleaned some of it out. As she did, she came upon a few hidden items. Pulling them out, she turned them in her hands: A carabiner with its gate frozen in place, a rusted steel piton and chock, and a small section of nylon climbing rope, now discolored but the tight weave still intact. She dusted away the gravel and returned the tokens to their place.

It was mid-morning before she settled herself on the thin blanket she had brought. Though the sun was not yet fully visible, the sky was bright, the brilliant blue background holding but a few puffs of white cloud. She lifted the purple case from her daypack. She always heard Debbie's voice whenever she opened the zipper. That voice brought its own source of comfort, different from the contents inside.

Most of the meds she left at the hotel. She brought only three: Metoclopramide to prevent her vomiting, Diazepam for anxiety, and the largest bag containing the Seconal powder she had emptied from the capsules. She closed the purple pack and placed it next to her. Lil looked at the three meds and took a long breath. It was time.

* * *

Light filtered through the fabric of the window curtain, filling the room at

Hotel Le Faucigny. Russell slowly opened his reluctant eyes, first his left, then his right. He was unprepared to transition from the dark of his sleep to the bright of the room. He shaded his eyes with one hand and reached out toward Lil with the other. He patted the bed several times, each time finding nothing but an empty mattress.

He shot up. His mind now more than fully awake. "Lil," he called in an act of desperate hope. He held his breath and listened. Perhaps she was in the shower and couldn't hear him. Silence but for the throb of his heart in his own ears. His mind conjured another hopeful flash even while his stomach roiled. Perhaps she went for a walk, to breathe the air and see the mountains, or to pick up some croissants and coffee to bring back to the room where they would sit across from one another on the small table holding hands while making plans for how they would enjoy this glorious day and all the other glorious days to come. The promise of comfort lasted less than a moment.

He saw the box, meticulously wrapped in lavender paper. The edges were perfectly creased, the way she always wrapped presents. A sprig of flowers braided into the bow, a card tucked under the ribbon that tightly hugged the box. Even from where he stood, he could read the crisp penmanship spread across two lines: "My Dearest Love, Russell."

He closed his eyes slowly and drew a deep breath. He imagined the scent of lavender and Lil and croissants and, in that infinite instant, all the other smells in the great wide world. He sat down on the bed, silently holding his head in his hands to prevent it from falling from his body, knowing his broken heart lay entombed in that purple box upon the bed.

* * *

The sun had edged above the ridge behind her. Lil opened the first med. She removed two tablets from the blister pack and tucked them into the corner of her mouth. They dissolved easily. The taste was mildly unpleasant – artificial lemon with an aftertaste of Stevia. Today she did not pucker her face. Instead, she honored the sensation. And rolled her tongue around the inside of her mouth, sucking out the saliva and holding the taste. She had heard stories about how chemo could ruin your sense of taste. As petty as it might sound, it was another on the long list of indignities and insults she had sought to avoid. She counted her continuing ability to savor as a small victory over the cancer that consumed her. After a few moments, she smiled and spat on the ground. "Enough of that," she said. She opened the bottle of wine she had brought, poured herself a quarter glass, and sipped it lovingly. "Much better," she said aloud, the wine increasing her gratitude for functioning taste buds.

Lil knew to wait 30 minutes for the antiemetic to take effect before ingesting the Seconal. Betsy had advised that while she was waiting, it was a good time to take the Diazepam. Lil reached toward the anxiety med she had placed on the front edge of the blanket, and paused. She checked in with her body. Her breathing was regular. She was not sweating. Good signs. She tightened and relaxed her shoulders, arms, and back. Moving to her lower body, Lil directed the tension down through her upper legs to her calves and finally away through her outstretched toes. She closed her eyes and waited. She felt the beat of her heart. The steady rhythm, her dependable companion for the past 67 years, was with her still. At least for a bit longer. She took stock of her thoughts. And at this moment, she did not feel anxious or worried or afraid. Lil recognized a familiar trace of melancholy, the sort of sadness she felt on the final day of an excellent vacation or when she arrived at the last pages of a good book. But she was not afraid. This tinge of sadness was overshadowed by a deep well of gratitude, and pride. Gratitude for a life of purpose filled with good people, for the opportunity to be a spouse, mother, and grandparent. Pride for a life's journey lived on her terms. As Lil approached the moment of her death, she was free from the trauma of regret. She put away the anxiety med, nibbled on her croissant, eyed the body bag of Seconal, and smiled.

* * *

Russell lifted his eyes and stared at the box. Though he had awoken only a few moments ago, it was a different lifetime, and he knew it. Gone were the options and the burden to act – Lil had taken those with her. Do I call her on her cell? She would not answer. Do I look for her? He would not find her. Do I scream and yell and pound on the wall? It would not matter. The only choice left was to open the envelope and unwrap the lavender box.

The paper quivered in his hand. He read it slowly, dwelling on every word. He was in no rush to read the next sentence. He already knew how the story ended.

My Dearest Love,

I hope you will, in time, forgive me for this selfish exit. For the past five months I told myself that I would spare you from the trauma, relieved of the temptation to save me. But the truth is I wanted to spare myself, and you have already saved me a hundred times over.

When I returned home that summer so long ago, I was lost. Finding you was, and remains, the greatest fortune in my life. You have been my anchor, my steadfast companion. And despite however flawed I remained, know it was you who allowed me to become my best self. Through the years I have wanted no life but our life together. I only hope I have given you a fraction of the love and happiness you have given me.

With every great adventure, you take something with you and you leave something behind. I chose this place because it was where the person I have become was truly first born. It was here I left Elizabetta behind and Lil began. My deepest hope is that this place and moment becomes the start of a new life for you. That is the gift I bequeath to you. It is my final wish that you will accept it.

With all my love,
Lil

* * *

It was time. She emptied the remaining water from her water bottle, filled it one-third full with some wine and added the complete contents of the plastic bag. She swished the bottle gently but much of the powder still floated on the top. She tried shaking it more vigorously but with little effect. Lil debated the merits of sipping versus chugging and could make an argument for either approach. She opted for a sip at first. As the film of powder entered her mouth, she felt herself starting to gag and spat the mixture back into the bottle. Nastier than I expected, she said to herself while taking a swig of straight wine. Best to chug this beast, she decided. She opened her mouth wide, poured a first gulp, and quickly swallowed. She followed this with a second and third. By the time she got to her fourth, the taste didn't seem quite as horrid. She moved to smaller sips until she emptied the entire bottle. She took a final swig of wine and again nibbled at the croissant.

Lil was curious what it would feel like. She had read several accounts of what to expect. Understandably, none of them were first-hand, so Lil treated them with suspicion. She had raised the question with Betsy but her description was too clinical. In the end, it was Debbie's words that Lil felt were closest to the truth: "Ms. Lil, in those final moments as they draw their last breath and truly pass, I believe most people die much like how they lived. Me, I'll be hearing trumpets and singing a song. You, Ms. Lil, you will be putting one sure foot in front of the other and push open that door as you become that shining light."

In her slowing breath she closed her eyes. Though she remained motionless on the blanket she felt sure she was walking still, passing by the places and people she had loved throughout her life, and at the very last moment, among the rustle of the leaves on the trees, she heard the wind call her name.

About the Author

Mike was born in the wonder-filled town of Hull, Massachusetts. After emigrating to Pennsylvania, he met his wife-to-be when the college fates assigned them both to the second floor of English House. For the past forty years, together they have raised their four children in Bucks County. Together, they enjoy hiking and Great Walks, especially when this includes a stop at a bakery! Beyond seeing the kids grow into kind and caring adults, his proudest accomplishment is being regularly awarded the nonsense crown by the grands for routinely telling fish stories generously sprinkled with malarkey.

www.ingramcontent.com/pod-product-compliance
Lightning Source LLC
Chambersburg PA
CBHW020436130626
46549CB00001B/174